Anonymous

The Spirit of Praise

a collection of hymns old and new

Anonymous

The Spirit of Praise
a collection of hymns old and new

ISBN/EAN: 9783337578565

Printed in Europe, USA, Canada, Australia, Japan

Cover: Foto ©Andreas Hilbeck / pixelio.de

More available books at **www.hansebooks.com**

THE
SPIRIT OF PRAISE

A Collection of Hymns

OLD AND NEW

SELECTED AND ARRANGED BY THE AUTHOR OF
GOLDEN THOUGHTS FROM GOLDEN FOUNTAINS

LONDON
FREDERICK WARNE AND COMPANY
BEDFORD STREET, COVENT GARDEN

NEW YORK: SCRIBNER, WELFORD, AND CO.

To the Original Edition.

AMONG the departments of popular literature which have been made the subject of illustrated art books, the wide field of Hymnology has as yet been unrepresented. While collections of "Hymns" and of "Psalms and Hymns" for congregational use have been indefininitely multiplied, hardly a year passing without bringing its contribution to the general stock, the works of individual authors only have been selected from among the writers of sacred poetry for publication in an illustrated form. It is believed that the want has been frequently felt of a book of this kind, that shall fairly represent the various authors who, from the twelfth to the present century, have built up the beautiful temple of sacred song that stands forth as the ornament and pride of our English literature.

To supply that want has been the object of the present volume.

The commencement of the era of modern hymn writing is coincident with that of the Reformation, and, like the Reformation, is associated with the name of Martin Luther. The great German reformer, anxious to spread among the people the tidings of better things that had arisen, wrote thirty-seven sacred songs, some founded on the Psalms, like the celebrated "*Eine feste Burg ist unser Gott*," others from old Latin hymns, others again from popular German songs, and not a few entirely original compositions. Thus he may be looked upon as the founder of congregational church singing; and in this, as in other departments of his work, he was assisted by the co-operation of a number of friends, and succeeded by many followers, such as Justus Jonas, Spengler, Kohler, Wehe, Mathesius, and others; and while the elders were thus enabled to express in song their belief and their aspirations, the younger lambs of the fold were not forgotten; witness the beautiful "Christmas Hymn for Children," written for the little ones by the great reformer himself.

The rise of Hymnology in England dates from a period considerably later. While the Latin hymns were banished from our churches, no attempt was made for a long time to supply their place by sacred songs in the language of the people; but in 1563 appeared "The Whole Book of Psalms: Collected into English Metre by Thomas Sternhold, John Hopkins, and Others;" and the importance of this kind of literature as a vehicle of Christian instruction is recognized in the quaint old title-page, which announces that these songs are "set forth, and allowed to be sung in all churches, of all the people together, before and after morning and evening prayer; and also before and after sermons, and moreover in private houses, for their godly solace and comfort; laying apart all ungodly songs and ballads, which tend only to the nourishing of vice and corrupting of youth." With all its ruggedness and old-fashioned quaintness, this version of the old translators is not destitute of a certain grandeur, as in the following stanza :

"The Lord descended from above, and bowed the heavens high,
And round about His feet He threw the darkness of the sky :
On cherub and on cherubim right royally He rode,
And on the wings of mighty winds came flying all abroad."

The Elizabethan era was unfavourable to the development of hymn writing, and thus very few of the productions of that period have been incorporated into our collections. The style of writing was too fanciful and allegorical to obtain favour with the people generally, and this species of composition remained the elegant pastime of the few rather than the vehicle of instruction for the many. In the latter half of the seventeenth century Milton led the way, in a style combining massive grandeur with polished elegance, to a more general appreciation of the value of Hymnology; and in the eighteenth and the present centuries the subject has been worthily treated by writers whose genius was quickened by true piety and a fervent desire for the promotion of what was good and holy.

Such writers were Ken, the faithful-minded bishop, Cowper, the gifted poet, the fervent Watts, the earnest-hearted Wesleys, and a multitude of others.

PREFACE.

This volume of selections from the treasures of British Hymnology is offered in the sincere hope that, as the before-mentioned quaint title-page has it, these hymns may be accepted in many "private houses, for their godly solace and comfort."

ADVERTISEMENT.

THE great success attendant upon the larger and more costly edition of the "Spirit of Praise" has induced the Publishers to offer the book in its present form; at the same time they avail themselves of the opportunity to considerably amplify the contents.

The Editor has to offer his best thanks to the Authors of some of the more modern hymns for the ready consent given in all cases where he has requested permission to insert various pieces; and also to those whose works he may have used without previously asking permission, which inadvertence has arisen only through ignorance of any existing copyright, or from inability to obtain the means of communication.

	PAGE
THE CREATOR	1
PRAYER	33
THE LORD'S DAY	65
FAITH	98
HOPE	137
LOVE	163
JOY	193
PATIENCE	214
MORNING	226
EVENING	247
NIGHT	271
SEEDTIME AND HARVEST	286
THE OLD AND NEW YEAR	311
DEATH AND THE GRAVE	325
THE JUDGMENT	345
THE NATIVITY	358
BAPTISM	377
THE LORD'S SUPPER	391
THE PASSION OF OUR LORD	411
THE CRUCIFIXION	420
THE RESURRECTION AND ASCENSION	429
THE KINGDOM OF CHRIST	456
HEAVEN	479
GENERAL HYMNS	517
INDEX	613

Praise ye the Lord. Sing unto the Lord a new song, and His praise in the congregation of saints.

Psalm cxlix. 1.

LIST OF ILLUSTRATIONS.

Engraved by the Brothers Dalziel.

SUBJECT.	ARTIST.	PAGE
Frontispiece	... J. BURLISON.	
PRAYER	... J. BURLISON.	
The spacious firmament on high ...	T. DALZIEL ...	1
View the broad sea's majestic plains	Ditto ...	7
Or the winter snow-flakes	Ditto ...	15
The moon shines full at His command	... J. W. NORTH	21
To fertile vales and dewy meads ...	... E. G. DALZIEL	23
All the flowers that gild the spring ..	... Ditto ...	27
Prayer is the simplest form of speech That infant lips can try	... G. DALZIEL	33
When at Thy footstool, Lord, I bend	... E. DALZIEL ...	39
Teach me to live by faith ...	... W. SMALLFIELD ...	45
Lord, Have mercy when we pray ...	G. J. PINWELL ...	49
Bowed down beneath a load of sin ...	... J. W. LAWSON ...	55
Teach our lips God's praise to sing ...	T. DALZIEL ...	65
Thine earthly Sabbaths, Lord, we love	Ditto	69
With willing steps Thy courts ascend	Ditto ...	75
Thy flocks meet in their several folds	Ditto ...	78
I love to stand within its walls	Ditto ...	83
Lord! our song ascends to Thee	... E. DALZIEL	89
When we join the world again	... J. W. NORTH	97
FAITH	... J. BURLISON	98
Can a woman's tender care ...	... G. DALZIEL	99

LIST OF ILLUSTRATIONS.

SUBJECT.	ARTIST.	PAGE
While the tempest still is high	J. W. NORTH	103
And when my dying hour draws near	W. SMALL	109
When sorrowing o'er some stone I bend	E. G. DALZIEL	115
Just as I am—poor, wretched, blind	A. B. HOUGHTON	119
Thy will be done!	Ditto	127
Though waves and storms go o'er my head	T. DALZIEL	131
From Egypt's bondage come	Ditto	137
I praised the sea, whose ample field	Ditto	143
Behold, how glorious is yon sky!	J. W. NORTH	149
The pilgrim faint, and nigh to sink	T. DALZIEL	155
All the depths of love express	G. DALZIEL	163
'T is manna to the hungry soul	A. W. BAYES	167
Have I something dearer still?	PAUL GRAY	173
Is He a rock? How firm He proves!	T. DALZIEL	177
Lo! the promise of a shower	J. W. NORTH	180
As the hart, with longing, looks	J. WOLF	185
The calm retreat, the silent shade	T. DALZIEL	193
The child leans on its mother's breast	W. SMALL	197
Rides upon the stormy sky	J. W. NORTH	201
There's not a bird, with lonely nest	J. WOLF	205
Calm as the evening ray	T. DALZIEL	210
PATIENCE	J. BURLISON	214
Rejoice though round thy pathway Is spread the gloom of night	J. W. NORTH	215
Still sink the spirits down?	G. J. PINWELL	219
MORNING	J. BURLISON	226
Christ, whose glory fills the skies	T. DALZIEL	227
My walks and works with me begin	G. J. PINWELL	231
The cheerful sun makes haste to rise	T. DALZIEL	235
Upon a rock-girt shore	Ditto	241
My voice ascending high	J. WOLF	246
Beginneth to decline below	T. DALZIEL	247
When round Thy wondrous works below	BIRKET FOSTER	253
Give to the sick, as Thy beloved, sleep	E. DALZIEL	259
For my parents dear I pray	Ditto	265
O, may my guardian, while I sleep	T. DALZIEL	270
Mid the silence of the night	Ditto	271
A thousand worlds of light	Ditto	275

LIST OF ILLUSTRATIONS.

SUBJECT.	ARTIST.	PAGE
Through the silent watches guard us	JOHN GILBERT	281
SEEDTIME AND HARVEST	J. BURLISON	286
The flowery Spring at Thy command	E. G. DALZIEL	287
The sower hid the grain	T. DALZIEL	291
By Him the birds are fed	J. WOLF	297
Autumn yields its ripened grain	W. SMALL	301
The sheaves brought safely home	T. DALZIEL	305
All is safely gathered in	BIRKET FOSTER	310
The opening year Thy mercy shows	E. G. DALZIEL	311
Storms are round us, hearts are quailing	J. W. NORTH	315
Welcome each closing year!	BIRKET FOSTER	319
In its narrow bed 't is sleeping!	G. DALZIEL	325
Weigh thy anchor, spread thy sail	T. DALZIEL	329
Thou art gone to the grave	Ditto	333
There, where the fathers sleep	J. W. NORTH	339
Hark! the trump of God is blown	T. DALZIEL	345
THE NATIVITY	E. DALZIEL	358
Hark! the herald angels sing	T. DALZIEL	359
We print the cross upon thee here	Ditto	377
Only there secure from harm	Ditto	383
Bread of the world in mercy broken	Ditto	391
The tokens of Thy dying love	W. SMALL	399
With grief and pain weighed down	T. DALZIEL	411
THE CRUCIFIXION	J. BURLISON	420
O world, behold upon the tree	T. DALZIEL	421
Jesus Christ is risen to-day	Ditto	429
How high, how strong, their raptures swell	A. B. HOUGHTON	437
God is gone up on high	P. HUNDLEY	447
THE KINGDOM OF CHRIST	E. DALZIEL	456
O'er earth's green fields	E. G. DALZIEL	457
Jesus the Saviour reigns	P. HUNDLEY	465
The sea send forth its song	T. DALZIEL	472
Once the big unbidden tear	Ditto	479
See, the streams of living waters	J. W. NORTH	487
There everlasting Spring abides	E. G. DALZIEL	497
These through fiery trials trod	E. DALZIEL	504
Praise ye the Lord, prepare your glad voice	F. A. FRASER	517
His flock to Him is dear	BIRKET FOSTER	524

LIST OF ILLUSTRATIONS.

SUBJECT.	ARTIST.	PAGE
For those in peril on the sea	T. Dalziel	533
As soars the eagle in the sky	J. Wolf	543
With waters sweet and clear	T. Sulmau	553
Come, visit every humble mind	Birket Foster	560
Haste, traveller, haste!	J. W. North	569
To the bare mountain-side	T. Sulmau	576
Our daily bread from day to day	T. Dalziel	583
There though the earth remove	T. Sulman	588
But birds and flowerets round us preach	J. Wolf	595
My tongue would bear her part	T. Dalziel	600
The leaves around me falling	Birket Foster	605
That life-giving stream	T. Sulman	609

Initial Letters and Ornamental Headings, &c., by P. Hundley.

Praise ye the Lord: for it is good to sing praises unto our God; for it is pleasant; and praise is comely.

Psalm cxlvii. 1.

The high and lofty One that inhabiteth eternity.
Isaiah, lvii. 15.

When thou prayest, enter into thy closet, and when thou hast shut thy door, pray to thy Father which is in secret; and thy Father which seeth in secret shall reward thee openly.
Matthew, vi. 6.

This is the day which the Lord hath made; we will rejoice and be glad in it. O give thanks unto the Lord; for He is good; for His mercy endureth for ever.
Psalm cxviii. 24, 29.

Remember now thy Creator in the days of thy youth.
Ecclesiastes, xii. 1.

THE CREATOR

The heavens declare the glory of God, and the firmament sheweth His handywork.

Psalm xix. 1.

THE spacious firmament on high,
With all the blue ethereal sky,
And spangled heavens, a shining frame,
Their great Original proclaim.

THE CREATOR.

Th' unwearied sun, from day to day,
Does his Creator's power display;
And publishes to every land
The work of an Almighty Hand.

Soon as the evening shades prevail,
The moon takes up the wondrous tale,
And nightly to the listening earth
Repeats the story of her birth;

Whilst all the stars that round her burn,
And all the planets in their turn,
Confirm the tidings as they roll,
And spread the truth from pole to pole.

What though in solemn silence all
Move round the dark terrestrial ball?
What though nor real voice nor sound
Amid their radiant orbs be found?

In Reason's ear they all rejoice,
And utter forth a glorious voice,
For ever singing as they shine,
"The HAND that made us is DIVINE."

ANDREW MARVEL.

THE CREATOR.

Make a joyful noise unto the Lord, all ye lands.
Psalm c. 1.

BEFORE Jehovah's awful throne,
  Ye nations, bow with sacred joy;
  Know that the Lord is God alone—
  He can create, and He destroy.

His sovereign power, without our aid,
Made us of clay, and formed us men;
And when, like wandering sheep, we strayed,
He brought us to His fold again.

We'll crowd Thy gates with thankful songs,
High as the heavens our voices raise;
And earth, with her ten thousand tongues,
Shall fill Thy courts with sounding praise.

Wide as the world is Thy command,
Vast as eternity Thy love!
Firm as a rock Thy truth shall stand
When rolling years shall cease to move.

                        ISAAC WATTS.

THE CREATOR.

> *For Thine is the kingdom, and the power, and the glory.*
> Matthew, vi. 13.

THINE, O Lord, is the kingdom,
  Thine the glory and power;
Thou hast kindled the starlight,
  Thou hast moulded the flower.

All things live by Thy presence,
  All things obey Thy will;
As the waters the ocean,
  Earth Thy glory shall fill.

Thou art Father of spirits;
  Thought is begotten of Thee:
In Thine image begotten,
  Glorious, boundless, and free!

When its freedom, transgressing,
  Out of Thy ways hath strayed,
Thou hast provided Redemption,
  Thou hast Atonement made.

Rolls this universe onward,
  Circling the foot of Thy throne;
Matter, and life, and spirit,
  Guided by Thee alone.

Therefore, in peril and sorrow,—
Therefore, in joy's bright hour,—
Thine, O Lord, is the kingdom,
Thine the glory and power!

DEAN ALFORD.

The earth is full of the goodness of the Lord.

Psalm xxxiii. 5.

THY goodness, Lord, our souls confess,
　Thy goodness we adore;
A spring, whose blessings never fail,
　A sea without a shore.

Sun, moon, and stars Thy love attest
　In every cheerful ray;
Love draws the curtain of the night,
　And love restores the day.

Thy bounty every season crowns
　With all the bliss it yields,
With joyful clusters bend the vines,
　With harvests wave the fields.

THE CREATOR.

But chiefly Thy compassions, Lord,
   Are in the Gospel seen;
There, like the sun, Thy mercy shines
   Without a cloud between.

THOMAS GIBBONS.

---

*Praise ye the Lord, for it is good to sing praises
unto our God.*
Psalm cxlvii. 1.

PRAISE the Lord, His glories show,
   Saints within His courts below,
   Angels round His throne above,
   All that see and share His love.
Earth to Heaven, and Heaven to earth,
Tell His wonders, sing His worth;
Age to age, and shore to shore,
Praise Him, praise Him, evermore!

Praise the Lord, His mercies trace;
Praise His providence and grace,
All that He for man hath done,
All He sends us through His Son:
Strings and voices, hands and hearts,
In the concert bear your parts;
All that breathe, your Lord adore,
Praise Him, praise Him, evermore!

HENRY FRANCIS LYTE.

His Name alone is excellent; His glory is above the earth and heaven.
                                        Psalm cxlviii. 13.

YE sons of men, with joy record
The various wonders of the Lord,
And let His power and goodness sound
Through all your tribes the earth around.

Let the high heavens your songs invite—
Those spacious fields of brilliant light,
Where sun, and moon, and planets roll,
And stars that glow from pole to pole.

THE CREATOR.

See earth in verdant robes arrayed,
Its herbs and flowers, its fruit and shade;
View the broad sea's majestic plains,
And think how wide its Maker reigns.

But O, that brighter world above,
Where lives and reigns Incarnate Love!
God's only Son, in flesh arrayed,
For man a bleeding victim made.

Thither, my soul, with rapture soar;
There in the land of praise adore.
This theme demands an angel's lay—
Demands an undeclining day.

PHILIP DODDRIDGE.

Let us come before His presence with thanksgiving, and make a joyful noise unto Him with psalms.
Psalm xcv. 2.

COME, O come! in pious lays
    Sound we God Almighty's praise;
    Hither bring, in one consent,
    Heart, and voice, and instrument;
Music add of every kind,
Sound the trump, the cornet wind,

Strike the viol, touch the lute,
Let not tongue nor string be mute;
Nor a creature dumb be found
That hath either voice or sound.

Let those things which do not live
In still music praises give:
Lowly pipe, ye worms that creep
On the earth or in the deep;
Loud aloft your voices strain,
Beasts and monsters of the main;
Birds, your warbling treble sing;
Clouds, your peals of thunder ring;
Sun and moon, exalted higher,
And, bright stars, augment the choir.

Come, ye sons of human race,
In this chorus take your place,
And amid the mortal throng
Be you masters of the song:
Angels and supernal powers,
Be the noblest tenor yours:
Let, in praise of God, the sound
Run a never-ending round,
That our song of praise may be
Everlasting, as is He.

From earth's vast and hollow womb,
Music's deepest bass may come;

Seas and floods, from shore to shore
Shall their counter-tenors roar:
To this concert when we sing,
Whistling winds, your descants bring;
That our song may over-climb
All the bounds of space and time,
And ascend from sphere to sphere,
To the great Almighty's ear.

So from Heaven on earth He shall
Let His gracious blessings fall;
And this huge wide orb we see
Shall one choir, one temple be;
Where in such a praiseful tone
We will sing what He hath done,
That the cursed fiends below
Shall thereat impatient grow:
Then, O come, in pious lays
Sound we God Almighty's praise!

GEORGE WITHER.

THE CREATOR.

O give thanks unto the Lord; for He is good: for His mercy endureth for ever.
Psalm cxxxvi. 1.

O God, ye choir above, begin
   A hymn so loud and strong,
That all the universe may hear
   And join the grateful song.

Praise Him, thou sun, who dwells unseen
   Amidst transcendent light,
Where thy refulgent orb would seem
   A spot as dark as night.

Thou silver moon, ye host of stars,
   The universal song
Through the serene and silent night
   To listening worlds prolong.

Sing Him, ye distant worlds and suns,
   From whence no travelling ray
Hath yet to us, through ages past,
   Had time to make its way.

Assist, ye raging storms, and bear
   On rapid wings His praise,
From north to south, from east to west,
   Through heaven, and earth, and seas.

THE CREATOR.

Exert your voice, ye furious fires
    That rend the watery cloud,
And thunder to this nether world
    Your Maker's words aloud.

Ye works of God that dwell unknown
    Beneath the rolling main;
Ye birds, that sing among the groves
    And sweep the azure plain;

Ye stately hills that rear your heads,
    And towering pierce the sky;
Ye clouds, that with an awful pace
    Majestic roll on high;

Ye insects small, to which one leaf
    Within its narrow sides
A vast extended world displays,
    And spacious realms provides;

Ye race still less than these, with which
    The stagnant water teems,
To which one drop, however small,
    A boundless ocean seems;

Whate'er ye are, where'er ye dwell,
    Ye creatures great or small,
Adore the wisdom, praise the power,
    That made and governs all.

And if ye want or sense or sounds,
    To swell the grateful noise,
Prompt mankind with that sense, and they
    Shall find for you a voice.

From all the boundless realms of space
    Let loud Hosannas sound;
Loud send, ye wondrous works of God,
    The grateful concert round.

PHILIP SKELTON.

---

*And God said, Let there be light:
and there was light.*
Genesis, i. 3.

THOU, whose almighty Word
    Chaos and darkness heard,
        And took their flight,
Hear us, we humbly pray,
And where the Gospel-day
Sheds not its glorious ray,
        Let there be light!

Thou, who didst come to bring
On Thy redeeming wing
    Healing and light,

Health to the sick in mind,
Sight to the inly blind,
O, now to all mankind
  Let there be light!

Spirit of truth and love,
Life-giving, holy Dove,
  Speed forth Thy flight;
Move on the waters' face,
Spreading the beams of grace,
And in earth's darkest place
  Let there be light!

Blessèd and Holy Three,
Glorious Trinity,
  Grace, Love, and Might:
Boundless as ocean's tide,
Rolling in fullest pride,
Through the world, far and wide,
  Let there be light!

JOHN MARRIOTT.

I am the Lord and there is none else; there is no God beside me.

Isaiah xlv. 5.

WHO can, on the sea-shore,
    Count the grains of sand?
Or the leaves in autumn,
    Whirling o'er the land?
Or the winter snow-flakes,
    Driving fierce and free?
Or the drops of water
    In the briny sea?

Who can measure ocean
    Where it deepest flows?

THE CREATOR.

Or the rays the sun darts
   When it brightest glows?
Who, than swiftest lightning,
   Faster yet can flee?
Name that wondrous Being—
   Greater none than He!

God is the unnumbered,
   Who no bound can know;
Suns and stars, before Him,
   Are as flakes of snow.
God is called the Boundless,
   Fathomless is He;
Swifter than the lightning,
   Deeper than the sea!

                DR. HENRY W. DULCKEN.

Thine is the kingdom, O Lord, and Thou reignest over all.
                I. Chronicles, xxix. 11, 12

JEHOVAH reigns, His throne is high,
His robes are light and majesty;
His glory shines with beams so bright,
No mortal can sustain the sight.

His terrors keep the world in awe;
His justice guards His holy law;

His love reveals a smiling face;
His truth and promise seal the grace.

Through all His works His wisdom shines,
And baffles Satan's deep designs;
His power is sovereign to fulfil
The noblest counsels of His will.

And will this glorious Lord descend
To be my Father and my Friend?
Then let my songs with angels' join;
Heaven is secure, if God be mine.

ISAAC WATTS.

O magnify the Lord with me, and let us exalt His Name together.
Psalm xxxiv. 3.

O WORSHIP the King,
   All glorious above;
O gratefully sing
   His power and His love;
Our Shield and Defender,
   The Ancient of Days,
Pavilioned in splendour
   And girded with praise.

THE CREATOR.

O tell of His might,
   O sing of His grace,
Whose robe is the light,
   Whose canopy space;
His chariots of wrath
   Deep thunder-clouds form,
And dark is His path
   On the wings of the storm.

The earth, with its store
   Of wonders untold,
Almighty, Thy power
   Hath founded of old,
Hath stablished it fast
   By a changeless decree,
And round it hath cast,
   Like a mantle, the sea.

Thy bountiful care
   What tongue can recite?
It breathes in the air,
   It shines in the light;
It streams from the hills,
   It descends to the plain,
And sweetly distils
   In the dew and the rain.

Frail children of dust,
   And feeble as frail,

In Thee do we trust,
   Nor find Thee to fail:
Thy mercies how tender!
   How firm to the end!
Our Maker, Defender,
   Redeemer, and Friend!

O measureless Might!
   Ineffable Love!
While angels delight
   To hymn Thee above,
The humbler creation,
   Tho' feeble their lays,
With true adoration
   Shall lisp to Thy praise.

SIR ROBERT GRANT.

The Lord shall reign for ever, even thy God,
   O Zion, unto all generations.
Psalm cxlvi. 10.

GOD moves in a mysterious way
   His wonders to perform;
He plants His footsteps in the sea,
   And rides upon the storm.

THE CREATOR.

Deep in unfathomable mines
    Of never-failing skill,
He treasures up His bright designs,
    And works His sov'reign will.

Ye fearful saints, fresh courage take;
    The clouds ye so much dread
Are big with mercy, and shall break
    In blessings on your head.

Judge not the Lord by feeble sense,
    But trust Him for His grace;
Behind a frowning Providence
    He hides a smiling face.

His purposes will ripen fast,
    Unfolding every hour:
The bud may have a bitter taste,
    But sweet will be the flower.

Blind unbelief is sure to err,
    And scan His work in vain:
God is His own interpreter,
    And He will make it plain.

WILLIAM COWPER.

Praise the Lord for His goodness, and for His wonderful works to the children of men.
                                               Psalm cvii. 15.

I SING th' almighty power of God,
    That made the mountains rise,
That spread the flowing seas abroad,
    And built the lofty skies.
I sing the wisdom that ordained
    The sun to rule the day:
The moon shines full at His command,
    And all the stars obey.

I sing the goodness of the Lord,
    That filled the earth with food;

He formed the creatures with His word,
  And then pronounced them good.
Lord, how Thy wonders are displayed
  Where'er I turn my eye,
If I survey the ground I tread,
  Or gaze upon the sky!

There's not a plant or flower below
  But makes Thy glories known;
And clouds arise, and tempests blow,
  By order from Thy throne.
Creatures, as num'rous as they be,
  Are subject to Thy care;
There's not a place where we can flee
  But God is present there.

In Heaven He shines with beams of love;
  With wrath in Hell beneath;
'T is on His earth I stand or move,
  And 't is His air I breathe.
His hand is my perpetual guard;
  He keeps me with His eye;
How should I then forget the Lord,
  Who is for ever nigh?

ISAAC WATTS.

The Lord is my shepherd : I shall not want. . . Goodness and mercy shall follow me all the days of my life.

Psalm xxiii. 1, 6.

THE Lord my pasture shall prepare,
    And feed me with a shepherd's care;
His presence shall my wants supply,
And guard me with a watchful eye;

My noonday walks He shall attend,
And all my midnight hours defend.

When in the sultry glebe I faint,
Or on the thirsty mountain pant,
To fertile vales and dewy meads
My weary, wandering steps He leads,
Where peaceful rivers, soft and slow,
Amid the verdant landscape flow.

Though in the paths of death I tread,
With gloomy horrors overspread,
My steadfast heart shall fear no ill,
For Thou, O Lord, art with me still;
Thy friendly crook shall give me aid,
And guide me through the dreadful shade.

Though in a bare and rugged way,
Through devious lonely wilds I stray,
Thy bounty shall my wants beguile;
The barren wilderness shall smile
With sudden greens and herbage crowned,
And streams shall murmur all around.

JOSEPH ADDISON.

*Thou art my Father, my God, and the
Rock of my salvation.*
                            Psalm lxxxix. 26.

GOD, my Strength and Fortitude,
  Of force I must love Thee;
Thou art my Castle and Defence
  In my necessity.

The Lord Jehovah is my God,
  My Rock, my Strength, my Wealth;
My strong Deliverer, and my Trust,
  My spirit's only Health.

In my distress I sought my God,
  I sought Jehovah's face:
My cry before Him came; He heard
  Out of His holy place.

The Lord descended from above,
  And bowed the heavens most high,
And underneath His feet He cast
  The darkness of the sky.

On cherub and on cherubim
  Full royally He rode,
And on the wings of mighty winds
  Came flying all abroad.

THE CREATOR.

The voice of God did thunder high,
    The lightnings answered keen;
The channels of the deep were bared,
    The world's foundation seen.

And so delivered He my soul.
    Who is a Rock but He?
He liveth—blessed be my Rock!
    My God exalted be!

THOMAS STERNHOLD.

Let everything that hath breath praise the Lord. Praise ye the Lord.
Psalm cl. 6.

HARK, my soul, how everything
    Strives to serve our bounteous King;
Each a double tribute pays,
    Sings its part, and then obeys.

Nature's chief and sweetest choir
Him with cheerful notes admire;
Chanting every day their lauds,
While the grove their song applauds.

Though their voices lower be,
Streams have too their melody;
Night and day they warbling run,
Never pause, but still sing on.

All the flowers that gild the spring
Hither their still music bring;
If Heaven bless them, thankful, they
Smell more sweet and look more gay.

Wake, for shame! my sluggish heart,
Wake, and gladly sing thy part;
Learn of birds, and springs, and flowers,
How to use thy nobler powers.

Call whole nature to thy aid,
Since 't was He whole nature made;
Join in one eternal song,
Who to one God all belong.

THE CREATOR.

Live for ever, glorious Lord!
Live, by all Thy works adored:
One in Three, and Three in One,
Thrice we bow to Thee alone!

       JOHN AUSTIN.

The earth is full of Thy riches, so is this great and wide sea.
       Psalm civ. 24, 25.

GOD! Thou knowest all our wants
 Long before we ask the boon;
Thy bounties ever go before:
 We seek—and, lo, the gift is done.

Thy tender love, O Father! God!
 Is boundless as Thy power:
Thou didst create the rolling sea,
 Thou dost paint the lily flower.

The lofty mountains Thou hast made,
 And all the stars in heaven;
All living things with life—and life
 To every blade of grass is given.

And Thou wilt deign to look on us,
 Humbly seeking help from Thee;
O! may we have Thy love on earth,
 Thy smile through all eternity!

       ANON.

THE CREATOR.

Praise ye the Lord, praise God in His sanctuary: praise Him in the firmament of His power.
Psalm cl. 1.

LET all the world in every corner sing,
  My God and King!

The heavens are not too high;
His praise may thither fly:
The earth is not too low;
His praises there may grow.

Let all the world in every corner sing,
  My God and King!

The Church with psalms must shout;
No door can keep them out:
But, above all, the heart
Must bear the longest part.

Let all the world in every corner sing,
  My God and King!

GEORGE HERBERT.

Serve the Lord with gladness: come before His presence with singing.
Psalm c. 2.

ALL people that on earth do dwell,
  Sing to the Lord with cheerful voice;
Him serve with fear, His praise forth tell;
  Come ye before Him and rejoice.

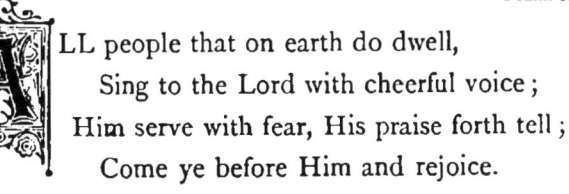

THE CREATOR.

Know ye, the Lord is God indeed;
    Without our aid He did us make;
We are His flock, He doth us feed,
    And for His sheep He doth us take.

O enter, then, His gates with praise,
    Approach with joy His courts unto;
Praise, laud, and bless His Name always,
    For it is seemly so to do.

For why? the Lord our God is good,
    His mercy is for ever sure;
His truth at all times firmly stood,
    And shall from age to age endure.

JOHN HOPKINS.

---

*The mercy of the Lord is from everlasting to everlasting
    upon them that fear Him.*
Psalm ciii. 17.

SERVANTS of God, in joyful lays,
    Sing ye the Lord Jehovah's praise;
His glorious Name let all adore,
    From age to age, for evermore.

Blest be that Name, supremely blest,
    From the sun's rising to its rest.
Above the heavens His power is known;
    Through all the earth His goodness shown.

THE CREATOR.

Who is like God?—so great, so high,
He bows Himself to view the sky;
And yet, with condescending grace,
Looks down upon the human race.

He hears the uncomplaining moan
Of those who sit and weep alone;
He lifts the mourner from the dust,
And saves the poor in Him that trust.

Servants of God, in joyful lays,
Sing ye the Lord Jehovah's praise;
His saving Name let all adore,
From age to age, for evermore.

JAMES MONTGOMERY.

They rest not day and night, saying, Holy, Holy, Holy, Lord God Almighty, which was, and is, and is to come.
Revelation, iv. 8.

HOLY, Holy, Holy! Lord God Almighty!
Early in the morning our song shall rise to Thee:
Holy, Holy, Holy! merciful and mighty;
God in Three Persons, blessèd Trinity!

Holy, Holy, Holy! all the saints adore Thee,
Casting down their golden crowns around the glassy sea;

THE CREATOR.

Cherubim and seraphim falling down before Thee,
Which wert, and art, and evermore shalt be.

Holy, Holy, Holy! though the darkness hide Thee,
Though the eye of sinful man Thy glory may not see,
Only Thou art Holy: there is none beside Thee
Perfect in power, in love, and purity.

Holy, Holy, Holy! Lord God Almighty!
All Thy works shall praise Thy Name, in earth, and sky, and sea:
Holy, Holy, Holy! merciful and mighty;
God in Three Persons, blessèd Trinity!

BISHOP REGINALD HEBER.

PRAYER

O Thou that hearest prayer, unto Thee shall all flesh come.
Psalm lxv. 2.

PRAYER is the soul's sincere desire,
    Uttered or unexpressed ;
The motion of a hidden fire
    That trembles in the breast.

PRAYER.

Prayer is the burthen of a sigh;
 The falling of a tear;
The upward glancing of an eye,
 When none but God is near.

Prayer is the simplest form of speech
 That infant lips can try;
Prayer, the sublimest strains that reach
 The Majesty on high.

Prayer is the contrite sinner's voice,
 Returning from his ways:
While angels in their songs rejoice,
 And cry, Behold, he prays!

Prayer is the Christian's vital breath,
 The Christian's native air;
His watchword at the gates of death:
 He enters Heaven with prayer.

The saints in prayer appear as one
 In word, and deed, and mind,
While with the Father and the Son
 Sweet fellowship they find.

Nor prayer is made on earth alone:
 The Holy Spirit pleads;
And Jesus, on the eternal throne,
 For sinners intercedes.

O Thou by whom we come to God,
  The Life, the Truth, the Way;
The path of prayer Thyself hast trod:
  Lord, teach us how to pray.

      JAMES MONTGOMERY.

Unto Thee, O Lord, do I lift up my soul.
      Psalm xxv. 1.

LORD, we come before Thee now;
  At Thy feet we humbly bow:
  O do not our suit disdain:
  Shall we seek Thee, Lord, in vain?

Lord, on Thee our souls depend;
  In compassion now descend:
  Fill our hearts with Thy rich grace;
  Tune our lips to sing Thy praise.

In Thine own appointed way,
  Now we seek Thee: here we stay:
  Lord, from hence we would not go,
  Till a blessing Thou bestow.

Send some message from Thy Word,
  That may joy and peace afford:

PRAYER.

Let Thy Spirit now impart
Full salvation to each heart.

Comfort those who weep and mourn;
Let the time of joy return;
Those that are cast down lift up;
Make them strong in faith and hope.

Grant that all may seek and find
Thee, a God supremely kind.
Heal the sick; the captive free;
Let us all rejoice in Thee.

WILLIAM HAMMOND.

By the things which He suffered.
Hebrews, v. 8.

SAVIOUR, when in dust to Thee
Low we bow the adoring knee;
When, repentant, to the skies
Scarce we lift our weeping eyes;
O, by all the pains and woe
Suffered once for man below,
Bending from Thy throne on high,
Hear our solemn Litany!

By Thy helpless infant years;
By Thy life of want and tears;
By Thy days of sore distress
In the savage wilderness;
By the dread mysterious hour
Of the insulting tempter's power;
Turn, O turn a favouring eye,
Hear our solemn Litany!

By the sacred griefs that wept
O'er the grave where Lazarus slept;
By the boding tears that flowed
Over Salem's loved abode;
By the anguished sigh that told
Treachery lurked within Thy fold!
From Thy seat above the sky,
Hear our solemn Litany!

By Thine hour of dire despair;
By Thine agony of prayer;
By the cross, the nail, the thorn,
Piercing spear, and torturing scorn;
By the gloom that veiled the skies
O'er the dreadful sacrifice ·
Listen to our humble cry,
Hear our solemn Litany!

By Thy deep expiring groan;
By the sad sepulchral stone;

PRAYER.

By the vault, whose dark abode
Held in vain the rising God;
O! from earth to Heaven restored,
Mighty re-ascended Lord,
Listen, listen to the cry
Of our solemn Litany.

SIR ROBERT GRANT.

Where two or three are gathered together in my Name, there am I in the midst of them.
Matthew, xviii. 20.

WHERE two or thee, with sweet accord,
 Obedient to their sovereign Lord,
 Meet to recount His acts of grace,
And offer solemn prayer and praise;

There, says the Saviour, will I be
 Amid that little company;
 To them unveil My smiling face,
And shed My glories round the place.

We meet at Thy command, dear Lord,
 Relying on Thy faithful word:
Now send Thy Spirit from above;
Now fill our hearts with heavenly love.

STENNETT.

The blood of Jesus Christ cleanseth us from all sin.

I. John, i. 7.

WHEN at Thy footstool, Lord, I bend,
    And plead with Thee for mercy there,
Think of the sinner's dying Friend,
    And for His sake receive my prayer.

O think not of my shame and guilt,
    My thousand stains of deepest dye;

Think of the blood which Jesus spilt,
    And let that blood my pardon buy.

Think, Lord, how I am still Thine own,
    The trembling creature of Thine hand;
Think how my heart to sin is prone,
    And what temptations round me stand.

O think upon Thy holy Word,
    And every plighted promise there;
How prayer should evermore be heard,
    And how Thy glory is to spare.

O think not of my doubts and fears,
    My strivings with Thy grace divine :
Think upon Jesus' woes and tears,
    And let His merits stand for mine.

Thine eye, Thine ear, they are not dull;
    Thine arm can never shortened be;
Behold me here; my heart is full;
    Behold, and spare, and succour me!

HENRY FRANCIS LYTE.

PRAYER.

What is thy petition? and it shall be granted thee.
— Esther, vii. 2.

COME, my soul, thy suit prepare;
Jesus loves to answer prayer:
He Himself has bid thee pray,
Therefore will not say thee nay.

Thou art coming to a King;
Large petitions with thee bring;
For His grace and power are such,
None can ever ask too much.

With my burden I begin :—
Lord, remove this load of sin;
Let Thy blood, for sinners spilt,
Set my conscience free from guilt.

Lord, I come to Thee for rest,
Take possession of my breast;
There Thy blood-bought right maintain,
And without a rival reign.

While I am a pilgrim here,
Let Thy love my spirit cheer;
As my Guide, my Guard, my Friend,
Lead me to my journey's end.

Show me what I have to do;
Every hour my strength renew.
Let me live a life of faith;
Let me die Thy people's death.

JOHN NEWTON.

O Thou that hearest prayer; unto Thee shall all flesh come.
Psalm lxv. 2.

WHEN in the hour of utmost need
   We know not where to look for aid,
   When days and nights of anxious thought
   Nor help nor counsel yet have brought

Then this our comfort is alone,
That we may meet before Thy throne,
And cry, O faithful God, to Thee
For rescue from our misery:

To Thee may raise our hearts and eyes.
Repenting sore, with bitter sighs,
And seek Thy pardon for our sin,
And respite from our griefs within.

For Thou hast promised graciously
So hear all those who cry to Thee,

PRAYER.

Through Him whose Name alone is great
Our Saviour and our Advocate.

And thus we come, O God, to-day,
And all our woes before Thee lay,
For tried, afflicted, lo! we stand,
Perils and foes on every hand.

Ah! hide not, for our sins, Thy face,
Absolve us through Thy boundless grace,
Be with us in our anguish still,
Free us at last from every ill.

That so with all our hearts may we
Once more with joy give thanks to Thee,
And walk obedient to Thy word,
And now and ever praise the Lord.

ANON.

God is our refuge and strength, a very present help in trouble.
Psalm xlvi. 1.

GOD of my life, to Thee I call,
Afflicted at Thy feet I fall;
When the great water-floods prevail,
Leave not my trembling heart to fail.

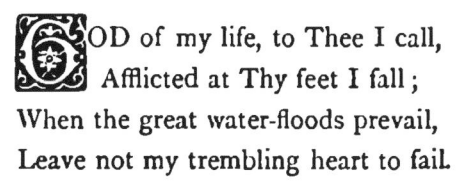

Friend of the friendless and the faint,
Where should I lodge my deep complaint?
Where but with Thee, whose open door
Invites the helpless and the poor?

Did ever mourner plead with Thee,
And Thou refuse that mourner's plea?
Does not the word still fixed remain,
That none shall seek Thy face in vain?

That were a grief I could not bear,
Didst Thou not hear and answer prayer;
But a prayer-hearing, answering God
Supports me under every load.

Fair is the lot that's cast for me;
I have an Advocate with Thee.
They whom the world caresses most,
Have no such privilege to boast.

Poor though I am, despised, forgot,
Yet God, my God, forgets me not.
And he is safe, and must succeed,
For whom the Lord vouchsafes to plead.

WILLIAM COWPER.

Let us therefore come boldly unto the throne of grace.
　　　　　　　　　　　　　　　　Hebrews, iv. 16.

BEHOLD the throne of grace,
　　The promise calls me near;
There Jesus shows a smiling face,
　　And waits to answer prayer.

That rich atoning blood,
　　Which sprinkled round I see,

Provides for those who come to God
  An all-prevailing plea.

My soul, ask what thou wilt,
  Thou canst not be too bold:
Since His own blood for thee He spilt,
  What else can He withhold?

Thine image, Lord, bestow,
  Thy presence and Thy love:
I ask to serve Thee here below,
  And reign with Thee above.

Teach me to live by faith;
  Conform my will to Thine;
Let me victorious be in death,
  And then in glory shine.

JOHN NEWTON.

I prayed unto the Lord my God, and made my confession.
Daniel, ix. 4.

LORD, when we bend before Thy throne,
  And our confessions pour,
Teach us to feel the sins we own,
  And hate what we deplore.

Our contrite spirits pitying see;
   True penitence impart;
Then let a healing ray from Thee
   Beam hope on every heart.

When we disclose our wants in prayer,
   May we our wills resign;
Let not a thought our bosom share
   Which is not wholly Thine.
Let faith each meek petition fill,
   And waft it to the skies;
And teach our hearts 't is goodness still
   That grants it or denies.

CARLISLE.

The eyes of the Lord are over the righteous, and His ears are open unto their prayers.
      I. Peter, iii. 12.

HAPPY the home when God is there,
   And love fills every breast;
Where one their wish, and one their prayer,
   And one their heavenly rest.
Happy the home where Jesus' name
   Is sweet to every ear;
Where children early lisp His fame,
   And parents hold Him dear.

Happy the home where prayer is heard,
    And praise is wont to rise;
Where parents love the sacred Word,
    And live but for the skies.
Lord, let us in our homes agree,
    This blessed peace to gain;
Unite our hearts in love to Thee,
    And love to all will reign.

ANON.

Jesus, thou Son of David, have mercy on me.
Luke, xviii. 38.

LORD, have mercy when we pray
  Strength to seek a better way;
When our wakening thoughts begin
  First to loathe our cherished sin;
When our weary spirits fail,
  And our aching brows are pale;
When our tears bedew Thy word,
  Then, O then, have mercy, Lord.

Lord, have mercy when we lie
  On the restless bed, and sigh;
Sigh for death, yet fear it still,
  From the thought of former ill;

When the dim advancing gloom
Tells us that our hour is come;
When is loosed the silver cord,
Then, O then, have mercy, Lord.

PRAYER.

Lord, have mercy when we know
First how vain this world below;
When our darker thoughts oppress,
Doubts perplex, and fears distress;
When the earliest gleam is given
Of Thy bright but distant Heaven;
Then Thy fostering grace afford,
Then, O then, have mercy, Lord.

HENRY HART MILMAN.

*The hand of our God is upon all them
for good that seek Him.*
Ezra, viii. 22.

LORD, another day is flown,
   And we, a feeble band,
Are met once more before Thy throne,
   To bless Thy fostering hand.

Thy heavenly grace to each impart;
   All evil far remove;
And shed abroad in every heart
   Thine everlasting love.

Our souls, obedient to Thy sway,
   In Christian bonds unite;
Let peace and love conclude the day,
   And hail the morning light.

Thus cleansed from sin, and wholly Thine,
    A flock by Jesus led,
The sun of righteousness shall shine
    In glory on our head.

O still restore our wandering feet,
    And still direct our way;
Till worlds shall fail, and faith shall greet
    The dawn of endless day.

H. KIRKE WHITE.

*Humble yourselves in the sight of the Lord,
  and He shall lift you up.*
James, iv. 10.

PRAYER is not heard through noisy sound,
    Solemn chaunt, nor organ pealing,
Nor all the glare that pomp can bring,
    Unless the heart is kneeling.

The highest flight of eloquence
    That lofty intellect may frame,
Can never form a prayer to meet
    The glory of God's holy Name.

'Tis from the humble heart alone,
    Bowed down in pious love and fear:

PRAYER.

The earnest prayer in Jesus' Name,
　　Our gracious God will deign to hear.

The wailing moan, the muttered cry,
　　The meek repentant sinner's tear,
The lisping of an infant's tongue,
　　Finds ready access to His ear.

Now, Father, fill our hearts with prayer,
　　Grant our sins be all forgiven,
That, with Thy help, we may prepare
　　And worthy be of Heaven.

There, holy, pure, and undefiled,
　　In light we may Thy face behold;
In seraph songs to sing Thy praise,
　　With music strung from harps of gold.

　　　　　　　　　　　　　　ANON.

Hear, O Lord, when I cry with my voice.
　　　　　　　　　　　Psalm xxvii. 7.

LORD, when I lift my voice to Thee,
　　To whom all praise belongs,
Thy justice and Thy love shall be
　　The subject of my songs.

Let wisdom o'er my heart preside,
  To lead my steps aright,
And make Thy perfect law my guide,
  Thy service my delight.

All sinful ways I will abhor,
  All wicked men forsake,
And only those who love Thy law,
  For my companions take.

Lord! that I may not go astray,
  Thy constant grace impart:
When wilt Thou come to point my way,
  And fix my roving heart?

WILLIAM HELEY BATHURST.

Give us this day our daily bread.
Matthew, vi. 11.

LORD of my life, whose tender care
  Hath led me on till now,
  Here lowly at the hour of prayer
Before Thy throne I bow;
I bless Thy gracious hand, and pray
Forgiveness for another day.

O! may I daily, hourly, strive
   In heavenly grace to grow;
To Thee and to Thy glory live,
   Dead else to all below;
Tread in the path my Saviour trod,
Though thorny, yet the path to God!

With prayer my humble praise I bring
   For mercies day by day;
Lord, teach my heart Thy love to sing,
   Lord, teach me how to pray!
All that I have, I am, to Thee
I offer through eternity!

ANON.

Come unto me, all ye that labour and are heavy laden, and I will give you rest.
Matthew, xi. 28.

APPROACH, my soul, the mercy-seat,
   Where Jesus answers prayer;
Then humbly fall before His feet,
   For none can perish there.

Thy promise is my only plea;
   With this I venture nigh.
Thou callest burdened souls to Thee,
   And such, O Lord, am I.

Bowed down beneath a load of sin,
By Satan sorely pressed,

By wars without and fears within,
   I come to Thee for rest.

Be Thou my shield and hiding-place,
   That, sheltered near Thy side,
I may my fierce accuser face,
   And tell him Thou hast died!

O wondrous love, to bleed and die,
   To bear the cross and shame,
That guilty sinners, such as I,
   Might plead Thy gracious Name!

                    JOHN NEWTON.

Lord, teach us to pray.
          Luke, xi. 1.

FATHER, when we bend the knee
   And supplicate before Thy throne;
When we raise our hearts to Thee,
   To make our poor petitions known;
O, let then our hearts' desire
   Be that which Thou canst well approve:
Touch our tongues with living fire,
   That words of life may ask Thy love.

That we may claim Thy promise still,
    All holy blessings from Thy hand;
Teach us, Lord, to do Thy will
    In all the ways Thou dost command.
Let our hearts be warm and true,
    Let our thoughts be pure and holy;
Make us, as Thy gifts renew,
    Thoughtful for the poor and lowly.

Fill our hearts with thankful love
    For blessings Thou dost aye bestow;
Fix our hearts on things above
    While we are dwelling here below.
Let us feel our Saviour's love
    To forgive all sins committed;
Guardian Angel, Heavenly Dove,
    Pardoning that which we've omitted.

ANON.

*Hear my prayer, O Lord, and let my
cry come unto Thee.*
Psalm cii. 1.

BLESSED Jesus, at Thy word
    We are gathered all to hear Thee;
Let our hearts and souls be stirred
    Now to seek and love and fear thee;
By Thy teachings, sweet and holy,
    Drawn from earth to love Thee solely.

All our knowledge, sense, and sight
   Lie in deepest darkness shrouded
Till Thy Spirit breaks our night,
   With the beams of truth unclouded;
Thou alone to God canst win us,
Thou must work all good within us.

Gracious Lord, Thyself impart!
   Light of light, from God proceeding,
Open Thou our ears and heart,
   Help us by Thy Spirit's pleading;
Hear the cry Thy people raises;
Hear, and bless our prayers and praises.

CATHERINE WINKWORTH,
FROM THE GERMAN OF CLAUSNITZER.

I will come into Thy house in the multitude of Thy mercy; and in Thy fear will I worship.
   Psalm v. 7.

WE would come before Thy throne,
   O God, with thankfulness;
We would kneel in humble prayer,
And ask Thee now to bless,
Keep, and prosper all our ways,
   To guard us with Thy might;

That every act, and each word,
    Find favour in Thy sight.

We would bow before Thy throne,
    And offer up our prayer
For those who will not pray to Thee,
    Nor seek to find a share
In the love which Jesus shows
    To those who do obey ;
Father, hear our humble prayer
    For those who will not pray.

Let us raise our voice again,
    O Father, unto Thee,
For those who lie in sickness,
    Or mental miserié :
Look in mercy on their state,
    And hear our voice to-day ;
O Jesus, hear our prayer now
    For those who cannot pray.
                              ANON.

Teach me Thy way, O Lord, and lead me in a plain path.
                                            Psalm xxvii. 11

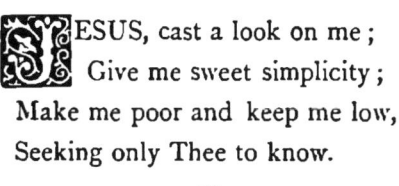

JESUS, cast a look on me ;
    Give me sweet simplicity ;
Make me poor and keep me low,
Seeking only Thee to know.

PRAYER.

Weanèd from my lordly self,
Weanèd from the miser's pelf,
Weanèd from the scorner's ways,
Weanèd from the lust of praise;

All that feeds my busy pride,
Cast it evermore aside;
Bid my will to Thine submit;
Lay me humbly at Thy feet.

Make me like a little child,
Of my strength and wisdom spoiled,
Seeing only in Thy light,
Walking only in Thy might;

Leaning on Thy loving breast,
Where a weary soul may rest;
Feeling well the peace of God
Flowing from Thy precious blood!

In this posture let me live,
And Hosannas daily give;
In this temper let me die,
And Hosannas ever cry!

JOHN BERRIDGE.

PRAYER.

Pray without ceasing.
I. Thessalonians, v. 17.

WHAT various hindrances we meet
In coming to the mercy-seat!
Yet who that knows the worth of prayer
But wishes to be often there?

Prayer makes the darkened cloud withdraw;
Prayer climbs the ladder Jacob saw;
Gives exercise to faith and love;
Brings every blessing from above.

Restraining prayer, we cease to fight;
Prayer makes the Christian's armour bright;
And Satan trembles when he sees
The weakest saint upon his knees.

While Moses stood with arms spread wide,
Success was found on Israel's side;
But when, through weariness, they failed,
That moment Amalek prevailed.

Have you no words? Ah! think again:
Words flow apace when you complain,
And fill your fellow-creature's ear
With the sad tale of all your care.

Were half the breath, thus vainly spent,
To Heaven in supplication sent,
Your cheerful song would oftener be,—
"Hear what the Lord hath done for me!"

WILLIAM COWPER.

When I saw Him, I fell at His feet as dead.
Revelation, i. 17.

GOD of mercy, God of might,
How should weak sinners bear the sight,
If, as Thy power is surely here,
Thine open glory should appear?

For now Thy people are allowed
To scale the mount, and pierce the cloud;
And faith may feed her eager view
With wonders Sinai never knew.

Fresh from the atoning sacrifice,
The world's Redeemer bleeding lies,
That man, His foe, for whom He bled,
May take Him for his daily bread.

O! agony of wavering thought,
When sinners first so near are brought:
It is my Maker—dare I stay?
My Saviour—dare I turn away?

PRAYER.

O Saviour, calm our troubled fears;
O Saviour, gather up our tears;
And let us in this solemn hour
Behold Thy glory, feel Thy power.

JOHN KEBLE.

Lord, teach us to pray.
Luke xi. 1.

LORD, teach us how to pray aright,
   With reverence and with fear:
Though dust and ashes in Thy sight,
   We may, we must draw near.

God of all grace, we come to Thee
   With broken, contrite hearts,
Give, what Thine eye delights to see,
   Truth in the inward parts.

Give deep humility; the sense
   Of godly sorrow give;
A strong, desiring confidence
   To hear Thy voice and live;

Faith in the only Sacrifice
   That can for sin atone;
To cast our hopes, to fix our eyes,
   On Christ, on Christ alone;

PRAYER.

Patience to watch and wait and weep,
    Though mercy long delay;
Courage, our fainting souls to keep,
    And trust Thee, though Thou slay.

Give these,—and then Thy will be done;
    Thus strengthened with all might,
We, by Thy Spirit, through Thy Son,
    Shall pray, and pray aright.

JAMES MONTGOMERY.

THE LORD'S DAY

Jesus was risen early the first day of the week.
Mark, xvi. 9.

HAIL, morning known among the blest!
    Morning of hope and joy and love;
Of heavenly peace and holy rest;
Pledge of the endless rest above.

Blessed be the Father of our Lord,
    Who from the dead hath brought His Son:

THE LORD'S DAY.

Hope to the lost was then restored,
   And everlasting glory won.

Scarce morning twilight had begun
   To chase the shades of night away,
When Christ arose—unsetting Sun—
   The dawn of joy's eternal day.

Mercy looked down with smiling eye
   When our Immanuel left the dead;
Faith marked His bright ascent on high,
   And Hope with gladness raised her head.

Descend, O Spirit of the Lord!
   Thy fire to every bosom bring;
Then shall our ardent hearts accord,
   And teach our lips God's praise to sing.

DR. WARDLAW.

Let me not be ashamed, O Lord; for I have called upon Thee.
Psalm xxxi. 17.

TO Thy temple I repair;
   Lord, I love to worship there,
When, within the veil, I meet
Christ before the mercy-seat.

THE LORD'S DAY.

Thou, through Him art reconciled,
I, through Him became Thy child;
Abba, Father! give me grace
In Thy courts to seek Thy face.

While Thy glorious praise is sung,
Touch my lips, unloose my tongue,
That my joyful soul may bless
Thee, the Lord my righteousness.

While the prayers of saints ascend,
God of love, to mine attend;
Hear me, for Thy Spirit pleads;
Hear, for Jesus intercedes.

While I hearken to Thy law,
Fill my soul with humble awe,
Till Thy Gospel bring to me
Life and immortality.

While Thy ministers proclaim
Peace and pardon in Thy Name,
Through their voice, by faith, may I
Hear Thee speaking from the sky.

From Thy house when I return,
May my heart within me burn,
And at evening let me say,—
I have walked with God to-day.

JAMES MONTGOMERY

THE LORD'S DAY.

Stand up and bless the Lord your God.
Nehemiah, ix. 5.

STAND up and bless the Lord,
  Ye people of His choice;
Stand up and bless the Lord your God,
  With heart and soul and voice.

Though high above all praise,
  Above all blessing high,
Who would not fear His holy Name,
  And laud and magnify?

O for the living flame
  From His own altar brought!
To touch our lips, our minds inspire,
  And wing to Heaven our thought!

There with benign regard
  Our hymns He deigns to hear:
Though unrevealed to mortal sense,
  The spirit feels Him near.

God is our strength and song,
  And His salvation ours;
Then be His love in Christ proclaimed
  With all our ransomed powers.

THE LORD'S DAY.

  Stand up and bless the Lord;
   The Lord your God adore:
  Stand up and bless His glorious Name,
   Henceforth for evermore.

      JAMES MONTGOMERY

My soul longeth, yea, even fainteth, for the courts of the Lord.
       Psalm lxxxiv. 2.

LORD of the Sabbath, hear our vows,
 On this Thy day, in this Thy house;
Accept, as grateful sacrifice,
The songs which from the desert rise.

Thine earthly Sabbaths, Lord, we love;
But there's a nobler rest above:
To that our labouring souls aspire,
With ardent hope and strong desire.

THE LORD'S DAY.

No more fatigue, no more distress;
No guilt the conscience to oppress;
No groans to mingle with the songs
Resounding from immortal tongues.

No rude alarms of raging foes,
No cares to break the long repose;
No midnight shade, no clouded sun
But sacred, high, eternal noon.

O long-expected day, begin!
Dawn on these realms of woe and sin.
Fain would we leave this weary road,
And sleep in death to rest with God.

PHILIP DODDRIDGE.

The Son of Man is Lord also of the Sabbath.
Mark, ii. 28.

DAY most calm, most bright!
  The fruit of this, the next world's bud;
  The endorsement of supreme delight,
Writ by a Friend, and with His blood;
The couch of time; care's balm and bay;
The week were dark, but for thy light;
  Thy torch doth show the way.

THE LORD'S DAY.

   The other days and thou
Make up one man; whose face thou
Knocking at Heaven with thy brow:
The working days are the back part;
The burden of the week lies there,
Making the whole to stoop and bow,
   Till Thy release appear.

   Man had straight forward gone
To endless death; but thou dost pull
And turn us round to look on One,
Whom, if we were not very dull,
We could not choose but look on still,
Since there is no place so alone,
   The which He doth not fill.

   Sundays the pillars are
On which Heav'n's palace archèd lies:
The other days fill up the spare
And hollow room with vanities:
They are the fruitful beds and borders
Of God's rich garden; that is bare
   Which parts their ranks and orders.

   The Sundays of man's life,
Threaded together on time's string,
Make bracelets to adorn the wife
Of the eternal glorious King:
On Sunday Heaven's gate stands ope;

THE LORD'S DAY.

Blessings are plentiful and rife,
  More plentiful than hope.

This day my Saviour rose,
And did enclose this light for His;
That, as each beast his manger knows,
Man might not of his fodder miss:
Christ hath took in this piece of ground,
And made a garden there, for those
  Who want herbs for their wound.

The rest of our Creation
Our great Redeemer did remove
With the same shake, which at His passion
Did th' earth, and all things with it, move:
As Samson bore the doors away,
Christ's hands, though nailed, wrought our salvation,
  And did unhinge that day.

The brightness of that day
We sullied by our foul offence;
Wherefore that robe we cast away.
Having a new at His expense,
Whose drops of blood paid the full price
That was required to make us gay,
  And fit for Paradise.

GEORGE HERBERT.

*I was glad when they said, Let us go into the
house of the Lord.*
                                    Psalm cxxii. 1.

'T is the Sabbath morning now,
  And we would come awhile apart,
    From the busy world away,
    From the toil of every day,
    And before our Maker lay
  The sacred longings of our heart.

We come into Thy house, O God,
  Humble thoughts our hearts possessing;
    At Thy throne low bending, there
    Casting every worldly care
    On Christ, who doth our sorrows share,
  And to meekly ask Thy blessing.

We come to read Thy holy book,
  To read Thy messages of love;
    How Thou wilt reward the good,
    Give them raiment, give them food:
    Blessings, more than understood,
With boundless mercies interwove.

We come to give Thee thanks and praise
For all the blessings Thou hast given;
    For the love our Saviour bore,
    Granting succour evermore;

THE LORD'S DAY.

O! we would now His Name adore
In shouts of joyful praise to Heaven.

Now we would lowly bend the knee,
And ask for strength in coming time,—
   Strength to battle in the fight,
   Light to see the wrong from right,
   Fearless, trusting in Thy might
To shelter us in every clime.

Now, Father, fill us with Thy love,
This holy day, the chief of days,
   From the world to stand apart:
   Let love for others fill our heart;
   Lead our footsteps where Thou art,
Where we may pray, and sing Thy praise.

ANON.

And from one Sabbath to another shall all flesh come to worship.
Isaiah, lxvi. 23.

THE festal morn, my God, is come,
  That calls me to Thy hallowed dome,
    Thy presence to adore;
  My feet the summons shall attend,
  With willing steps Thy courts ascend,
    And tread the sacred floor.

What joy while thus I view the day
That warns my thirsting soul away!
What transports fill my breast!

THE LORD'S DAY.

For, lo ! my great Redeemer's power
Unfolds the everlasting door,
   And leads me to His rest.

E'en now, to my expecting eyes,
The heaven-built towers of Salem rise ;
   E'en now with glad survey
I view her mansions, that contain
The angelic forms, an awful train,
   And shine with cloudless day.

Hither, from earth's remotest end,
Lo ! the redeemed of God ascend,
   Their tribute hither bring ;
Here crowned with everlasting joy,
In hymns of praise their tongues employ,
   And hail the Immortal King.

JAMES MERRICK.

They shall hallow my Sabbaths.
Ezekiel, xliv. 24.

THOU who art enthroned above,
  Thou by whom we live and move,
O how sweet, with joyful tongue,
To proclaim thy praise in song !

THE LORD'S DAY.

When the morning paints the skies,
When the sparkling stars arise,
All Thy favours to rehearse,
And give thanks in grateful verse.

Sweet the day of sacred rest,
When devotion fills the breast,
When we dwell within Thy house,
Hear Thy word and pay our vows:
Notes to Heaven's high mansions raise;
Fill its courts with joyful praise;
With repeated hymns proclaim
Great Jehovah's awful Name.

From Thy works our joys arise,
O Thou only good and wise!
Who Thy wonders can express?
All Thy thoughts are fathomless.
Warm our hearts with sacred fire;
Grateful fervours still inspire;
All our powers with all their might,
Ever in Thy praise unite.

SANDYS.

He shall feed His flock like a shepherd.
Isaiah, xl. 11.

MY Lord, my love was crucified,
    He all the pains did bear;
But in the sweetness of His rest
    He makes His servants share.
How sweetly rest Thy saints above
    Which in Thy bosom lie!
The Church below doth rest in hope
    Of that felicity.

Thou, Lord, who daily feed'st Thy sheep,
    Mak'st them a weekly feast;
Thy flocks meet in their several folds
    Upon this day of rest:
Welcome and dear unto my soul
    Are these sweet feasts of love;

THE LORD'S DAY.

But what a Sabbath shall I keep
   When I shall rest above!

I bless Thy wise and wondrous love,
   Which binds us to be free;
Which makes us leave our earthly snares,
   That we may come to Thee.
I come, I wait, I hear, I pray!
   Thy footsteps, Lord, I trace!
I sing to think this is the way
   Unto my Saviour's face!

JOHN MASON.

They sang praises with gladness.
II. Chronicles, xxix. 30.

COME, Thou Almighty King,
   Help us Thy Name to sing,
     Help us to praise;
Father all-glorious,
O'er all victorious,
Come and reign over us,
   Ancient of days.

Jesus, our Lord, arise;
Scatter our enemies,

THE LORD'S DAY.

And make them fall;
Let thine almighty aid
Our sure defence be made,
Our souls on Thee be stayed :
　Lord, hear our call.

Come, Thou Incarnate Word,
Gird on Thy mighty sword,
　Our prayer attend ;
Come, and Thy people bless,
And give Thy Word success ;
Spirit of holiness,
　On us descend.

Come, holy Comforter,
Thy sacred witness bear,
　In this glad hour :
Thou, who almighty art,
Now rule in every heart,
And ne'er from us depart,
　Spirit of power !

To the Great One in Three
Eternal praises be,
　Hence evermore :
His sovereign majesty,
May we in glory see,
And to eternity
　Love and adore.

MARTIN MADAN.

THE LORD'S DAY.

Where two or three are gathered together in my Name, there am I in the midst of them.
Matthew, xviii. 20.

JESUS, where'er Thy people meet,
There they behold Thy mercy-seat;
Where'er they seek Thee, Thou art found,
And every place is hallowed ground.

For Thou, within no walls confined,
Inhabitest the humble mind;
Such ever bring Thee where they come,
And going, take Thee to their home.

Dear Shepherd of Thy chosen few,
Thy former mercies here renew;
Here to our waiting hearts proclaim
The sweetness of Thy saving Name.

Here may we prove the power of prayer
To strengthen faith and sweeten care,
To teach our faint desires to rise,
And bring all Heaven before our eyes.

Behold, at Thy commanding word,
We stretch the curtain and the cord;
Come Thou, and fill this wider space,
And bless us with a large increase.

THE LORD'S DAY.

Lord, we are few, but Thou art near;
Nor short Thine arm, nor deaf Thine ear;
O rend the heavens, come quickly down,
And make a thousand hearts Thine own!

WILLIAM COWPER.

The Son of Man is Lord also of the Sabbath.

Mark, ii. 28.

WELCOME, sweet day of rest,
   That saw the Lord arise;
Welcome to this reviving breast
   And these rejoicing eyes.

The King Himself comes near,
   And feasts His saints to-day;
Here we may sit, and see Him here,
   And love and praise and pray.

One day amidst the place
   Where my dear Lord hath been,
Is sweeter than ten thousand days
   Of pleasurable sin.

My willing soul would stay
   In such a frame as this,
And sit and sing herself away
   To everlasting bliss.

ISAAC WATTS.

In the midst of the church will I sing praise unto Thee.
Hebrews, ii. 12.

SWEET is the solemn voice that calls
　　The Christian to the house of prayer:
　　I love to stand within its walls,
For Thou, O Lord, art present there.

I love to tread the hallowed courts
Where two or three for worship meet;
For thither Christ Himself resorts,
And makes the little band complete.

THE LORD'S DAY.

'T is sweet to raise the common song,
To join in holy praise and love,
And imitate the blessed throng
That mingle hearts and songs above.

Within these walls may peace abound,
May all our hearts in one agree:
Where brethren meet, where Christ is found,
May peace and concord ever be.

HENRY FRANCIS LYTE.

*In His temple doth every one speak
of His glory.*
Psalm xxix. 9.

THE day of rest once more comes round,
    A day to all believers dear;
The silver trumpets seem to sound
    That call the tribes of Israel near.
      Ye people all,
      Obey the call,
And in Jehovah's courts appear.

Obedient to Thy summons, Lord,
    We to Thy sanctuary come;
Thy gracious presence here afford,
    And send Thy people joyful home.

THE LORD'S DAY.

    Of Thee, our King,
      O may we sing,
And none with such a theme be dumb!

O hasten, Lord, the day when those
  Who know Thee here, shall see Thy face;
When suffering shall for ever close,
  And they shall reach their destined place;
    Then shall they rest
    Supremely blest,
Eternal debtors to Thy grace!

THOMAS KELLY.

In every place incense shall be offered unto my Name.
Malachi, i. 11.

THOU to whom, in ancient time,
  The lyre of Hebrew bards was strung;
Whom kings adored in song sublime,
  And prophets praised with glowing tongue;

Not now on Zion's height alone,
  Thy favoured worshippers may dwell,
Nor where at sultry noon Thy Son
  Sat, weary, by the patriarch's well:

THE LORD'S DAY.

From every place below the skies
    The grateful song, the fervent prayer,
The incense of the heart, may rise
    To Heaven, and find acceptance there.

To Thee shall age with snowy hair,
    And strength and beauty, bend the knee;
And childhood lisp, with reverent air,
    Its praises and its prayers to Thee.

O Thou to whom, in ancient time,
    The lyre of prophet-bards was strung,—
To Thee, at last, in every clime
    Shall temples rise, and praise be sung.

                                   PIERPOINT.

The Sabbath was made for man.
                                Mark, ii. 27

HOW welcome to the saints, when press'd
    With six days' noise and care and toil,
Is the returning day of rest,
    Which hides them from the world awhile!

Now, from the throng withdrawn away,
    They seem to breathe a different air:
Composed and softened by the day,
    All things another aspect wear.

With joy they hasten to the place
Where they their Saviour oft have met;
And while they feast upon His grace,
Their burdens and their griefs forget.

We thank Thee for Thy day, O Lord:
Here we Thy promised presence seek:
Open Thy hand with blessings stored,
And give us manna for the week.

JOHN NEWTON.

Surely the Lord is in this place.
Genesis, xxviii. 16.

O! God is here! Let us adore,
  And own, how dreadful is this place!
Let all within us feel His power
  And silent bow before His face.
Who know His power, His grace who prove,
Serve Him with awe, with reverence love.

Lo! God is here! Him day and night
  Th' united choirs of angels sing:
To Him, enthroned above all height,
  Heaven's hosts their noblest praises bring:
Disdain not, Lord, our meaner song,
Who praise Thee with a stammering tongue!

THE LORD'S DAY.

Gladly the toys of earth we leave,
   Wealth, pleasure, fame, for Thee alone:
To Thee our will, soul, flesh, we give;
   O take, O seal them for Thine own.
Thou art the God! Thou art the Lord!
Be Thou by all Thy works adored.

Being of beings, may our praise
   Thy courts with grateful fragrance fill;
Still may we stand before Thy face,
   Still hear and do Thy sovereign will;
To Thee may all our thoughts arise,
Ceaseless, accepted sacrifice!

In Thee we move; all things of Thee
   Are full, Thou source and life of all!
Thou vast, unfathomable Sea!
   Fall prostrate, lost in wonder fall,
Ye sons of men; for God is Man!
All may we lose, so Thee we gain!

As flowers their opening leaves display,
   And glad drink in the solar fire,
So may we catch Thy every ray,
   So may Thy influence us inspire;
Thou Beam of the eternal Beam!
Thou purging Fire! thou quickening Flame!

                      JOHN WESLEY.
                  FROM GERHARD TERSTEEGEN.

Blessed is the man that keepeth the Sabbath from polluting it.
                                                Isaiah, lvi 2

ERE another Sabbath's close,
Ere again we seek repose,
Lord! our song ascends to Thee;
At Thy feet we bow the knee.

THE LORD'S DAY.

For the mercies of the day,
For this rest upon our way,
Thanks to Thee alone be given,
Lord of earth, and King of Heaven!

Cold our services have been;
Mingled every prayer with sin;
But Thou canst and will forgive:
By Thy grace alone we live.

Whilst this thorny path we tread,
May Thy love our footsteps lead!
When our journey here is past,
May we rest with Thee at last!

Let these earthly Sabbaths prove
Foretastes of our joys above;
While their steps Thy pilgrims bend
To the rest which knows no end.

GERARD THOMAS NOEL.

Speak, Lord; for Thy servant heareth.
I. Samuel, iii. 9.

IN Thy Name, O Lord, assembling,
    We, Thy people, now draw near;
Teach us to rejoice with trembling,
    Speak, and let Thy servants hear,—

THE LORD'S DAY.

  Hear with meekness;
 Hear Thy word with godly fear.

While our days on earth are lengthened,
 May we give them, Lord, to Thee;
Cheered by hope, and daily strengthened,
 May we run, nor weary be,
  Till Thy glory
 Without cloud in Heaven we see.

There in worship purer, sweeter,
 All Thy people shall adore;
Tasting of enjoyment greater
 Than they could conceive before:
  Full enjoyment;
 Full, unmixed for evermore.

THOMAS KELLY.

And God blessed the seventh day and sanctified it; because that in it He had rested from all His work.
Genesis, ii. 3.

AGAIN returns the day of holy rest
 Which, when He made the world, Jehovah blest;
When, like His own, He bade our labours cease,
 And all be piety, and all be peace.

THE LORD'S DAY.

Let us devote this consecrated day
To learn His will, and all we learn obey;
In pure religion's hallowed duties share,
And join in penitence, and join in prayer.

So shall the God of mercy, pleased, receive
That only tribute man has power to give;
So shall He hear, while fervently we raise
Our choral harmony in hymns of praise.

Father of Heaven, in whom our hopes confide,
Whose power defends us and whose precepts guide;
In life our Guardian and in death our Friend,
Glory supreme be Thine till time shall end.

JOHN MASON.

Blessed is the people that know the joyful sound.
Psalm lxxxix. 15.

HOW blest the congregation
   Who the Gospel know and prize!
Joyful tidings of salvation
   Brought by Jesus from the skies:
     He is near them,
   Knows their wants and hears their cries.

In His Name rejoicing ever,
   Walking in His light and love,

And foretasting in His favour
  Something here of bliss above;
    Happy people!
  Who shall harm them? what shall move?

By His righteousness exalted,
  On from strength to strength they go;
By ten thousand ills assaulted,
  Yet preserved from every foe;
    On to glory,
  Safe they speed through all below.

God will keep His own anointed;
  Nought shall harm them, none condemn:
All their trials are appointed,
  All must work for good to them:
    All shall help them
  To their heavenly diadem.

HENRY FRANCIS LYTE.

Blessed is the man that keepeth the Sabbath from polluting it.
Isaiah, lvi. 2.

WELCOME, sacred day of rest!
  Sweet repose from worldly care;
  Day above all days the best,
  When our souls for Heaven prepare;

THE LORD'S DAY.

Day when our Redeemer rose
Victor o'er the hosts of hell.
Thus He vanquished all our foes :
Let our lips His glories tell.

Gracious Lord, we love this day,
When we hear Thy holy Word,
When we sing Thy praise and pray :
Earth can no such joys afford.
But a better rest remains,
Heavenly Sabbaths, happier days ;
Rest from sin and rest from pains ;
Endless joys and endless praise.

Call the Sabbath a delight, the holy of the Lord.
Isaiah, lviii. 13.

AWAKE, ye saints, awake !
  And hail this sacred day ;
In loftiest songs of praise
  Your joyful homage pay :
Come, bless the day that God hath blest,
The type of Heaven's eternal rest.

On this auspicious morn
  The Lord of Life arose ;
He burst the bars of death,
  And vanquished all our foes ;

And now He pleads our cause above,
And reaps the fruit of all His love.

All hail, triumphant Lord!
 Heaven with Hosannas rings,
And earth, in humbler strains,
 Thy praise responsive sings,—
Worthy the Lamb that once was slain,
Through endless years to live and reign.

Great King! gird on Thy sword,
 Ascend Thy conquering car,
While justice, power, and love
 Maintain the glorious war:
This day let sinners own Thy sway,
And rebels cast their arms away.

HENRY FRANCIS LYTE.

Mine house shall be called an house of prayer for all people.
Isaiah, lvi. 7.

GREAT Father of mankind,
 We bless that wondrous grace
 Which could for Gentiles find
 Within Thy courts a place.
  How kind the care
   Our God displays,
  For us to raise
  A house of prayer!

THE LORD'S DAY.

Though once estranged far,
We now approach the throne;
For Jesus brings us near,
And makes our cause His own:
  Strangers no more,
    To Thee we come,
    And find our home
  And rest secure.

To Thee our souls we join,
And love Thy sacred Name;
No more our own, but Thine,
We triumph in Thy claim:
  Our Father-King,
    Thy covenant grace
    Our souls embrace,
  Thy titles sing.

May all the nations throng
To worship in Thy house,
And Thou attend the song,
And smile upon their vows;
  Indulgent still,
    Till earth conspire
    To join the choir
  On Zion's hill.

PHILIP DODDRIDGE.

THE LORD'S DAY.

For the Lord Jesus Christ's sake, and for the love of the Spirit.
Romans, xv. 30.

OF Thy love some gracious token
    Grant us, Lord, before we go;
Bless Thy word which has been spoken;
    Life and peace on all bestow!
When we join the world again,
Let our hearts with Thee remain:
    O direct us
    And protect us,
Till we gain the heavenly shore,
Where Thy people want no more!

THOMAS KELLY.

Hast thou faith? have it to thyself before God.
Romans, xiv. 22.

Behold what manner of love the Father hath bestowed upon us, that we should be called the sons of God.
I. John, iii. 1.

In Thy presence is fulness of joy; at Thy right hand there are pleasures for evermore.
Psalm xvi. 11.

Why art thou cast down, O my soul? Hope thou in God.
Psalm xlii. 5.

FAITH

Lovest thou me?
John, xxi. 15.

HARK, my soul! it is the Lord,
'T is thy Saviour, hear His word:
Jesus speaks, and speaks to thee:
"Say, poor sinner, lov'st thou me?

I delivered thee when bound,
And, when bleeding, healed thy wound;
Sought thee wandering, set thee right,
Turned thy darkness into light.

" Can a woman's tender care
Cease toward the child she bare?
Yes, she may forgetful be
Yet will I remember thee.
Mine is an unchanging love.
Higher than the heights above.
Deeper than the depths beneath.
Free and faithful, strong as death.

" Thou shalt see my glory soon,
When the work of grace is done;
Partner of my throne shalt be:
Say, poor sinner, lov'st thou me?"
Lord! it is my chief complaint
That my love is weak and faint;
Yet I love Thee and adore,
O! for grace to love Thee more!

WILLIAM COWPER.

Though your sins be as scarlet, they shall be as white as snow.
Isaiah, i. 18.

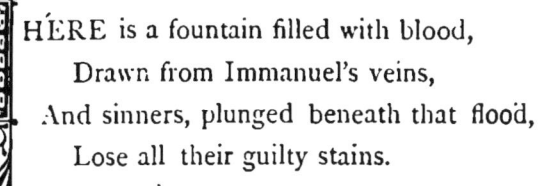

THERE is a fountain filled with blood,
 Drawn from Immanuel's veins,
And sinners, plunged beneath that flood,
 Lose all their guilty stains.

The dying thief rejoiced to see
 That fountain in his day;
And there have I, as vile as he,
 Washed all my sins away.

Dear dying Lamb, Thy precious blood
 Shall never lose its power
Till all the ransomed Church of God
 Be saved, to sin no more.

E'er since, by faith, I saw the stream
 Thy flowing wounds supply,
Redeeming love has been my theme,
 And shall be till I die.

Then in a nobler, sweeter song,
 I'll sing Thy power to save,
When this poor lisping stamm'ring tongue
 Lies silent in the grave.

FAITH.

Lord, I believe thou hast prepared
   (Unworthy though I be)
For me a blood-bought free reward,
   A golden harp for me:

'T is strung and tuned for endless years,
   And formed by power divine,
To sound, in God the Father's ears,
   No other name but Thine.

WILLIAM COWPER.

My grace is sufficient for thee.
II. Corinthians, xii. 9.

JESU, lover of my soul,
   Let me to Thy bosom fly,
While the nearer waters roll,
   While the tempest still is high!
Hide me, O my Saviour, hide,
   Till the storm of life is past,
Safe into the haven guide;
   O receive my soul at last!

Other refuge have I none;
   Hangs my helpless soul on Thee;
Leave, ah! leave me not alone,
   Still support and comfort me!

All my trust on Thee is stayed,
    All my help from Thee I bring:
Cover my defenceless head
    With the shadow of Thy wing!

FAITH.

Wilt Thou not regard my call?
   Wilt Thou not accept my prayer?
Lo! I sink, I faint, I fall!
   Lo! on Thee I cast my care!
Reach me out Thy gracious hand!
   While I of Thy strength receive,
Hoping against hope I stand,
   Dying, and behold I live!

Thou, O Christ, art all I want;
   More than all in Thee I find:
Raise the fallen, cheer the faint,
   Heal the sick, and lead the blind!
Just and holy is Thy Name;
   I am all unrighteousness;
False and full of sin I am,
   Thou art full of truth and grace.

Plenteous grace with Thee is found,
   Grace to cover all my sin:
Let the healing streams abound;
   Make and keep me pure within!
Thou of Life the Fountain art,
   Freely let me take of Thee;
Spring Thou up within my heart!
   Rise to all eternity!

                           CHARLES WESLEY.

FAITH.

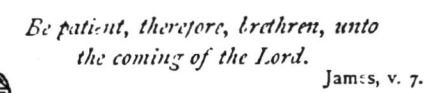

> *Be patient, therefore, brethren, unto
> the coming of the Lord.*
> James, v. 7.

WHEN languor and disease invade
   This trembling house of clay,
'T is sweet to look beyond the cage,
   And long to fly away

Sweet to look inward, and attend
   The whispers of His love;
Sweet to look upward to the place
   Where Jesus pleads above.

Sweet to look back, and see my name
   In life's fair book set down;
Sweet to look forward, and behold
   Eternal joys my own.

Sweet to reflect, how grace divine
   My sins on Jesus laid;
Sweet to remember that His blood
   My debt of sufferings paid.

Sweet on His righteousness to stand
   Which saves from second death;
Sweet to experience, day by day,
   His Spirit's quickening breath.

Sweet on His faithfulness to rest
   Whose love can never end;
Sweet on His covenant of grace
   For all things to depend.

Sweet, in the confidence of faith,
   To trust His firm decrees;
Sweet to lie passive in His hand,
   And know no will but His.

Sweet to rejoice in lively hope,
   That, when my change shall come,
Angels will hover round my bed,
   And waft my spirit home.

There shall my disimprisoned soul
   Behold Him and adore;
Be with His likeness satisfied,
   And grieve and sin no more.

Shall see Him wear that very flesh
   On which my guilt was lain;
His love intense, His merit fresh,
   As though but newly slain.

Soon, too, my slumbering dust shall hear
   The trumpet's quickening sound;
And, by my Saviour's power rebuilt,
   At His right hand be found.

These eyes shall see Him in that day,
    The God that died for me!
And all my rising bones shall say,
    Lord, who is like to Thee?

If such the views which grace unfolds,
    Weak as it is below,
What raptures must the Church above
    In Jesus' presence know!

If such the sweetness of the streams,
    What must the fountain be?
Where saints and angels draw their bliss
    Immediately from Thee!

O! may the unction of these truths
    For ever with me stay,
Till, from her sinful cage dismissed,
    My spirit flies away.

AUGUSTUS M. TOPLADY.

He is able to save them to the uttermost.
Hebrews, vii. 25.

LEAVE all to God,
    Forsaken one, and stay thy tears;
For the Highest knows thy pain,
    Sees thy sufferings and thy fears:
Thou shalt not wait His help in vain,
    Leave all to God.

FAITH.

Be still and trust!
For His strokes are strokes of love,
  Thou must for thy profit bear;
He thy filial fear would move:
  Trust thy Father's loving care,
    Be still and trust!

Know, God is near!
Though thou think Him far away,
  Though His mercy long have slept,
He will come and not delay,
  When His child enough hath wept,
    For God is near!

O teach Him not
When and how to hear thy prayers;
  Never doth our God forget:
He the cross who longest bears,
  Finds his sorrows' bounds are set;
    Then teach Him not.

If thou love Him,
Walking truly in His ways,
  Then no trouble, cross, or death,
E'er shall silence faith and praise:
  All things serve thee here beneath,
    If thou love God!

CATHERINE WINKWORTH.
TRANSLATED FROM ANTON ULRICH,
DUKE OF BRUNSWICK.

An advocate with the Father.
I. John, ii. 1.

THOU, the contrite sinners' Friend,
Who, loving, lov'st them to the end,
On this alone my hopes depend,
That Thou wilt plead for me.

When, weary in the Christian race,
Far off appears my resting-place,
And fainting I mistrust Thy grace,
Then, Saviour, plead for me!

When I have erred and gone astray,
Afar from Thine and Wisdom's way,
And see no glimmering guiding ray,
   Still, Saviour, plead for me!

When Satan, by my sins made bold,
Strives from Thy Cross to loose my hold,
Then with Thy pitying arms enfold,
   And plead, O, plead for me!

And when my dying hour draws near,
Darkened with anguish, guilt, and fear,
Then to my fainting sight appear,
   Pleading in Heaven for me!

When the full light of heavenly day
Reveals my sin in dread array,
Say Thou hast washed them all away;
   O! say Thou plead'st for me!

CHARLOTTE ELLIOTT.

Faith toward our Lord Jesus Christ.
Acts, xx. 21.

FAITH! 'tis a precious grace,
   Where'er it is bestowed;
It boasts of a celestial birth
   And is the gift of God.

Jesus it owns a King,
    An all-atoning Priest :
It claims no merit of its own,
    But looks for all in Christ.

On Him it safely leans
    In times of deep distress ;
Flies to the fountain of His blood,
    And trusts His righteousness.

All through the wilderness
    It is our strength and stay ;
Nor can we miss the heavenly road
    While faith directs our way.

Since 't is Thy work alone,
    And that divinely free,
Lord, send the Spirit of Thy Son,
    To work that faith in me.

                    BENJAMIN BEDDOME.

Lo, we have left all and have followed Thee.
                                Mark, x. 28.

JESUS, I my cross have taken,
    All to leave, and follow Thee ;
Destitute, despised, forsaken,
Thou, from hence, my all shalt be.

FAITH.

Perish every fond ambition,
    All I 've sought, or hoped, or known;
Yet how rich is my condition!
    God and Heaven are still my own!

Let the world despise and leave me,
    They have left my Saviour too;
Human hearts and looks deceive me:
    Thou art not, like them, untrue;
And, while Thou shalt smile upon me,
    God of wisdom, love, and might,
Foes may hate and friends may shun me;
    Show Thy face, and all is bright!

Go, then, earthly fame and treasure!
    Come, disaster, scorn, and pain!
In Thy service, pain is pleasure,
    With Thy favour, loss is gain!
I have called Thee Abba, Father!
    I have stayed my heart on Thee!
Storms may howl and clouds may gather,
    All must work for good to me.

Man may trouble and distress me,
    'T will but drive me to Thy breast;
Life with trials hard may press me,
    Heaven will bring me sweeter rest!
O! 't is not in grief to harm me,
    While Thy love is left to me!

FAITH.

O! 't were not in joy to charm me,
    Were that joy unmixed with Thee!

Take, my soul, thy full salvation!
    Rise o'er sin, and fear, and care;
Joy to find, in every station,
    Something still to do or bear:
Think what Spirit dwells within thee!
    What a Father's smile is thine!
What a Saviour died to win thee!
    Child of Heaven, shouldst thou repine?

Haste, then, on from grace to glory,
    Armed by faith and winged by prayer;
Heaven's eternal day's before thee,
    God's own hand shall guide thee there!
Soon shall close thy earthly mission,
    Swift shall pass thy pilgrim days;
Hope soon change to glad fruition,
    Faith to sight, and prayer to praise!

                    HENRY FRANCIS LYTE.

He is able to succour them that are tempted.
                    Hebrews, ii. 18.

WHEN gathering clouds around I view,
    And days are dark and friends are few,
      On Him I lean who not in vain
Experienced every human pain:

FAITH.

He sees my wants, allays my fears,
And counts and treasures up my tears.

If aught should tempt my soul to stray
From heavenly wisdom's narrow way,
To fly the good I would pursue,
Or do the sin I would not do,
Still He who felt temptation's power
Shall guard me in that dangerous hour.

If wounded love my bosom swell,
Deceived by those I prized too well,
He shall His pitying aid bestow,
Who felt on earth severer woe,—
At once betrayed, denied, or fled
By those who shared His daily bread.

If vexing thoughts within me rise,
And, sore dismayed, my spirit dies,
Still He who once vouchsafed to bear
The sickening anguish of despair,
Shall sweetly soothe, shall gently dry,
The throbbing heart, the streaming eye.

When sorrowing o'er some stone I bend,
Which covers what was once a friend,
And from his voice, his hand, his smile,
Divides me for a little while,
Thou, Saviour, mark'st the tears I shed,
For Thou didst weep o'er Lazarus dead.

And O! when I have safely past
Through every conflict but the last,
Still, still unchanging, watch beside
My painful bed, for Thou hast died!
Then point to realms of cloudless day,
And wipe the latest tear away!

      SIR ROBERT GRANT.

FAITH.

Lord, save us : we perish.
Matthew, viii. 25.

O ! the storms of life are breaking,
Faithless fears our hearts are shaking
For our succour undertaking,
    Lord and Saviour, help us.

Lo ! the world, from Thee rebelling,
Round Thy Church in pride is swelling;
With Thy word their madness quelling,
    Lord and Saviour, help us.

On Thine own command relying,
We our onward task are plying,
Unto Thee for safety sighing,
    Lord and Saviour, help us.

Steadfast we, in faith abiding,
In Thy secret presence hiding,
In Thy love and grace confiding,
    Lord and Saviour, help us.

By Thy birth, Thy cross, Thy passion,
By Thy tears of deep compassion,
By Thy mighty intercession,
    Lord and Saviour, help us.

DEAN ALFORD.

FAITH.

O Lord, my strength and my refuge.
                                        Jeremiah, xvi. 19.

HOLY Saviour, Friend unseen,
The faint, the weak, on Thee may lean:
Help me, throughout life's varying scene,
    By faith to cling to Thee!

Blest with communion so divine,
Take what Thou wilt, shall I repine,
When, as the branches to the vine,
    My soul may cling to Thee?

Far from her home, fatigued, opprest,
Here she has found a place of rest,
An exile still, yet not unblest
    While she can cling to Thee!

Without a murmur I dismiss
My former dreams of earthly bliss;
My joy, my recompense be this,
    Each hour to cling to Thee!

What though the world deceitful prove,
And earthly friends and joys remove?
With patient uncomplaining love
    Still would I cling to Thee!

Oft when I seem to tread alone
Some barren waste with thorns o'ergrown,
A voice of love, in gentlest tone,
   Whispers, "Still cling to me!"

Though faith and hope awhile be tried,
I ask not, need not, aught beside:
How safe, how calm, how satisfied,
   The souls that cling to Thee!

They fear not life's rough storms to brave,
Since Thou art near, and strong to save;
Nor shudder e'en at death's dark wave;
   Because they cling to Thee!

Blest is my lot, whate'er befall:
What can disturb me, who appal,
While as my strength, my rock, my all,
   Saviour! I cling to Thee?

CHARLOTTE ELLIOTT.

Him that cometh to me I will in no wise cast out.
John, vi. 37.

JUST as I am—without one plea,
  But that Thy blood was shed for me,
And that Thou bidd'st me come to Thee,
   O Lamb of God, I come.

Just as I am—and waiting not
To rid my soul of one dark blot;

To Thee, whose blood can cleanse each spot,
    O Lamb of God, I come.

Just as I am—though tossed about
With many a conflict, many a doubt,
Fightings within, and fears without,
    O Lamb of God, I come.

Just as I am—poor, wretched, blind;
Sight, riches, healing of the mind,
Yea, all I need, in Thee to find,
    O Lamb of God, I come.

Just as I am—Thou wilt receive,
Wilt welcome, pardon, cleanse, relieve;
Because Thy promise I believe,
    O Lamb of God, I come.

Just as I am—Thy love unknown
Has broken every barrier down;
Now to be Thine, yea, Thine alone,
    O Lamb of God, I come.

Just as I am—of that free love,
The breadth, length, depth, the height to prove;
Here for a season, then above,
    O Lamb of God, I come.

CHARLOTTE ELLIOTT.

FAITH.

Give ear to my words, O Lord, consider my meditation.
Psalm v. 1.

WHEN I survey life's varied scene,
    Amid the darkest hours
Sweet rays of comfort shine between,
    And thorns are mixed with flowers.

Lord, teach me to adore Thy hand,
    From whence my comforts flow,
And let me in this desert land
    A glimpse of Canaan know.

And O! whate'er of earthly bliss
    Thy sovereign hand denies,
Accepted at Thy throne of grace
    Let this petition rise:

Give me a calm, a thankful heart,
    From every murmur free;
The blessings of Thy grace impart,
    And let me live to Thee.

Let the sweet hope, that Thou art mine,
    My path of life attend,
Thy presence through my journey shine,
    And bless its happy end!

ANNE STEELE.

FAITH.

Whether we live, we live unto the Lord; and whether we die, we die unto the Lord.
Romans, xiv. 8.

NOW it belongs not to my care
    Whether I die or live;
To love and serve Thee is my share,
    And this Thy grace must give.

If death shall bruise this springing seed
    Before it come to fruit,
The will with Thee goes for the deed,
    Thy life was in the root.

Would I long bear my heavy load,
    And keep my sorrows long?
Would I long sin against my God,
    And His dear mercy wrong?

How much is sinful flesh my foe,
    That doth my soul pervert
To linger here in sin and woe,
    And steals from God my heart!

Christ leads me through no darker rooms
    Than He went through before;
He that unto God's kingdom comes
    Must enter by this door.

FAITH.

Come, Lord, when grace hath made me meet
    Thy blessed face to see;
For, if Thy work on earth be sweet,
    What will Thy glory be?

Then I shall end my sad complaints,
    And weary sinful days,
And join with the triumphant saints
    That sing Jehovah's praise.

My knowledge of that life is small;
    The eye of faith is dim;
But it's enough that Christ knows all,
    And I shall be with Him.

RICHARD BAXTER.

Unite my heart to fear Thy Name.
Psalm lxxxvi. 11.

JESU, my strength, my hope,
    On Thee I cast my care,
With humble confidence look up,
    And know Thou hear'st my prayer.
Give me on Thee to wait
    Till I can all things do.
On Thee, Almighty to create!
    Almighty to renew!

I want a sober mind,
   A self-renouncing will,
That tramples down and casts behind
   The baits of pleasing ill;
   A soul inured to pain,
   To hardship, grief, and loss;
Bold to take up, firm to sustain,
   The consecrated Cross.

I want a godly fear,
   A quick-discerning eye,
That looks to Thee when sin is near,
   And sees the tempter fly;
   A spirit still prepared,
   And armed with jealous care,
For ever standing on its guard,
   And watching unto prayer.

I want a heart to pray,
   To pray and never cease,
Never to murmur at Thy stay,
   Or wish my sufferings less;
   This blessing above all,
   Always to pray, I want,
Out of the deep on Thee to call,
   And never, never faint.

Give me a true regard,
   A single, steady aim,

FAITH.

Unmoved by threatening or reward,
   To Thee and Thy great Name;
   A jealous, just concern,
   For Thine immortal praise;
A pure desire that all may learn
   And glorify Thy grace.

I rest upon Thy word;
   The promise is for me;
My succour and salvation, Lord,
   Shall surely come from Thee.
   But let me still abide,
   Nor from my hope remove,
Till Thou my patient spirit guide
   Into Thy perfect love.

CHARLES WESLEY.

I live by the faith of the Son of God, who loved me, and gave Himself for me.
Galatians, ii. 20.

MY faith looks up to Thee,
   Thou Lamb of Calvary,
     Saviour divine:
   Now hear me while I pray;
   Take all my guilt away;
   O let me from this day
     Be wholly Thine.

FAITH.

May Thy rich grace impart
Strength to my fainting heart,
    My zeal inspire:
As Thou hast died for me,
O may my love to Thee
Pure, warm, and changeless be,
    A living fire.

While life's dark maze I tread,
And griefs around me spread,
    Be Thou my Guide;
Bid darkness turn to day,
Wipe sorrow's tears away,
Nor let me ever stray
    From Thee aside.

When ends life's transient dream,
When death's cold, sullen stream
    Shall o'er me roll,
Blest Saviour, then, in love,
Fear and distrust remove;
O bear me safe above—
    A ransomed soul!

RAY PALMER.

Thy will be done.
　　　　　　Matthew, vi. 10.

MY God and Father, while I stray
Far from my home, on life's rough way,
O teach me from my heart to say,
　　Thy will be done!

Though dark my path and sad my lot,
Let me be still and murmur not,
Or breathe the prayer divinely taught,
　　Thy will be done!

What though in lonely grief I sigh
For friends beloved, no longer nigh?

Submissive still would I reply,
    Thy will be done!

Though Thou hast called me to resign
What I most prized, it ne'er was mine,
I have but yielded what was Thine;
    Thy will be done!

Should grief or sickness waste away
My life in premature decay,
My Father, still I strive to say,
    Thy will be done!

Let but my fainting heart be blest
With Thy sweet Spirit for its guest,
My God, to Thee I leave the rest;
    Thy will be done!

Renew my will from day to day;
Blend it with Thine; and take away
All that now makes it hard to say,
    Thy will be done!

Then, when on earth I breathe no more,
The prayer, oft mixed with tears before,
I'll sing upon a happier shore,
    Thy will be done!

CHARLOTTE ELLIOTT.

> *This is a faithful saying, that Christ Jesus
> came into the world to save sinners.*
> I Timothy, i. 15.

AND can it be, that I should gain
    An interest in the Saviour's blood?
Died He for me, who caused His pain,
    For me, who Him to death pursued?
Amazing love! how can it be,
That Thou, my God, shouldst die for me?

'T is mystery all! Th' Immortal dies!
    Who can explore His strange design?
In vain the first-born seraph tries
    To sound the depths of love divine.
'T is mercy all! Let earth adore!
Let angel minds inquire no more!

He left His Father's throne above,
    (So free, so infinite His grace!)
Emptied Himself of all but love,
    And bled for Adam's helpless race.
'T is mercy all, immense and free!
For O, my God! it found out me!

Long my imprisoned spirit lay
    Fast bound in sin and Nature's night;
Thine eye diffused a quickening ray;
    I woke: the dungeon flamed with light;

FAITH.

My chains fell off, my heart was free,
I rose, went forth, and followed Thee!

Still the small inward voice I hear,
   That whispers all my sins forgiven;
Still the atoning blood is near,
   That quenched the wrath of hostile Heaven:
I feel the life His wounds impart;
I feel my Saviour in my heart.

No condemnation now I dread;
   Jesus, and all in Him, is mine!
Alive in Him, my living Head,
   And clothed in righteousness divine,
Bold I approach th' eternal throne,
And claim the crown, through Christ my own.

CHARLES WESLEY.

An anchor of the soul.
Hebrews, vi. 19.

NOW I have found the ground wherein
   Sure my soul's anchor may remain;
The wound of Jesus, for my sin,
   Before the world's foundation slain;
Whose mercy shall unshaken stay
When Heaven and earth are fled away.

Father, Thine everlasting grace
    Our scanty thought surpasses far;
Thy heart still melts with tenderness;
    Thine arms of love still open are,
Returning sinners to receive,
That mercy they may taste and live.

O Love! thou bottomless abyss!
    My sins are swallowed up in thee;
Covered is my unrighteousness,
    Nor spot of guilt remains on me:
While Jesus' blood, through earth and skies,
Mercy—free, boundless mercy—cries.

With faith I plunge me in this sea;
   Here is my hope, my joy, my rest;
Hither, when Hell assails, I flee,
   I look into my Saviour's breast:
Away, sad doubt and anxious fear!
Mercy is all that's written there.

Though waves and storms go o'er my head;
   Though strength, and health, and friends be gone;
Though joys be withered all and dead;
   Though every comfort be withdrawn;
On this my steadfast soul relies,—
Father! Thy mercy never dies.

Fixed on this ground will I remain,
   Though my heart fail and flesh decay;
This anchor shall my soul sustain
   When earth's foundations melt away:
Mercy's full power I then shall prove,
Loved with an everlasting love.

JOHN WESLEY.
FROM ZINZENDORF.

Whether we live or die, we are the Lord's.
Romans, xiv 8.

BLEST be Thy love, dear Lord,
   That taught us this sweet way,
Only to love Thee for Thyself,
   And for that love obey.

FAITH.

O Thou, our souls' chief hope!
   We to Thy mercy fly;
Where'er we are, Thou canst protect,
   Whate'er we need, supply.

Whether we sleep or wake,
   To Thee we both resign;
By night we see, as well as day,
   If Thy light on us shine.

Whether we live or die,
   Both we submit to Thee;
In death we live, as well as life,
   If Thine in death we be.

JOHN AUSTIN.

---

*Hear the voice of my supplications when
I cry unto Thee.*
Psalm xxviii 2

HERE behold me as I cast me
   At Thy throne, O glorious King!
Tears fast thronging, childlike longing,
   Son of Man, to Thee I bring.
Let me find Thee ! let me find Thee!
   Me a poor and worthless thing.

Look upon me, Lord, I pray Thee,
   Let Thy Spirit dwell in mine;

FAITH.

Thou hast sought me, Thou hast bought me,
    Only Thee to know I pine.
Let me find Thee! let me find Thee!
    Take my heart, and grant me Thine.

Nought I ask for, nought I strive for,
    But Thy grace so rich and free,
That Thou givest whom Thou lovest,
    And who truly cleave to Thee.
Let me find Thee! let me find Thee!
    He hath all things who hath Thee.

Earthly treasure, mirth and pleasure,
    Glorious name, or richest hoard,
Are but weary, void and dreary,
    To the heart that longs for Thee;
Let me find Thee! let me find Thee!
    I am ready, mighty Lord.

        TRANSLATED BY CATHERINE WINKWORTH.

*To Him who is able to keep you from falling be glory and majesty,
dominion and power, for ever.*
                                  Jude, i. 24.

TO God the only wise,
    Our Saviour and our King,
Let all the saints below the skies
    Their humble praises bring.

FAITH.

'T is His almighty love,
   His counsel and His care,
Preserve us safe from sin and death,
   And every hurtful snare.

He will present our souls,
   Unblemished and complete,
Before the glory of His face,
   With joys divinely great.

Then all the chosen race
   Shall meet around the throne,
Shall bless the conduct of His grace,
   And make His wonders known.

To our Redeemer, God,
   Wisdom and power belong,
Immortal crowns of majesty,
   And Heaven's eternal song.

ISAAC WATTS.

That rock was Christ.
I. Corinthians, x. 4.

ROCK of ages, cleft for me,
   Let me hide myself in Thee
   Let the water and the blood,
   From Thy riven side which flowed,
Be of sin the double cure,
Cleanse me from its guilt and power.

FAITH.

Not the labours of my hands
Can fulfil Thy law's demands:
Could my zeal no respite know,
Could my tears for ever flow,
All for sin could not atone;
Thou must save, and Thou alone.

Nothing in my hand I bring;
Simply to Thy cross I cling:
Naked, come to Thee for dress;
Helpless, look to Thee for grace;
Foul, I to the fountain fly:
Wash me, Saviour, or I die.

Whilst I draw this fleeting breath—
When my eye-strings break in death—
When I soar through tracts unknown—
See Thee on Thy judgment throne—
Rock of Ages, cleft for me,
Let me hide myself in Thee.

AUGUSTUS M. TOPLADY.

HOPE.

They shall ask the way to Zion.
Jeremiah, l. 5.

FROM Egypt's bondage come,
    Where death and darkness reign,
We seek our new, our better home,
    Where we our rest shall gain.
        Hallelujah!
    We are on our way to God.

To Canaan's sacred bound
We haste with songs of joy,

HOPE.

Where peace and liberty are found,
    And sweets that never cloy.
        Hallelujah!
    We are on our way to God.

There sin and sorrow cease,
    And every conflict's o'er;
There we shall dwell in endless peace,
    Nor thirst nor hunger more.
        Hallelujah!
    We are on our way to God.

There, in celestial strains
    Enraptured myriads sing;
There love in every bosom reigns,
    For God Himself is King.
        Hallelujah!
    We are on our way to God.

We soon shall join the throng,
    Their pleasure we shall share,
And sing the everlasting song,
    With all the ransomed there.
        Hallelujah!
    We are on our way to God.

How bright the prospect is!
    It cheers the pilgrim's breast.
We're journeying through the wilderness,

But soon shall gain our rest.
Hallelujah!
We are on our way to God.

THOMAS KELLY.

*Learn of me, for I am meek and
lowly of heart.*
Matthew, xi. 29.

FIERCE passions discompose the mind,
    As tempests vex the sea;
But calm content and peace we find,
    When, Lord, we turn to Thee.

In vain by reason and by rule
    We try to bend the will;
For none but in the Saviour's school
    Can learn the heavenly skill.

Since at His feet my soul has sat,
    His gracious words to hear,
Contented with my present state,
    I cast on Him my care.

Art thou a sinner, soul?" He said;
    "Then How canst thou complain?
How light thy troubles here, if weighed
    With everlasting pain.

"If thou of murmuring would'st be cured,
 Compare thy griefs with mine:
Think what my love for thee endured,
 And thou wilt not repine.

"'T is I appoint thy daily lot,
 And I do all things well;
Thou soon shalt leave this wretched spot,
 And rise with Me to dwell.

" In life my grace shall strength supply
 Proportioned to thy day ;
At death thou still shalt find me nigh,
 To wipe thy tears away."

Thus I, who once my wretched days
 In vain repinings spent,
Taught in my Saviour's school of grace,
 Have learnt to be content.
WILLIAM COWPER.

For the hope which is laid up for you in Heaven.
Colossians, i. 5.

WHO would not leave this world below,
 To meet the promise given?
To go where tears do cease to flow,
 To die and go to Heaven!

To die and go to Heaven, Lord!
   There to mingle with the blest;
"Where the wicked cease from troubling,
   And the weary are at rest."

Dear Lord! on Thee we rest our hope,
   When with temptation riven;
Grant us to feel Thy Spirit's love,
   Then—die and go to Heaven.

ANON.

And again they said, Alleluia.
Revelation, xix. 3.

HALLELUJAH! song of gladness,
   Song of everlasting joy;
Hallelujah! song the sweetest
   That can angel hosts employ;
Hymning in God's holy presence
   Their high praise eternally.

Hallelujah! Church victorious,
   Thou may'st lift this joyful strain;
Hallelujah! songs of triumph
   Will befit the ransomed train:
We our song must raise with sadness,
   While in exile we remain.

Hallelujah! strains of gladness
  Suit not souls with anguish torn;
Hallelujah! notes of sadness
  Best befit our state forlorn;
For, in this dark world of sorrow,
  We with tears our sin must mourn.

But our earnest supplication,
  Holy God, we raise to Thee;
Bring us to Thy blissful presence,
  Make us all Thy joys to see;
Then we'll sing our Hallelujah,—
  Sing to all eternity.

THIRTEENTH CENTURY.

---

*Set your affection on things above, not
  on things on the earth.*
Colossians, iii. 2.

I PRAISED the earth, in beauty seen,
  With garlands gay of various green;
I praised the sea, whose ample field
  Shone glorious as a silver shield;
  And earth and ocean seemed to say,
  "Our beauties are but for a day."

I praised the sun, whose chariot rolled
On wheels of amber and of gold;

I praised the moon, whose softer eye
Gleamed sweetly through the summer sky;

HOPE.

And moon and sun in answer said,
"Our days of light are numberèd."

O God! O Good beyond compare!
If thus Thy meaner works are fair,
If thus Thy bounties gild the span
Of ruined earth and sinful man,
How glorious must the mansion be
Where Thy redeemed shall dwell with Thee!

BISHOP REGINALD HEBER.

Guide our feet into the way of peace.
Luke, i. 79.

FAIN would my thoughts fly up to Thee,
   Thy peace, sweet Lord, to find;
But when I offer, still the world
   Lays clogs upon my mind.

Sometimes I climb a little way,
   And thence look down below;
How nothing, there, do all things seem
   That here make such a show.

Then round about I turn my eyes,
   To feast my hungry sight;
I meet with Heaven in everything,
   In everything delight.

HOPE.

I see Thy wisdom ruling all,
   And it with joy admire;
I see myself among such hopes
   As set my heart on fire.

When I have thus triumphed awhile,
   And think to build my nest,
Some cross conceits come fluttering by,
   And interrupt my rest.

Then to the earth again I fall,
   And from my low dust cry,
'Twas not in my wing, Lord, but Thine,
   That I got up so high.

And now, my God, whether I rise,
   Or still lie down in dust,
Both I submit to Thy blest will;
   In both, on Thee I trust.

Guide Thou my way, who art Thyself
   My everlasting end,
That every step, or swift or slow,
   Still to Thyself may tend.

To Father, Son, and Holy Ghost,
   One consubstantial Three,
All highest praise, all humblest thanks,
   Now and for ever be! Amen.

JOHN AUSTIN.

I cried with my whole heart, hear me, O Lord!
Psalm cxix. 145.

O up, go up, my heart,
    Dwell with thy God above;
For here thou canst not rest,
    Nor here give out thy love.

Go up, go up, my heart,
    Be not a trifler here;
Ascend above these clouds,
    Dwell in a higher sphere.

Let not thy love flow out
    To things so soiled and dim;
Go up to Heaven and God,
    Take up thy love to Him.

Waste not thy precious stores
    On creature-love below;
To God that wealth belongs,
    On Him that wealth bestow.

Go up, reluctant heart,
    Take up thy rest above;
Arise, earth-clinging thoughts;
    Ascend, my lingering love!

HORATIUS BONAR.

HOPE.

> *Hear me, when I call, O God; have mercy upon me, and hear my prayer.*
> Psalm iv. 1.

HEAR, gracious God! a sinner's cry,
For I have nowhere else to fly;
My hope, my only hope's in Thee:
O God, be merciful to me!

To Thee I come, a sinner poor,
And wait for mercy at Thy door;
Indeed, I've nowhere else to flee:
O God, be merciful to me!

To Thee I come, a sinner weak,
And scarce know how to pray or speak:
From fear and weakness set me free:
O God, be merciful to me!

To Thee I come, a sinner vile;
Upon me, Lord, vouchsafe to smile!
Mercy alone I make my plea:
O God, be merciful to me!

To Thee I come, a sinner great,
And well Thou knowest all my state;
Yet full forgiveness is with Thee:
O God, be merciful to me!

HOPE.

To Thee I come, a sinner lost,
Nor have I ought wherein to trust;
But where Thou art, Lord, I would be:
O God, be merciful to me!

To glory bring me, Lord, at last;
And there, when all my fears are past,
With all the saints I'll then agree,
God has been merciful to me!

SAMUEL MEDLEY.

The Lord hath prepared His throne in the heavens.
Psalm ciii. 19.

BEHOLD! how glorious is yon sky.
Lo! there the righteous never die,
But dwell in peace for ever:
Then who would wear this earthly clay,
When bid to cast life's chains away,
And win Thy gracious favour?
Holy, Holy, O forgive us;
And receive us, heavenly Father,
When around Thy throne we gather.

Confiding in Thy sacred Word,
Our Saviour is our hope, O Lord,

The guiding star before us;
Our Shepherd, leading us the way,
If from Thy paths our footsteps stray,

To Thee He will restore us.
 Holy, Holy, ever hear us,
And receive us, while we gather
 Round Thy throne, Almighty Father.

NICOLAI.

In my Father's house are many mansions.
John, xiv. 2.

WHEN I can read my title clear
 To mansions in the skies,
I bid farewell to every fear,
 And wipe my weeping eyes.

Should Death against my soul engage,
 And hellish darts be hurled,
Then I can smile at Satan's rage,
 And face a frowning world.

Should cares like a wild deluge come,
 And storms of sorrow fall,
May I but safely reach my home,
 My God, my Heaven, my all;

There shall I bathe my weary soul
 In seas of heavenly rest,
And not a wave of trouble roll
 Across my peaceful breast.

ISAAC WATTS.

For here have we no continuing city.
Hebrews, xiii. 14.

WE 'VE no abiding city here:
    This may distress the worldling's mind,
But should not cost the saint a tear,
    Who hopes a better rest to find.

We 've no abiding city here:
    Sad truth! were this to be our home!
But let this thought our spirits cheer—
    We seek a city yet to come.

We 've no abiding city here;
    Then let us live as pilgrims do!
Let not the world our rest appear,
    But let us haste from all below.

We 've no abiding city here:
    We seek a city out of sight;
Zion its name,—the Lord is there,—
    It shines with everlasting light!

Zion! Jehovah is her strength;
    Secure she smiles at all her foes;
And weary travellers at length
    Within her sacred walls repose.

O sweet abode of peace and love,
   Where pilgrims, freed from toil, are blest;
Had I the pinions of a dove,
   I'd fly to thee, and be at rest!

THOMAS KELLY.

Where I am, there ye may be also.

John, xiv. 3.

LET me be with Thee where Thou art,
   My Saviour, my eternal Rest;
Then only will this longing heart
   Be fully and for ever blest!

Let me be with Thee where Thou art,
   Thy unveiled glory to behold;
Then only will this wandering heart
   Cease to be treacherous, faithless, cold.

Let me be with Thee where Thou art,
   Where spotless saints Thy Name adore;
Then only will this sinful heart
   Be evil and defiled no more!

Let me be with Thee where Thou art,
   Where none can die, where none remove;
There neither death nor life will part
   Me from Thy presence and Thy love.

CHARLOTTE ELLIOTT.

HOPE.

The Lord Jehovah is everlasting strength.
Isaiah, xxvi. 4.

I NEED Thee, precious Jesu,
    For I am very poor:
A stranger and a pilgrim,
    I have no earthly store;
I need the love of Jesus
    To cheer me on my way,
To guide my doubting footsteps,
    To be my strength and stay.

I need Thee, precious Jesu,
    I need a friend like Thee,
A friend to soothe and pity,
    A friend to care for me;
I need the heart of Jesus
    To feel each anxious care,
To tell my every trial,
    And all my sorrows share.

I need Thee, precious Jesu,
    I need Thee, day by day,
To fill me with Thy fulness,
    To lead me on my way.
I need Thy Holy Spirit
    To teach me what I am,
To show me more of Jesus,
    To point me to the Lamb.

I need Thee, precious Jesu,
   And hope to see Thee soon,
Encircled with the rainbow,
   And seated on Thy throne;
There, with Thy blood-bought children,
   My joy shall ever be
To sing Thy praises, Jesu,
   To gaze, my Lord, on Thee.

ANON.

A spring of water, whose waters fail not.
Isaiah, lviii. 11.

THERE is a pure and tranquil wave,
   That rolls around the throne of love,
Whose waters gladden as they lave
   The peaceful shores above.

While streams, which on that tide depend,
   Steal from those heavenly shores away,
And on this desert world descend
   O'er weary lands to stray.

The pilgrim faint, and nigh to sink
   Beneath his load of earthly woe,
Refreshed beside their verdant brink,
   Rejoices in their flow.

There, O my soul, do thou repair,
And hover o'er the hallowed spring,
To drink the crystal wave, and there
   To lave thy wearied wing.

HOPE.

There droop that wing, when far it flies
From human care, and toil, and strife,
And feed by those still streams, that rise
   Beneath the Tree of Life.

It may be that the breath of love
Some leaves on their pure tide have driven,
Which, passing from the shores above,
   Have floated down from Heaven.

So shall thy wounds and woes be healed
By the blest virtue that they bring;
So thy parched lips shall be unsealed,
   Thy Saviour's praise to sing.

WILLIAM BALL.

Lay hold on eternal life.
I. Timothy, vi. 19.

WHERE shall rest be found,
   Rest for the weary soul?
'T were vain the ocean depths to sound
   Or pierce to either pole.
   The world can never give
   The bliss for which we sigh;
'T is not the whole of life, to live,
   Nor all of death, to die.

HOPE.

  Beyond this vale of tears
   There is a life above,
 Unmeasured by the flight of years,
   And all that life is love.
   There is a death, whose pang
   Outlasts the fleeting breath;
 O, what eternal horrors hang
   Around the second death!

   Lord God of truth and grace,
   Teach us that death to shun,
 Lest we be banished from Thy face,
   And evermore undone.
   Here would we end our quest;
   Alone are found in Thee
 The life of perfect love—the rest
   Of immortality.
      JAMES MONTGOMERY.

Arise ye, and depart; for this is not your rest.
        Micah, ii. 10.

RISE, my soul, and stretch thy wings;
  Thy better portion trace;
 Rise from transitory things,
Towards Heaven, thy native place.

Sun and moon and stars decay;
Time shall soon this earth remove:
Rise, my soul, and haste away
   To seats prepared above.

Rivers to the ocean run,
   Nor stay in all their course;
Fire ascending seeks the sun;
   Both speed them to their source.
So a soul that's born of God
Pants to view His glorious face;
Upwards tends to His abode,
   To rest in His embrace.

Cease, ye pilgrims, cease to mourn,
   Press onward to the prize;
Soon your Saviour will return
   Triumphant in the skies.
Yet a season, and we know
Happy entrance will be given;
All our sorrows left below,
   And earth exchanged for Heaven.

MARTIN MADAN.

The things which are not seen are eternal.
II. Corinthians, iv. 13.

MY thoughts surmount these lower skies,
    And look within the veil;
There springs of endless pleasure rise,
    The waters never fail.

There I behold, with sweet delight,
    The blessed Three in One,
And strong affections fix my sight
    On God's incarnate Son.

His promise stands for ever firm,
    His grace shall ne'er depart;
He binds my name upon His arm,
    And seals it on His heart.

Light are the pains that nature brings;
    How short our sorrows are
When with eternal future things
    The present we compare!

I would not be a stranger still
    To that celestial place
Where I for ever hope to dwell
    Near my Redeemer's face.

ISAAC WATTS.

The time of my departure is at hand: I have finished my course.
II. Timothy, iv. 6, 7

THE hour of my departure's come;
I hear the voice that calls me home.
At last, O Lord, let troubles cease,
And let Thy servant die in peace.

The race appointed I have run,
The fight is o'er, the prize is won;
And now my witness is on high,
And now my record's in the sky.

Not in mine innocence I trust;
I bow before Thee in the dust,
And through my Saviour's blood alone
I look for mercy at Thy throne.

I leave the world without a tear,
Save for the friends I held so dear;
To heal their sorrows, Lord, descend,
And to the friendless prove a friend.

I come, I come, at Thy command,
I yield my spirit to Thy hand;
Stretch forth Thine everlasting arms,
And shield me in the last alarms.

The hour of my departure's come;
I hear the voice that calls me home
Now, O my God, let troubles cease,
Now let Thy servant die in peace.

MICHAEL BRUCE.

We have seen His star in the east.
Matthew, ii. 2.

BRIGHTEST and best of the sons of the morning,
    Dawn on our darkness, and lend us thine aid!
Star of the east, the horizon adorning,
    Guide where our infant Redeemer is laid!

Cold on His cradle the dew-drops are shining,
    Low lies His head with the beasts of the stall;
Angels adore Him in slumber reclining,
    Maker, and Monarch, and Saviour of all!

Say, shall we yield Him, in costly devotion
    Odours of Edom and offerings divine,
Gems of the mountain and pearls of the ocean,
    Myrrh from the forest and gold from the mine?

Vainly we offer each ample oblation,
    Vainly with gifts would His favour secure;
Richer by far is the heart's adoration,
    Dearer to God are the prayers of the poor.

BISHOP REGINALD HEBER.

O God, Thou art my God: my soul thirsteth for Thee.
Psalm lxiii. 1.

FAR from my heavenly home,
   Far from my Father's breast,
Fainting I cry, "Blest Spirit! come,
   And speed me to my rest!"

Upon the willows long
My harp has silent hung:
   How should I sing a cheerful song
   Till Thou inspire my tongue?

My spirit homeward turns,
   And fain would thither flee;
My heart, O Zion, droops and yearns
   When I remember thee.

To thee, to thee I press,
   A dark and toilsome road:
When shall I pass the wilderness,
   And reach the saints' abode?

God of my life, be near!
   On Thee my hopes I cast:
O guide me through the desert here,
   And bring me home at last!

            HENRY FRANCIS LYTE.

LOVE

The God of patience and consolation grant you to be like minded one toward another according to Christ Jesus.

Romans, xv. 5.

JESUS, Lord, we look to Thee:
Let us in Thy Name agree;
Show Thyself the Prince of Peace;
Bid all strife for ever cease.

Make us of one heart and mind,
Courteous, pitiful, and kind;
Lowly, meek in thought and word,—
Altogether like our Lord.

Let us for each other care,
Each the other's burden bear;
To Thy Church the pattern give,
Show how true believers live.

Free from anger and from pride,
Let us thus in Thee abide;
All the depths of love express,
All the heights of holiness:

Let us then with joy remove
To Thy family above;
And with faith and comfort high,
Prove how true believers die.

CHARLES WESLEY.

Love not the world, neither the things that are in the world.
I. John, ii. 15.

CHRIST, my hidden life, appear,
Soul of my inmost soul!
Light of life, the mourner cheer,
And make the sinner whole!

LOVE.

Now in me Thyself display;
   Surely Thou in all things art;
I from all things turn away,
   To seek Thee in my heart!

Open, Lord, my inward ear,
   And bid my heart rejoice!
Bid my quiet spirit hear
   Thy comfortable voice;
Never in the whirlwind found,
   Or where earthquakes rock the place;
Still and silent is the sound,
   The whisper of Thy grace!

From the world of sin, and noise,
   And hurry, I withdraw;
For the small and inward voice
   I wait with humble awe;
Silent am I now and still,
   Dare not in Thy presence move;
To my waiting soul reveal
   The secret of Thy love!

Thou hast undertook for me;
   For me to death wast sold;
Wisdom in a mystery
   Of bleeding love unfold!
Teach the lesson of Thy Cross;
   Let me die, with Thee to reign!

LOVE.

All things let me count but loss,
  So I may Thee regain!

Show me, as my soul can bear,
  The depth of inbred sin:
All the unbelief declare,
  The pride that lurks within:
Take me, whom Thyself hast bought!
  Bring into captivity
Every high aspiring thought,
  That would not stoop to Thee!

Lord, my time is in Thy hand;
  My soul to Thee convert!
Thou canst make me understand
  Though I am slow of heart.
Thine, in whom I live and move,
  Thine the work, the power is Thine!
Thou art Wisdom, Power, and Love;
  And all Thou art is mine!

CHARLES WESLEY.

Unto you therefore which believe He is precious.
I. Peter, ii. 7.

HOW sweet the Name of Jesus sounds
  In a believer's ear!
It soothes his sorrows, heals his wounds,
  And drives away his fear.

It makes the wounded spirit whole,
    And calms the troubled breast;
'T is manna to the hungry soul,
    And to the weary rest.

Dear Name! the rock on which I build,
   My shield and hiding-place;
My never-failing treas'ry, filled
   With boundless stores of grace.

Jesus, my Shepherd, Guardian, Friend,
   My Prophet, Priest, and King;
My Lord, my Life, my Way, my End,
   Accept the praise I bring.

Weak is the effort of my heart,
   And cold my warmest thought;
But when I see Thee as Thou art,
   I'll praise Thee as I ought.

Till then I would Thy love proclaim
   With ev'ry fleeting breath;
And may the music of Thy Name,
   Refresh my soul in death.

                      JOHN NEWTON.

If ye love me, keep my commandments.
                      John, xiv. 15.

JESUS, my all, to Heaven is gone,
   He whom I fix my hopes upon;
His track I see, and I'll pursue
The narrow way, till Him I view.

The way the holy prophets went;
The road that leads from banishment;
The King's highway of holiness
I'll go, for all His paths are peace.

No stranger may proceed therein,
No lover of the world and sin;
No lion, no devouring care,
No ravenous tiger shall be there.

No: nothing may go up thereon
But travelling souls; and I am one:
Wayfaring men, to Canaan bound,
Shall only in the way be found.

Nor fools, by carnal men esteemed,
Shall err therein; but they, redeemed
In Jesus' blood, shall show their right
To travel there, till Heaven's in sight.

This is the way I long have sought,
And mourned because I found it not;
My grief, my burden long have been
Because I could not cease from sin.

The more I strove against its power,
I sinned and stumbled but the more;
Till late I heard my Saviour say,
"Come hither, soul! for I'm the Way!"

Lo! glad I come; and Thou, dear Lamb,
Shall take me to Thee, as I am:
Nothing but sin I Thee can give;
Yet help me, and Thy praise I'll live!

I'll tell to all poor sinners round
What a dear Saviour I have found;
I'll point to Thy redeeming blood,
And say, "Behold the Way to God!"

JOHN CENNICK.

I will walk before the Lord in the land of the living.
Psalm cxvi. 9.

FOR a closer walk with God!
    A calm and heavenly frame,
A light to shine upon the road
    That leads me to the Lamb!

Where is the blessedness I knew
    When first I saw the Lord?
Where is the soul-refreshing view
    Of Jesus and His Word?

What peaceful hours I once enjoyed!
    How sweet their mem'ry still!
But they have left an aching void
    The world can never fill.

Return, O holy Dove! return,
    Sweet messenger of rest:
I hate the sins that made Thee mourn,
    And drove Thee from my breast.

The dearest idol I have known,
    Whate'er that idol be,
Help me to tear it from Thy throne,
    And worship only Thee.

So shall my walk be close with God,
    Calm and serene my frame;
So purer light shall mark the road
    That leads me to the Lamb.

WILLIAM COWPER.

Lord, Thou knowest that I love Thee.
John, xxi. 16.

DO not I love Thee, O my Lord?
    Behold my heart, and see;
And turn each cherished idol out,
    That dares to rival Thee.

Do not I love Thee from my soul?
    Then let me nothing love;
Dead be my heart to every joy,
    When Jesus cannot move.

LOVE.

Is not Thy Name melodious still
    To mine attentive ear?
Doth not each pulse with pleasure bound
    My Saviour's voice to hear?

Hast Thou a lamb in all Thy flock
    I would disdain to feed?
Hast thou a foe before whose face
    I fear Thy cause to plead?

Would not mine ardent spirit vie
    With angels round the throne,
To execute Thy sacred will
    And make Thy glory known?

Thou know'st I love Thee, dearest Lord,
    But, Oh! I long to soar
Far from the sphere of mortal joys,
    And learn to love Thee more.

PHILIP DODDRIDGE.

All things are yours; and ye are Christ's; and Christ is God's.
I. Corinthians, iii. 21, 23.

SOVEREIGN Ruler of the skies,
    Ever gracious, ever wise,
    All my times are in Thy hand,
All events at Thy command.

His decree, who formed the earth,
Fixed my first and second birth;
Parents, native place, and time,
All appointed were by Him.

LOVE.

He that formed me in the womb,
He shall guide me to the tomb;
All my times shall ever be
Ordered by His wise decree.

Times of sickness, times of health,
Times of penury and wealth;
Times of trial and of grief,
Times of triumph and relief;

Times the tempter's power to prove,
Times to taste a Saviour's love;
All must come, and last, and end,
As shall please my heavenly Friend.

Plagues and deaths around me fly;
Till He bids I cannot die:
Not a single shaft can hit
Till the God of love sees fit.

O Thou Gracious, Wise, and Just!
In Thy hands my life I trust:
Have I something dearer still?
I resign it to Thy will.

May I always own Thy hand:
Still to the surrender stand;
Know that Thou art God alone:
I and mine are all Thine own.

LOVE.

Thee at all times will I bless;
Having Thee, I all possess;
How can I bereavèd be,
Since I cannot part with Thee?

JOHN RYLAND.

---

*O come, let us worship and bow down, let us kneel
before the Lord our Maker, for He is our God.*
Psalm xcv. 6, 7

O, worship at Immanuel's feet;
See in His face what wonders meet:
Earth is too narrow to express
His worth, His glory, or His grace!

The whole creation can afford
But some faint shadows of my Lord;
Nature, to make His beauties known,
Must mingle colours not her own.

Is He compared to Wine or Bread?
Dear Lord, our souls would thus be fed:
That flesh, that dying blood of Thine,
Is Bread of Life, is heavenly Wine.

Is He a Tree? The world receives
Salvation from His healing leaves:
That righteous Branch, that fruitful Bough,
Is David's root and offspring too.

LOVE.

Is He a Rose? Not Sharon yields
Such fragrancy in all her fields;
Or if the Lily He assume,
The valleys bless the rich perfume.

Is He a Vine? His heavenly root
Supplies the boughs with life and fruit:
O let a lasting union join
My soul the branch to Christ the Vine!

Is He the Head? Each member lives,
And owns the vital power He gives;
The saints below and saints above
Joined by His Spirit and His love.

Is He a Fountain? There I bathe,
And heal the plague of sin and death;
These waters all my soul renew,
And cleanse my spotted garments too.

Is He a Fire? He'll purge my dross,
But the true gold sustains no loss:
Like a Refiner shall He sit,
And tread the refuse with His feet.

Is He a Rock? How firm He proves!
The Rock of Ages never moves;
Yet the sweet streams that from Him flow
Attend us all the desert through.

Is He a Way?   He leads to God;
The path is drawn in lines of blood:
There would I walk with hope and zeal,
Till I arrive at Sion's hill.

Is He a Door?   I'll enter in:
Behold the pastures large and green!
A Paradise divinely fair;
None but the sheep have freedom there.

Is He designed a Corner-stone,
For men to build their Heaven upon?
I'll make Him my Foundation too,
Nor fear the plots of hell below.

LOVE.

Is He a Temple? I adore
The indwelling majesty and power;
And still to His Most Holy Place,
Whene'er I pray, I turn my face.

Is He a Star? He breaks the night,
Piercing the shades with dawning light.
I know His glories from afar,
I know the bright, the Morning Star!

Is He a Sun? His beams are grace,
His course is joy and righteousness:
Nations rejoice when He appears
To chase their clouds and dry their tears.

O! let me climb those higher skies
Where storms and darkness never rise!
There He displays His powers abroad,
And shines and reigns, th' incarnate God.

Nor earth, nor seas, nor sun, nor stars,
Nor heaven His full resemblance bears:
His beauties we can never trace
Till we behold Him face to face.

ISAAC WATTS.

That the Word of the Lord may be glorified.
                                II. Thessalonians, iii. 1

SEE how great a flame aspires,
Kindled by a spark of grace!
Jesus' love the nations fires,
Sets the kingdoms on a blaze:
To bring fire on earth He came;
Kindled in some hearts it is:
O that all might catch the flame,
All partake the glorious bliss!

When He first the work begun,
Small and feeble was His day;
Now the Word doth swiftly run,
Now it wins its widening way:
More and more it spreads and grows,
Ever mighty to prevail;
Sin's strongholds it now o'erthrows,
Shakes the trembling gates of hell.

Sons of God, your Saviour praise:
He the door hath opened wide;
He hath given the word of grace,—
Jesus' word is glorified.
Jesus, mighty to redeem,
He alone the work hath wrought;

LOVE.

Worthy is the work of Him,—
Him who spake a world from nought.

Saw ye not the cloud arise,
Little as a human hand?
Now it spreads along the skies,
Hangs o'er all the thirsty land.

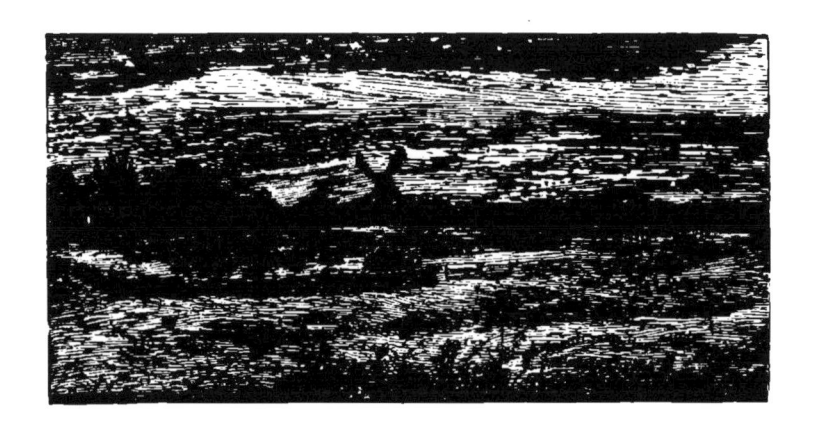

Lo! the promise of a shower
Drops already from above,
But the Lord will shortly pour
All the Spirit of His love.

CHARLES WESLEY.

LOVE.

> *Blessed are the poor in spirit, for theirs
> is the kingdom of Heaven.*
> Matthew, v. 3.

THERE is a dwelling-place above;
  Thither, to meet the God of love,
    The poor in spirit go;
  There is a Paradise of rest;
  For contrite hearts and souls distrest
    Its streams of comfort flow.

There is a goodly heritage,
Where earthly passions cease to rage;
    The meek that haven gain;
There is a board, where they who pine,
Hungry, athirst, for grace divine,
    May feast, nor crave again.

There is a voice to mercy true;
To them who mercy's path pursue
    That voice shall bliss impart;
There is a sight from man concealed;
That sight, the face of God revealed,
    Shall bless the pure in heart.

There is a name, in Heaven bestowed:
That name which hails them sons of God,
    The friends of peace shall know;
There is a kingdom in the sky,

LOVE.

Where they shall reign with God on high
    Who serve Him best below.

Lord! be it mine like them to choose
The better part, like them to use
    The means Thy love hath given!
Be holiness my aim on earth,
That death be welcomed as a birth
    To life and bliss in Heaven!

                      BISHOP RICHARD MANT.

The love of Christ constraineth us.
                II. Corinthians, v. 14.

JESUS, Thy boundless love to me
    No thought can reach, no tongue declare;
O knit my thankful heart to Thee,
    And reign without a rival there:
Thine wholly, Thine alone I am;
Lord, with Thy love my heart inflame.

O grant that nothing in my soul
    May dwell, but Thy pure love alone:
O may Thy love possess me whole,
    My joy, my treasure, and my crown;
All coldness from my heart remove,—
May every act, word, thought, be love.

LOVE.

O love, how cheering is thy ray!
    All pain before thy presence flies;
Care, anguish, sorrow melt away
    Where'er thy healing beams arise:
O Jesus, nothing may I see,
Nothing desire, or seek, but Thee.

In suffering, be Thy love my peace;
    In weakness, be Thy love my power;
And when the storms of life shall cease,
    Jesus, in that important hour,
In death, in life, be Thou my Guide,
And save me, who for me hast died.

PAUL GERHARD.

Thou compassest my path and my lying down, and art acquainted with all my ways.
Psalm cxxxix. 3.

LORD, in the day Thou art about
    The paths wherein I tread;
And in the night, when I lie down,
    Thou art about my bed.

While others in God's prisons lie,
    Bound with affliction's chain,
I walk at large, secure and free
    From sickness and from pain.

'T is Thou dost crown my hopes and plans
   With good success each day:
This crown, together with myself,
   At Thy blest feet I lay.

O let my house a temple be,
   That I and mine may sing
Hosanna to Thy Majesty,
   And praise our heavenly King!

JOHN HAMPDEN GURNEY.
FROM JOHN MASON.

---

*As the hart panteth after the water brooks,
so panteth my soul after Thee, O God.*
Psalm xlii. 1.

SOURCE of good, whose power controls
   Every movement of our souls;
   Wind that quickens where it blows;
Comforter of human woes
Lamp of God, whose ray serene
In the darkest night is seen;
Come, inspire my feeble strain,
That I may not sing in vain!

God's own Finger, skilled to teach
Tongues of every land and speech;
Balsam of the wounded soul,
Binding up, and making whole;

Flame of pure and holy love;
Strength of all that live and move,
Come! Thy gifts and fire impart;
Make me love Thee from the heart!

LOVE.

As the hart, with longing, looks
For refreshing water-brooks,
Heated in the burning chase,
So my soul desires Thy grace:
So my heavy-laden breast,
By the cares of life opprest,
Longs Thy cooling streams to taste
In this dry and barren waste.

Mighty Spirit! by whose aid
Man a living soul was made,
Everlasting God! whose fire
Kindles chaste and pure desire,
Grant, in every grief and loss,
I may calmly bear the cross,
And surrender all to Thee,
Comforting and strengthening me!

Let not hell, with frowns or smiles,
Open force or cunning wiles,
Snap the thread of my brief days;
But, when gently life decays,
Take to Heaven Thy servant dear,
Who hath loved and served Thee here;
There eternal hymns to raise,
Mighty Spirit! to Thy praise!

RICHARD MASSIE.
FROM JOHN FRANK.

Blessed are the poor in spirit: for theirs is the kingdom of Heaven.
Matthew, v. 3.

BLEST are the humble souls that see
Their emptiness and poverty;
Treasures of grace to them are given,
And crowns of joy laid up in Heaven.

Blest are the men of broken heart
Who mourn for sin with inward smart;
The blood of Christ divinely flows,
A healing balm for all their woes.

Blest are the meek, who stand afar
From rage and passion, noise and war;
God will secure their happy state,
And plead their cause against the great.

Blest are the souls that thirst for grace,
Hunger and long for righteousness;
They shall be well supplied and fed
With living streams and living bread.

Blest are the men whose bowels move
And melt with sympathy and love;
From Christ the Lord shall they obtain
Like sympathy and love again.

LOVE.

Blest are the pure, whose hearts are clean
From the defiling power of sin;
With endless pleasure they shall see
A God of spotless purity.

Blest are the men of peaceful life,
Who quench the coals of growing strife;
They shall be called the heirs of bliss,
The sons of God, the God of peace.

Blest are the sufferers, who partake
Of pain and shame for Jesus' sake;
Their souls shall triumph in the Lord.
Glory and joy are their reward.

ISAAC WATTS.

The love which passeth knowledge.
Ephesians, iii 19.

LOVE divine, all love excelling,
   Joy of Heaven, to earth come down;
Fix in us Thy humble dwelling;
   All Thy faithful mercies crown.
Jesus, Thou art all compassion;
   Pure, unbounded love Thou art:
Visit us with Thy salvation;
   Enter every longing heart.

LOVE.

Come, almighty to deliver,
    Let us all Thy grace receive;
Suddenly return, and never,
    Never more Thy temples leave.
Thee we would be always blessing,
    Serve Thee as Thy hosts above;
Pray and praise Thee without ceasing;
    Glory in Thy precious love.

Finish, then, Thy new creation:
    Pure, unspotted may we be;
Let us see our whole salvation
    Perfectly secured by Thee;
Changed from glory into glory,
    Till in Heaven we take our place;
Till we cast our crowns before Thee,
    Lost in wonder, love, and praise.

                          CHARLES WESLEY.

Brethren, by love serve one another.
                          Galatians, v. 13.

HOW sweet, how heavenly is the sight,
    When those that love the Lord
In one another's peace delight,
    And so fulfil His word!

When each can feel his brother's sigh,
    And with him bear a part;

LOVE.

When sorrow flows from eye to eye,
    And joy from heart to heart;

When, free from envy, scorn, and pride,
    Our wishes all above,
Each can his brother's failings hide,
    And show a brother's love;

When love in one delightful stream
    Through every bosom flows;
When union sweet, and dear esteem
    In every action glows.

Love is the golden chain that binds
    The happy souls above;
And he's an heir of Heaven that finds
    His bosom glow with love.

JOSEPH SWAIN.

In the likeness of man He humbled Himself, and became obedient unto death.
Philippians, ii. 7.

THOU Son of God and Son of man,
    Beloved, adored Immanuel!
Who didst, before all time began,
    In glory with Thy Father dwell:

We sing Thy love, who didst in time
    For us humanity assume,

LOVE.

To answer for the sinner's crime,
To suffer in the sinner's room.

The ransomed Church Thy glory sings;
The hosts of Heaven Thy will obey;
And, Lord of lords and Kings of kings,
We celebrate Thy blessed sway.

A servant's form Thou didst sustain,
And with delight the law obey;
Thou didst endure amazing pain,
While all our sorrows on Thee lay.

Blest Saviour, we are wholly Thine,
So freely loved, so dearly bought;
Our souls to Thee would we resign,
To Thee subject our every thought.

ANON.

The fruit of the Spirit is love, joy, peace.
Galatians, v. 22.

COMPARED with Christ, in all beside
    No comeliness I see;
The one thing needful, dearest Lord,
    Is to be one with Thee.

The sense of Thy expiring love
    Into my soul convey;

LOVE.

Thyself bestow: for Thee alone
   I absolutely pray.

Whatever else Thy will withholds,
   Here grant me to succeed!
O let Thyself my portion be,
   And I am blest indeed!
Less than Thyself will not suffice
   My comfort to restore;
More than Thyself I cannot have,
   And Thou canst give no more.

Loved of my God, for Him again
   With love intense I burn;
Chosen of Thee ere time began,
   I choose Thee in return!
Whate'er consists not with Thy love,
   O teach me to resign!
I'm rich to all th' intents of bliss,
   If Thou, O God, art mine!

AUGUSTUS M. TOPLADY.

JOY.

Go forth into the plain, and I will there talk with thee.
                                                    Ezekiel, iii. 22.

FAR from the world, O Lord, I flee,
    From strife and tumult far;
From scenes where Satan wages still
    His most successful war.

JOY.

The calm retreat, the silent shade,
   With prayer and praise agree,
And seem by Thy sweet bounty made
   For those who follow Thee.

There, if Thy Spirit touch the soul,
   And grace her mean abode,
  with what peace, and joy, and love,
   She communes with her God!

There, like the nightingale, she pours
   Her solitary lays,
Nor asks a witness of her song,
   Nor thirsts for human praise.

Author and Guardian of my life,
   Sweet Source of light divine,
And, all harmonious names in one,
   My Saviour! Thou art mine!

What thanks I owe Thee, and what love!
   A boundless, endless store
Shall echo through the realms above,
   When time shall be no more!

WILLIAM COWPER.

JOY.

Although the fig tree shall not blossom,
yet I will rejoice in the Lord.
Habakkuk, iii. 17, 18.

SOMETIMES a light surprises
   The Christian while he sings;
It is the Lord, who rises
   With healing in His wings:
When comforts are declining,
   He grants the soul again
A season of clear shining,
   To cheer it after rain.

In holy contemplation
   We sweetly then pursue
The theme of God's salvation,
   And find it ever new:
Set free from present sorrow,
   We cheerfully can say,
E'en let the unknown morrow
   Bring with it what it may.

It can bring with it nothing
   But He will bear us through;
Who gives the lilies clothing
   Will clothe His people too;
Beneath the spreading heavens
   No creature but is fed;

And He who feeds the ravens
  Will give His children bread.

Though vine nor fig tree neither
  Their wonted fruit shall bear,
Though all the field should wither,
  Nor flocks nor herds be there;
Yet, God the same abiding,
  His praise shall tune my voice;
For, while in Him confiding,
  I cannot but rejoice.

WILLIAM COWPER.

Let the heart of them rejoice that seek the Lord.
Psalm cv. 3.

THE child leans on its mother's breast,
  Leaves there its cares, and is at rest;
The bird sits singing by his nest,
      And tells aloud
His trust in God, and so is blest
      'Neath every cloud.

He has no store, he sows no seed,
Yet sings aloud, and doth not heed;
By flowing stream or grassy mead
      He sings to shame
Men, who forget, in fear of need,
      A Father's Name.

The heart that trusts for ever sings,
And feels as light as it had wings;

JOY.

A well of peace within it springs:
    Come good or ill,
Whate'er to day, to-morrow brings,
    It is His will!

      ISAAC WILLIAMS.

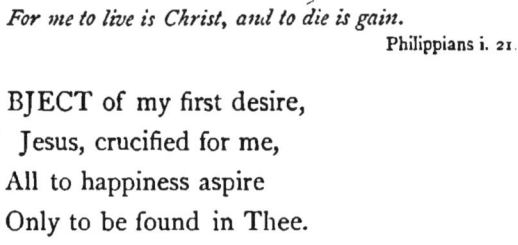

For me to live is Christ, and to die is gain.
      Philippians i. 21.

OBJECT of my first desire,
 Jesus, crucified for me,
All to happiness aspire
 Only to be found in Thee.
Thee to praise and Thee to know,
Constitute our bliss below;
Thee to see and Thee to love,
Constitute our bliss above.

Lord, it is not life to live,
If Thy presence Thou deny;
Lord, if Thou Thy presence give,
'T is no longer death to die.
Source and Giver of repose,
Singly from Thy smile it flows;
Peace and happiness are Thine,
Mine they are, if Thou art mine.

JOY.

While I feel Thy love to me,
Every object teems with joy;
Here, O! may I walk with Thee,
Then into Thy presence die.
Let me but Thyself possess—
Total sum of happiness!—
Real bliss I then shall prove,
Heaven below and Heaven above.

AUGUSTUS M. TOPLADY.

My spirit hath rejoiced in God my Saviour.
Luke i. 47.

JESUS, the very thought of Thee
   With sweetness fills my breast,
But sweeter far Thy face to see,
   And in Thy presence rest.

Nor voice can sing, nor heart can frame,
   Nor can the memory find
A sweeter sound than Thy blest Name,
   O Saviour of mankind.

O hope of every contrite heart!
   O joy of all the meek!
To those who fall how kind Thou art!
   How good to those who seek!

But what to those who find? Ah, this
    Nor tongue nor pen can show;
The love of Jesus—what it is
    None but His loved ones know.

Jesus, our only joy be Thou,
    As Thou our crown wilt be;
Jesus, be Thou our glory now
    And through eternity.

ST. BERNARD.

O come, let us sing unto the Lord: let us make a joyful noise to the Rock of our salvation.

Psalm xcv. 1.

COME, we that love the Lord,
    And let our joys be known;
Join in a song with sweet accord,
    And thus surround the throne.
The sorrows of the mind
    Be banished from the place:
Religion never was designed
    To make our pleasures less.

Let those refuse to sing
    That never knew our God;
But children of the heavenly King
    May speak their joys abroad.

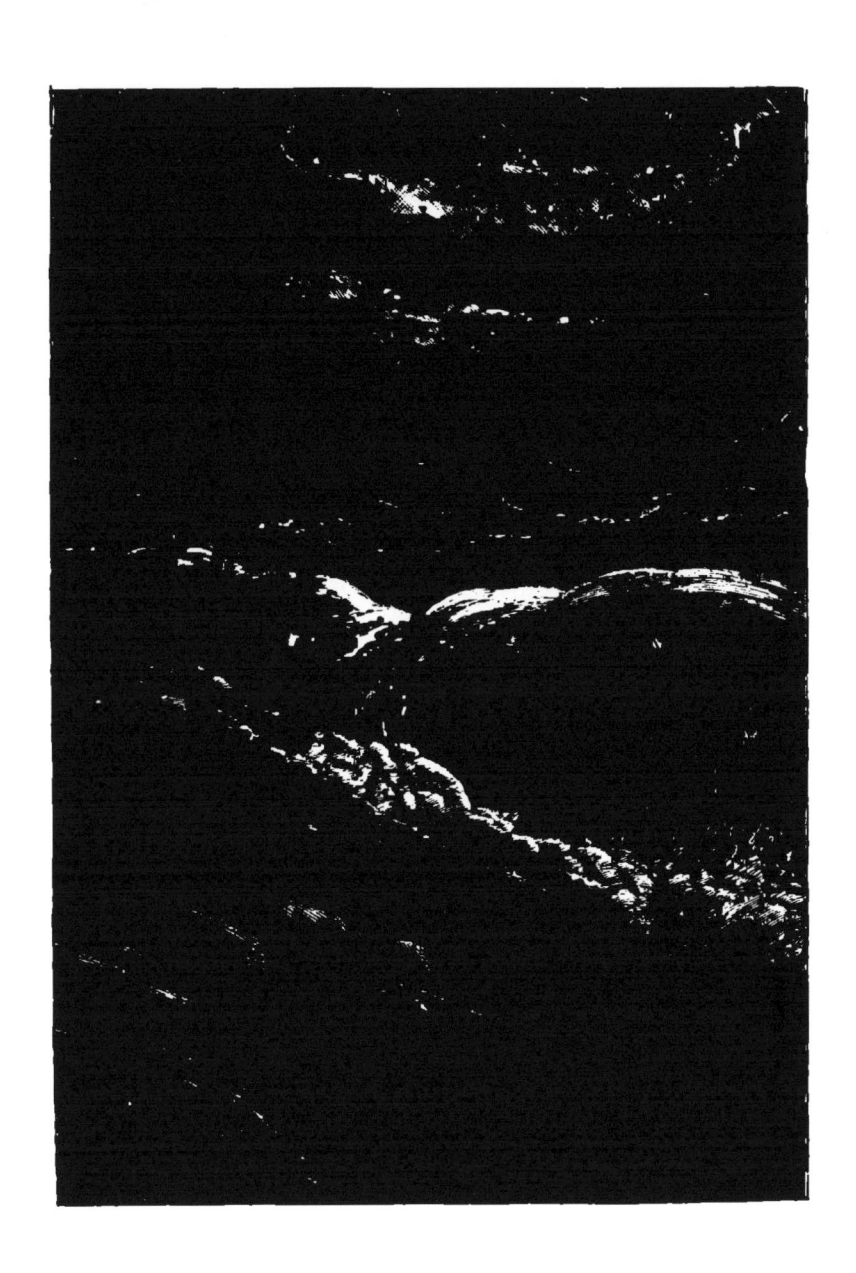

The God that rules on high,
And thunders when He please,

JOY.

 That rides upon the stormy sky,
  And manages the seas;

 This awful God is ours,
  Our Father and our love;
He shall send down His heavenly powers
  To carry us above.
  There shall we see His face,
  And never, never sin;
There, from the rivers of His grace,
  Drink endless pleasures in.

 Yes, and before we rise
  To that immortal state,
The thoughts of such amazing bliss
  Should constant joys create.
  The men of grace have found
  Glory begun below:
Celestial fruits on earthly ground
  From faith and hope may grow.

 The hill of Zion yields
  A thousand sacred sweets,
Before we reach the heavenly fields,
  Or walk the golden streets.
  Then let our songs abound,
  And every tear be dry
We're marching through Immanuel's ground,
  To fairer worlds on high.

       ISAAC WATTS.

JOY.

All things are yours: things present or things to come; all are yours.
I. Corinthians, iii. 21, 22.

HOW vast the treasure we possess!
How rich Thy bounty, King of grace!
This world is ours, and worlds to come;
Earth is our lodge, and Heaven our home.

All things are ours, the gifts of God,
The purchase of a Saviour's blood;
While the good Spirit shows us how
To use and to improve them too.

If peace and plenty crown my days,
They help me, Lord, to speak Thy praise;
If bread of sorrows be my food,
Those sorrows work my lasting good.

I would not change my blest estate
For all the world calls good or great;
And, while my faith can keep her hold,
I envy not the sinner's gold.

Father, I wait Thy daily will;
Thou shalt divide my portion still:
Grant me on earth what seems Thee best,
Till death and Heaven reveal the rest.

ISAAC WATTS.

JOY.

Whom having not seen, ye love; in whom, though now ye see Him not, yet believing, ye rejoice with joy unspeakable and full of glory.
I. Peter, i. 8.

MY God, the spring of all my joys,
    The life of my delights,
The glory of my brightest days,
    And comfort of my nights.

In darkest shades if He appear,
    My dawning is begun;
He is my soul's sweet Morning Star,
    And He my rising Sun.

The opening heavens around me shine
    With beams of sacred bliss,
While Jesus shows His heart is mine,
    And whispers I am His.

My soul would leave this heavy clay
    At that transporting word,
Run up with joy the shining way,
    T' embrace my dearest Lord.

Fearless of Hell and ghastly death,
    I'd break through every foe;
The wings of love and arms of faith
    Should bear me conqueror through.

ISAAC WATTS.

Humble yourselves therefore, that He may exalt you : casting all your care upon Him ; for He careth for you.

I. Peter, v. 6, 7.

THERE'S not a bird, with lonely nest
In pathless wood or mountain crest,
Nor meaner thing, which does not share,
O God ! in Thy paternal care.

There's not a being now accurst,
Who did not taste Thy goodness first ;

JOY.

And every joy the wicked see
Received its origin from Thee.

Each barren crag, each desert rude,
Holds Thee within its solitude;
And Thou dost bless the wanderer there,
Who makes His solitary prayer.

In busy mart and crowded street,
No less than in the still retreat,
Thou, Lord, art near, our souls to bless
With all a parent's tenderness.

And every moment still doth bring
Thy blessings on its loaded wing;
Widely they spread through earth and sky,
And last to all eternity!

Through all creation let Thy Name
Be echoed with a glad acclaim!
That let the grateful Churches sing,
With that let Heaven for ever ring!

And we, where'er our lot is cast,
While life and thought and feeling last,
Through all our years, in every place,
Will bless Thee for Thy boundless grace!

BAPTIST WRIOTHESLEY NOEL.

JOY.

*Happy art thou, O Israel: who is like unto
thee, O people saved by the Lord.*
Deuteronomy, xxxiii. 29.

ISRAEL, blest beyond compare!
Unrivalled all thy glories are!
Jehovah deigns to fill thy throne,
And calls thine interests His own.

He is thy Saviour, He thy Lord:
His shield is thine, and thine His sword;
Review in ecstacy of thought
The grand redemption He has wrought.

From Satan's yoke He sets thee free;
Opens thy passage through the sea;
He through the desert is thy guide,
And Heaven for Canaan will provide.

Not Jacob's sons of old could boast
Such favours to their chosen host;
Their glories, which through ages shine,
Are but dim shades and types of thine.

Celestial Spirit, teach our tongue
Sublimer strains than Moses sung,
Proportioned to the sweeter Name
Of God, the Saviour, and the Lamb.

PHILIP DODDRIDGE.

JOY.

The joy of the Lord is your strength.

Nehemiah, viii. 10.

JOY is a fruit that will not grow
 In nature's barren soil;
All we can boast, till Christ we know,
 Is vanity and toil.

But where the Lord has planted grace,
 And made His glories known,
There fruits of heavenly joy and peace
 Are found, and there alone.

A bleeding Saviour seen by faith,
 A sense of pardoning love,
A hope that triumphs over death,
 Give joys like those above.

To take a glimpse within the veil,
 To know that God is mine,
Are springs of joy that never fail,
 Unspeakable, divine!

These are the joys which satisfy
 And sanctify the mind,
Which make the spirit mount on high,
 And leave the world behind.

JOHN NEWTON.

JOY.

Sing praises to the Lord, which dwelleth in Zion.

Psalm ix. 11

IS Heaven begun below
 To hear Christ's praises flow
In Zion, where His Name is known:
 What will it be above
 To sing redeeming love,
And cast our crowns before His throne!

 When we adore Him there,
 We shall be void of fear,
Nor faith, nor hope, nor patience need:
 Love will absorb us quite,
 Love in the midst of light,
On God's eternal love shall feed.

 O! what sweet company
 We then shall hear and see!
What harmony will there abound!
 When souls unnumbered sing
 The praise of Zion's King,
Nor one dissenting voice is found!

 With everlasting joy,
 Such as will never cloy,
We shall be filled, nor wish for more,

JOY.

Bright as meridian day,
Calm as the evening ray,
Full as a sea without a shore.

Till that blest period come,
Zion shall be my home;
And may I never thence remove,
Till from the Church below
To Heaven at once I go,
And there commune in perfect love!

JOSEPH SWAIN.

The Lord is my strength and my shield; therefore my heart greatly rejoiceth; and with my song will I praise Him.
Psalm xxviii. 7.

I WILL praise Thee every day,
Now Thine anger's turned away:
Comfortable thoughts arise
From the bleeding sacrifice.

JOY.

Here, in the fair Gospel-field,
Wells of free salvation yield
Streams of life, a plenteous store,
And my soul shall thirst no more.

Jesus is become at length
My salvation and my strength;
And His praises shall prolong,
While I live, my pleasant song.

Praise ye, then, His glorious Name,
Publish His exalted fame;
Still His worth your praise exceeds,
Excellent are all His deeds.

Raise again the joyful sound,
Let the nations roll it round.
Zion, shout, for this is He:
God the Saviour dwells in thee.

WILLIAM COWPER.

Therefore will I give thanks unto Thee, O Lord, and sing praises unto Thy Name.
Psalm xviii. 49.

AWAKE, my soul, in joyful lays,
And sing the great Redeemer's praise:
He justly claims a song from me,—
His loving-kindness, O how free!

He saw me ruined in the fall,
Yet loved me, notwithstanding all;
He saved me from my lost estate:
His loving-kindness, O how great!

When trouble, like a gloomy cloud,
Has gathered thick and thundered loud,
He near my soul has ever stood:
His loving-kindness, O how good!

Soon shall I pass the gloomy vale;
Soon all my mortal powers must fail;
O may my last expiring breath
His loving-kindness sing in death.

Then let me mount and soar away
To the bright world of endless day,
And sing, with rapture and surprise,
His loving-kindness in the skies.

SAMUEL MEDLEY.

Sing unto the Lord a new song; sing unto the Lord, all the earth.
Psalm xcvi. 1.

AWAKE, and sing the song
    Of Moses and the Lamb,
Wake every heart and every tongue
    To praise the Saviour's Name.

JOY.

Sing of His dying love;
   Sing of His rising power;
Sing how He intercedes above
   For those whose sins He bore.

Sing, till we feel our hearts
   Ascending with our tongues;
Sing, till the love of sin departs,
   And grace inspires our songs.

Sing on your heavenly way,
   Ye ransomed sinners, sing;
Sing on, rejoicing every day
   In Christ the eternal King.

Soon shall ye hear Him say,
   Ye blessed children, come;
Soon will He call you hence away,
   And take His wanderers home.

MARTIN MADAN.
VARIATION FROM WILLIAM HAMMOND.

Ye have need of patience.
Hebrews, x. 36.

Tribulation worketh patience; and patience, experience; and experience, hope; and hope maketh not ashamed.
Romans, v. 3, 4, 5.

Now the God of patience and consolation grant you to be likeminded one toward another, according to Christ Jesus.
Romans, xv. 5.

Be patient therefore, brethren, unto the coming of the Lord.
James, v. 7.

PATIENCE

Rejoice in the Lord, O ye righteous.
                    Psalm xxxiii. 1.

REJOICE, though storms assail thee;
    Rejoice, when skies are bright;
Rejoice, though round thy pathway
    Is spread the gloom of night:
If the good hope be in thee
    That all at last is well,
Then let thy happy spirit
    With joyful feelings swell!

Look back on early childhood,
    And let thy soul rejoice!

Who then upheld thy goings,
  And tuned thy feeble voice?
Look back on youth's gay visions
  When life one glory seemed:
Who poured those rays of gladness
  Which on thy prospect beamed?

Recall the hours of anguish,
  And let thy soul rejoice,
Though wave on wave of sorrow
  Rush on with fearful noise:
Was not the bow of promise
  Still seen amidst the gloom,
Shedding its hallowed lustre
  E'en round the silent tomb?

Rejoice, rejoice for ever,
  Though earthly friends be gone!
For silently and swiftly
  The wheels of time roll on;
And still they bear thee forward
  Nearer that happy shore,
While the triumphant song is,
  "Rejoice for evermore!"

ANON.

Whom have I in Heaven but Thee?
                                    Psalm lxxiii. 25.

NEARER, my God to Thee,
    Nearer to Thee!
E'en though it be a cross
    That raiseth me;
Still all my song shall be,
Nearer, my God, to Thee,
    Nearer to Thee!

Though like the wanderer,
    The sun gone down,
Darkness be over me,
    My rest a stone;
Yet in my dreams I'd be
Nearer, my God, to Thee,
    Nearer to Thee!

There let the way appear
    Steps unto Heaven;
All that Thou send'st to me
    In mercy given;
Angels to beckon me
Nearer, my God, to Thee,
    Nearer to Thee!

Then with my waking thoughts
  Bright with Thy praise,
Out of my stony griefs
  Bethel I'll raise;
So by my woes to be
Nearer, my God, to Thee,
  Nearer to Thee!

Or if on joyful wing
  Cleaving the sky,
Sun, moon, and stars forgot,
  Upwards I fly,
Still all my song shall be,
Nearer, my God, to Thee,
  Nearer to Thee!

SARAH FLOWER ADAMS.

In all thy ways acknowledge Him, and He shall direct thy paths.
Proverbs, iii. 6.

COMMIT thou all thy griefs
  And ways into His hands,
To his sure truth and tender care
  Who earth and Heaven commands;

Who points the clouds their course,
Whom winds and seas obey;

He shall direct thy wandering feet,
He shall prepare thy way.

Thou on the Lord rely,
  So safe shalt thou go on;
Fix on His work thy steadfast eye,
  So shall thy work be done.

No profit canst thou gain
  By self-consuming care;
To Him commend thy cause; His ear
  Attends the softest prayer.

Thy everlasting truth,
  Father! Thy ceaseless love,
Sees all Thy children's wants, and knows
  What best for each will prove.

And whatsoe'er Thou will'st
  Thou dost, O King of kings;
What Thy unerring wisdom chose,
  Thy power to being brings.

Thou everywhere hast sway,
  And all things serve Thy might;
Thy every act pure blessing is,
  Thy path unsullied light.

When Thou arisest, Lord,
  Who shall Thy work withstand?
When all Thy children want Thou giv'st,
  Who, who shall stay Thy hand?

PATIENCE.

Give to the winds thy fears;
Hope and be undismayed;
God hears thy sigh and counts thy tears,
God shall lift up thy head.

Through waves and clouds and storms,
He gently clears thy way;
Wait thou His time; so shall this night
Soon end in joyous day.

Still heavy is thy heart?
Still sink thy spirits down?
Cast off the weight, let fear depart,
And every care be gone.

What though thou rulest not?
Yet Heaven and earth and Hell
Proclaim, God sitteth on the throne,
And ruleth all things well!

Leave to His sovereign sway
To choose and to command;
So shalt thou wondering own, His way
How wise, how strong His hand!

Far, far above thy thought
His counsel shall appear,
When fully He the work hath wrought
That caused thy needless fear.

PATIENCE.

Thou seest our weakness, Lord!
Our hearts are known to Thee:
O! lift Thou up the sinking hand,
Confirm the feeble knee!

Let us, in life, in death,
Thy steadfast truth declare,
And publish, with our latest breath,
Thy love and guardian care!

JOHN WESLEY.
FROM PAUL GERHARDT.

So shall we ever be with the Lord.
I. Thessalonians, iv. 17.

FOR ever with the Lord!
   Amen! so let it be!
Life from the dead is in that word,
   And immortality!

Here in the body pent,
   Absent from Him I roam,
Yet nightly pitch my moving tent
   A day's march nearer home.

My Father's house on high,
   Home of my soul! how near,
At times, to faith's foreseeing eye,
   Thy golden gates appear!

PATIENCE.

Ah! then my spirit faints
  To reach the land I love,
The bright inheritance of saints,
  Jerusalem above!

Yet clouds will intervene,
  And all my prospect flies;
Like Noah's dove, I flit between
  Rough seas and stormy skies.

Anon the clouds depart,
  The winds and waters cease;
While sweetly o'er my gladdened heart
  Expands the bow of peace!

Beneath its glowing arch,
  Along the hallowed ground,
I see cherubic armies march,
  A camp of fire around.

I hear at morn and even,
  At noon and midnight hour,
The choral harmonies of Heaven
  Earth's Babel tongues o'erpower.

Then, then I feel that He
  Remembered or forgot,
The Lord, is never far from me
  Though I perceive Him not.

JAMES MONTGOMERY.

PATIENCE.

*The angel of the Lord encampeth round
about them that fear Him.*
Psalm xxxiv. 7.

O N silent wings an angel
  Through all the land is borne,
  Sent by the gracious Father
To comfort them that mourn.
There's blessing in his glances,
Peace dwells where'er he came,
O! follow when he calls thee,
For *Patience* is his name.

Through earthly care and sorrow
He'll smooth the thorny way,
And speak with hopeful courage
Of brighter, happier day;
And when thy weakness falters,
His strength is firm and fast;
He'll help to bear thy burden,
He'll lead thee home at last.

Thy tears he never chideth,
When comfort he'd impart;
Rebuking not, he quiets
The longings of thy heart;
And when, in stormy sorrow,
Thou murmuring askest "Why?"

PATIENCE.

He, silent yet, but smiling,
Points upward to the sky.

He will not always answer
Each question that's addrest;
His maxim is "Endure thou,
And after toil comes rest."
Through life, if thou wilt love him,
Thus by thy side he'll wend,
Oft silent, ever hopeful,
Still looking to the end.

DR. H. W. DULCKEN.

Evening, and morning, and at noon, will I pray.
Psalm lv. 17.

My voice shalt Thou hear in the morning, O Lord; in the morning will I direct my prayer unto Thee, and will look up.
Psalm v. 3.

And God called the light Day, and the darkness He called Night. And the evening and the morning were the first day.
Genesis i. v.

With my soul have I desired Thee in the night.
Isaiah, xxvi 9.

MORNING.

His compassions fail not; they are new every morning.
Lamentations, iii. 22, 23.

CHRIST, whose glory fills the skies,
    Christ, the true, the only Light,
Sun of Righteousness, arise,
    Triumph o'er the shades of night!
Day-spring from on high, be near!
Day-star, in my heart appear!

MORNING.

Dark and cheerless is the morn
   Unaccompanied by Thee;
Joyless is the day's return
   Till Thy mercy's beams I see;
Till they inward light impart,
Glad my eyes and warm my heart.

Visit then this soul of mine,
   Pierce the gloom of sin and grief!
Fill me, Radiancy Divine,
   Scatter all my unbelief!
More and more Thyself display,
Shining to the perfect day.

CHARLES WESLEY.

The Lord's mercies . . are new every morning.
Lamentations, iii. 22, 23.

O TIMELY happy, timely wise,
Hearts that with rising morn arise;
Eyes that the beams celestial view,
Which evermore makes all things new.

New every morning is the love
Our wakening and uprising prove;
Through sleep and darkness safely brought,
Restored to life, and power, and thought.

MORNING.

New mercies, each returning day,
Hover around us while we pray;
New perils past, new sins forgiven,
New thoughts of God, new hopes of Heaven.

If, on our daily course, our mind
Be set to hallow all we find,
New treasures still, of countless price,
God will provide for sacrifice.

Old friends, old scenes, will lovelier be,
As more of Heaven in each we see;
Some softening gleam of love and prayer
Shall dawn on every cross and care.

As for some dear familiar strain
Untired we ask, and ask again,
Ever, in its melodious store,
Finding a spell unheard before;

Such is the bliss of souls serene,
When they have sworn, and steadfast mean,
Counting the cost, in all t' espy
Their God, in all themselves deny.

O could we learn that sacrifice,
What lights would all around us rise!
How would our hearts with wisdom talk
Along life's dullest, dreariest walk!

MORNING.

We need not bid, for cloistered cell,
Our neighbour and our work farewell,
Nor strive to wind ourselves too high
For sinful man beneath the sky:

The trivial round, the common task,
Will furnish all we ought to ask,—
Room to deny ourselves; a road
To bring us daily nearer God.

Seek we no more: content with these,
Let present rapture, comfort, ease,
As Heaven shall bid them, come and go;
The secret this of rest below.

Only, O Lord, in Thy dear love,
Fit us for perfect rest above;
And help us, this and every day,
To live more nearly as we pray.

JOHN KEBLE.

In the morning shall my prayer prevent Thee.
Psalm lxxxviii. 13.

SINCE Thou hast added now, O God,
    Unto my life another day,
And giv'st me leave to walk abroad,
    And labour in my lawful way;

My walks and works with me begin,
Conduct me forth and bring me in.

MORNING.

In every power my soul enjoys
   Internal virtues to improve;
In every sense that she employs
   In her external works to move;
Bless her, O God, and keep me sound
From outward harm and inward wound.

Let sin nor Satan's fraud prevail
   To make mine eye of reason blind,
Or faith, or hope, or love to fail,
   Or any virtues of the mind;
But more and more let them increase,
And bring me to mine end in peace.

Lewd courses let my feet forbear;
   Keep Thou my hands from doing wrong;
Let not ill counsels pierce mine ear,
   Nor wicked words defile my tongue;
And keep the windows of each eye,
That no strange lust climb in thereby.

But guard Thou safe my heart in chief,
   That neither hate, revenge, nor fear,
Nor vain desire, vain joy or grief,
   Obtain command or dwelling there:
And, Lord! with every saving grace,
Still true to Thee maintain that place!

So till the evening of this morn
   My time shall then so well be spent,

MORNING.

That when the twilight shall return
I may enjoy it with content,
And to Thy praise and honour say
That this hath proved a happy day.

GEORGE WITHER.

The Lord shall guide thee continually, and satisfy thy soul.
Isaiah, lviii. 11.

THROUGH all the dangers of the night
    Preserved, O Lord, by Thee,
Again we hail the cheerful light,
    Again we bow the knee.

Preserve us, Lord, throughout the day,
    And guide us by Thine arm;
For they are safe, and only they,
    Whom Thou preserv'st from harm.

Let all our words and all our ways
    Declare that we are Thine,
That so the light of truth and grace
    Before the world may shine.

Let us ne'er turn away from Thee;
    O Saviour, hold us fast,
Till with unclouded eyes we see
    Thy glorious face at last.

ANON.

The darkness and the light are both alike to Thee.
Psalm cxxxix. 12.

LORD God of morning and of night,
We thank Thee for Thy gift of light:
As in the dawn the shadows fly,
We seem to find Thee now more nigh.

Fresh hopes have wakened in our hearts,
Fresh energy to do our parts;
Thy thousand sleeps our strength restore,
A thousandfold to serve Thee more.

Yet whilst Thy will we would pursue,
Oft what we would we cannot do;
The sun may stand in zenith skies,
But on the soul thick midnight lies.

O Lord of lights! 'tis Thou alone
Canst make our darkened hearts Thine own:
Though this new day with joy we see,
O Dawn of God! we cry for Thee!

Praise God, our Maker and our Friend!
Praise Him through time till time shall end!
Till psalm and song His Name adore
Through Heaven's great day of Evermore!

FRANCIS TURNER PALGRAVE.

My voice shalt Thou hear in the morning.
                                    Psalm v. 3.

GOD of the morning, at whose voice
    The cheerful sun makes haste to rise,
  And like a giant doth rejoice
    To run his journey through the skies;

From the fair chambers of the east
    The circuit of his race begins,
And, without weariness or rest,
    Round the whole earth he flies and shines;

O, like the sun, may I fulfil
    Th' appointed duties of the day,
With ready mind and active will
    March on, and keep my heavenly way!

MORNING.

But I shall rove and lose the race,
   If God, my Sun, should disappear,
And leave me in this world's wide maze
   To follow every wandering star.

Lord, Thy commands are clean and pure,
   Enlightening our beclouded eyes;
Thy threatenings just, Thy promise sure;
   Thy Gospel makes the simple wise.

Give me Thy counsel for my guide,
   And then receive me to Thy bliss:
All my desires and hopes beside
   Are faint and cold, compared with this!

ISAAC WATTS.

In the morning will I direct my prayer unto Thee, and will look up.
Psalm v. 3.

AWAKE, my soul, and with the sun
Thy daily stage of duty run;
Shake off dull sloth, and joyful rise
To pay thy morning sacrifice.

Thy precious time misspent redeem;
Each present day thy last esteem;
Improve thy talent with due care;
For the great day thyself prepare.

In conversation be sincere;
Keep conscience as the noontide clear;
Think how all-seeing God thy ways
And all thy secret thoughts surveys.

By influence of the light divine
Let thy own light to others shine;
Reflect all Heaven's propitious ways,
In ardent love and cheerful praise.

Wake up and lift thyself, my heart,
And with the angels bear thy part,
Who all night long unwearied sing
High praise to the Eternal King.

Awake! awake, ye heavenly choir!
May your devotion me inspire,
That I, like you, my age may spend,
Like you may on my God attend!

May I, like you, in God delight,
Have all day long my God in sight;
Perform, like you, my Maker's will;
O, may I never more do ill!

Had I your wings, to Heaven I'd fly;
But God shall that defect supply,
And my soul, winged with warm desire.
Shall all day long to Heaven aspire.

MORNING.

All praise to Thee, who safe hast kept,
And hast refreshed me whilst I slept.
Grant, Lord, when I from death shall wake,
I may of endless light partake!

I would not wake, nor rise again,
Ev'n Heaven itself I would disdain,
Wert Thou not there to be enjoyed,
And I in hymns to be employed.

Heaven is, dear Lord, where'er Thou art;
O, never then from me depart!
For to my soul 't is Hell to be
But for one moment void of Thee.

Lord, I my vows to Thee renew;
Disperse my sins as morning dew;
Guard my first springs of thought and will,
And with Thyself my spirit fill.

Direct, control, suggest, this day,
All I design, or do, or say;
That all my powers, with all their might,
In Thy sole glory may unite.

Praise God, from whom all blessings flow;
Praise Him, all creatures here below!
Praise Him above, ye heavenly host;
Praise Father, Son, and Holy Ghost!

BISHOP THOMAS KEN.

MORNING.

> *Sing unto the Lord, all the earth; shew forth from day to day His salvation.*
> I. Chronicles, xvi. 23

JESU, Lord of heavenly grace,
  Thou brightness of Thy Father's face,
Thou fountain of eternal light,
Whose beams disperse the shades of night!

Come, heavenly Sun of heavenly love,
Shower down Thy radiance from above,
And to our inward hearts convey
The Holy Spirit's cloudless ray!

And we the Father's help will claim,
And sing the Father's glorious Name;
His powerful succour we implore,
That we may stand, to fall no more.

May He our actions deign to bless,
And loose the bonds of wickedness;
From sudden falls our feet defend,
And bring us to a prosperous end!

May faith, deep rooted in the soul,
Subdue our flesh, our minds control;
May guile depart, and discord cease,
And all within be joy and peace!

And Christ shall be our daily food,
Our daily drink His precious blood;
And thus the Spirit's calm excess
Shall fill our souls with holiness.

O hallowed be the approaching day!
Let meekness be our morning ray,
And faithful love our noonday light,
And hope our sunset, calm and bright!

O Christ, with each returning morn
Thine image to our hearts is borne:
O, may we ever clearly see
Our Saviour and our God in Thee!

JOHN CHANDLER.
FROM ST. AMBROSE.

I will pay my vows unto the Lord now.
Psalm cxvi. 18.

GOD, we thank Thee for the love
    And care Thou dost bestow
Upon us in our sleeping hours,
    And all the hours we know.

And now the gladsome morning sun
    Lights all the land and sea,
And we, refreshed by blessed sleep,
    Rise up to worship Thee.

All glorious is Thy holy Name,
　　All wondrous is Thy might;
Creator of the sunlit day
　　And of the starry night.

If Thou, O God, dost grant thy love,
　　The world shall hurt no more,

MORNING.

Though sin may chafe, as doth the sea
   Upon a rock-girt shore.

O shield us in temptation's hour!
   O guard us night and day!
O give us Thy protecting love!
   And hear us when we pray.

ANON.

And Samuel lay until the morning.
I. Samuel, iii. 15.

LORD, from my bed again I rise
   To offer up the sacrifice
     Of praise and prayer to Thee:
   I laid me down to sleep at night;
   I trusted in Thine arm of might:
     Thine arm protected me.

Uphold Thy servant through the day;
Direct my steps in wisdom's way,
   Let me not turn aside;
Let me not walk where scorners walk,
And sinful men profanely talk:
   Still be my God and Guide.

BARTHOLOMEW.

MORNING.

Whatsoever ye do, do all to the glory of God.
I. Corinthians, x. 31.

FORTH in Thy Name, O Lord, I go,
My daily labour to pursue,
Thee, only Thee, resolved to know,
In all I think, or speak, or do.

The task Thy wisdom has assigned,
O let me cheerfully fulfil;
In all Thy works Thy presence find,
And prove Thy good and perfect will

Thee may I set at my right hand,
Whose eyes my inmost substance see,
And labour on at Thy command,
And offer all my works to Thee.

Give me to bear Thine easy yoke,
And every moment watch and pray;
And still to things eternal look,
And hasten to Thy glorious day.

For Thee delightfully employ
Whate'er Thy bounteous grace hath given,
And run my even course with joy,
And closely walk with Thee to Heaven.

CHARLES WESLEY.

MORNING.

*Day unto day uttereth speech, and night unto
night sheweth knowledge.* Psalms xix. 2.

ONCE more, my soul, the rising day
   Salutes thy waking eyes;
Once more, my voice, thy tribute pay
   To Him that rules the skies.

Night unto night His Name repeats,
   The day renews the sound
Wide as the heaven on which He sits,
   To turn the seasons round.

'T is He supports my mortal frame,
   My tongue shall speak His praise;
My sins would rouse His wrath to flame,
   And yet His wrath delays.

Great God, let all my hours be Thine,
   Whilst I enjoy the light,
Then shall my sun in smiles decline,
   And bring a pleasant night.
ISAAC WATTS.

Every good gift and every perfect gift is from above.
James, i. 17.

FATHER of life and light,
   To Thee our song we raise:
For all the mercies of the night
   Accept our humble praise.

MORNING.

Thy providential care
Our morning board has spread;
O may our souls Thy favour share,
And eat the living bread.

Thus strengthened by Thy voice
In duty's path to run,
Our faith and hope in Christ we place,
And say, Thy will be done

And when the vesper's peal
From toil recalls us home,
Before Thy mercy-seat we'll kneel,
And pray, Thy kingdom come!

S. FLETCHER.

I will praise Thy Name for ever and ever.
Psalm cxlv. 2.

LORD, in the morning Thou shalt hear
   My voice ascending high;
To Thee will I direct my prayer,
   To Thee lift up mine eye—

Up to the hills where Christ is gone
   To plead for all His saints,
Presenting at His Father's throne
   Our songs and our complaints.

MORNING.

Thou art a God before whose sight
    The wicked shall not stand;
Sinners shall ne'er be Thy delight,
    Nor dwell at Thy right hand.

But to Thy house will I resort,
    To taste Thy mercies there;
I will frequent Thy holy court,
    And worship in Thy fear.

O, may Thy Spirit guide my feet
    In ways of righteousness;
Make every path of duty straight
    And plain before my face.

ISAAC WATTS.

EVENING.

Hear me when I call, O God.

Psalm iv. 1.

BEHOLD, the sun, that seemed but now
  Enthronèd overhead,
Beginneth to decline below
  The globe whereon we tread;

And he, whom yet we look upon
  With comfort and delight,

EVENING.

Will quite depart from hence anon,
   And leave us to the night.

Thus time, unheeded, steals away
   The life which Nature gave;
Thus are our bodies every day
   Declining to the grave;

Thus from us all our pleasures fly
   Whereon we set our heart;
And when the night of death draws nigh,
   Thus will they all depart.

Lord, though the sun forsake our sight,
   And mortal hopes are vain,
Let still Thine everlasting light
   Within our souls remain!

And in the nights of our distress
   Vouchsafe those rays divine,
Which from the Sun of righteousness
   For ever brightly shine!

GEORGE WITHER.

EVENING.

I will sing unto the Lord, because He hath dealt bountifully with me.

Psalm xiii. 6.

ACCEPT, my God, my evening song,
    Like incense let it fragrant rise;
Stir up my heart, and tune my tongue,
    And let the music reach the skies.

Thou hast my kind Protector been
    Through all the dangers of the day;
My Guardian to defend from sin,
    My Guide to choose me out my way.

The flowing spring of all my good,
    Still pouring blessings from on high,
Thine hand hath dealt me out my food,
    For every want a kind supply.

Unceasing, Lord, Thy bounty flowed;
    Each moment brought me in fresh aid;
But what returns of love to God
    Have I for all His kindness made?

What have I done for Him who died
    To save myself from endless woe?
How much have I His patience tried
    From whom all my enjoyments flow!

Fast as my flying minutes pass,
   My faults augment the former sum!
Forgive the past, and by Thy grace
   Prevent the like for time to come!

Dear Saviour, to Thy Cross I'll fly,
   And there my guilty head recline,
And my whole soul, that sin may die,
   Yield up to influence divine!

Then, sprinkled with atoning blood,
   I'll lay me down and take my rest,
Trust the protection of my God,
   And sleep as on my Saviour's breast.

SIMON BROWNE,
VARIATION FROM ISAAC WATTS.

Abide with us: the day is far spent.
Luke, xxiv. 29.

ABIDE with me! fast falls the eventide;
The darkness deepens; Lord, with me abide!
When other helpers fail and comforts flee,
Help of the helpless, O abide with me!

Swift to its close ebbs out life's little day;
Earth's joys grow dim, its glories pass away;
Change and decay in all around I see:
O Thou who changest not, abide with me!

EVENING.

Not a brief glance I beg, a passing word;
But, as Thou dwell'st with Thy disciples, Lord,
Familiar, condescending, patient, free,
Come, not to sojourn, but abide, with me!

Come not in terrors, as the King of kings,
But kind and good, with healing in Thy wings;
Tears for all woes, a heart for every plea;
Come, Friend of sinners, and thus 'bide with me!

Thou on my head in early youth didst smile;
And, though rebellious and perverse meanwhile,
Thou hast not left me, oft as I left Thee:
On to the close, O Lord, abide with me!

I need Thy presence every passing hour:
What but Thy grace can foil the tempter's power?
Who like Thyself my Guide and Stay can be?
Through cloud and sunshine, O abide with me!

I fear no foe, with Thee at hand to bless:
Ills have no weight and tears no bitterness:
Where is Death's sting? where, Grave, thy victory?
I triumph still, if Thou abide with me!

Hold then Thy Cross before my closing eyes!
Shine through the gloom, and point me to the skies!
Heaven's morning breaks, and earth's vain shadows flee;
In life and death, O Lord, abide with me!

HENRY FRANCIS LYTE.

EVENING.

He shall give His angels charge concerning Thee.
Matthew, iv 6.

HEAR my prayer, O heavenly Father,
    Ere I lay me down to sleep:
Bid Thine angels, pure and holy,
    Round my bed their vigil keep.

My sins are heavy, but Thy mercy
    Far outweighs them every one;
Down before Thy Cross I cast them,
    Trusting in Thy help alone.

Keep me, through this night of peril,
    Underneath its boundless shade;
Take me to Thy rest, I pray Thee,
    When my pilgrimage is made!

None shall measure out Thy patience
    By the span of human thought;
None shall bound the tender mercies
    Which Thy Holy Son hath bought.

Pardon all my past transgressions;
    Give me strength for days to come;
Guide and guard me with Thy blessing
    Till Thine angels bid me home!

HARRIETT PARR.

EVENING.

He giveth His beloved sleep.
Psalm cxxvii. 2.

SUN of my soul, Thou Saviour dear,
It is not night if Thou be near;
O! may no earth-born cloud arise
To hide Thee from Thy servant's eyes!

When round Thy wondrous works below
My searching rapturous glance I throw,
Tracing out wisdom, power, and love,
In earth or sky, in stream or grove;

EVENING.

Or, by the light Thy words disclose,
Watch time's full river as it flows,
Scanning Thy gracious Providence,
Where not too deep for mortal sense;

When with dear friends sweet talk I hold,
And all the flowers of life unfold,
Let not my heart within me burn
Except in all I Thee discern!

When the soft dews of kindly sleep
My wearied eyelids gently steep,
Be my last thought, How sweet to rest
For ever on my Saviour's breast!

Abide with me from morn till eve,
For without Thee I cannot live!
Abide with me when night is nigh,
For without Thee I dare not die!

Thou Framer of the light and dark,
Steer through the tempest Thine own ark!
Amid the howling wintry sea
We are in port if we have Thee.

The rulers of this Christian land,
'Twixt Thee and us ordained to stand,
Guide Thou their course, O Lord, aright!
Let all do all as in Thy sight!

EVENING.

O! by Thine own sad burthen, borne
So meekly up the hill of scorn,
Teach Thou Thy priests their daily cross
To bear as Thine, nor count it loss!

If some poor wandering child of Thine
Have spurned, to-day, the voice divine,
Now, Lord, the gracious work begin;
Let him no more lie down in sin.

Watch by the sick; enrich the poor
With blessings from Thy boundless store;
Be every mourner's sleep to-night
Like infant's slumbers, pure and light!

Come near and bless us when we wake,
Ere through the world our way we take:
Till, in the ocean of Thy love,
We lose ourselves in Heaven above!

JOHN KEBLE.

Into Thine hand I commit my spirit.
Psalm xxxi. 5.

THE sun is sinking fast,
　　The daylight dies;
Let love awake and pay
　　Her evening sacrifice.

EVENING.

As Christ upon the cross
   His head inclined
And to His Father's hands
His parting soul resigned;

So now herself my soul
   Would wholly give
Into His sacred charge,
In whom all spirits live;

So now beneath His eye
   Would calmly rest,
Without a wish or thought
Abiding in the breast;

Save that His will be done,
   Whate'er betide;
Dead to herself, and dead
In Him to all beside.

Thus would I live: yet now
   Not I, but He
In all His power and love
Henceforth alive in me.

One Sacred Trinity!
   One Lord Divine!
May I be ever His,
And He for ever mine.

ANON.

EVENING.

All things were made by Him; and the Life was the Light of men.
John, i. 3, 4.

LIGHT, whose beams illumine all
  From twilight dawn to perfect day,
Shine Thou before the shadows fall
That lead our wandering feet astray;
At morn and eve Thy radiance pour,
That youth may love and age adore.

O Way, through whom our souls draw near
To yon eternal Home of peace,
Where perfect love shall cast out fear,
And earth's vain toil and wandering cease;
In strength or weakness may we see
Our heavenward path, O Lord, through Thee.

O Truth, before whose shrine we bow,
Thou priceless pearl for all who seek,
To Thee our earliest strength we vow,
Thy love will bless the pure and meek;
When dreams or mists beguile our sight,
Turn Thou our darkness into light.

O Life, the well that ever flows
To slake the thirst of those that faint,
Thy power to bless what seraph knows?

EVENING.

Thy joy supreme what words can paint?
In earth's last hour of fleeting breath
Be Thou our Conqueror over death.

O Light, O Way, O Truth, O Life,
O Jesu, born mankind to save,
Give Thou Thy peace in deadliest strife,
Shed Thou Thy calm on stormiest wave;
Be Thou our hope, our joy, our dread,
Lord of the living and the dead.

ANON.

Casting all your care upon Him, for He careth for you.
I. Peter, v. 7.

THE night is come, wherein at last we rest,
God order this and all things for the best!
Beneath His blessing fearless we may lie
    Since He is nigh.

Drive evil thoughts and spirits far away,
Master, watch o'er us till the dawning day,
Body and soul alike from harm defend,
    Thine angel send.

Let holy prayers and thoughts our latest be,
Let us awake with joy, still close to Thee,

In all serve Thee, in every deed and thought
>   Thy praise be sought.

Give to the sick, as Thy beloved, sleep.
And help the captive, comfort those who weep,
Care for the widows' and the orphans' woe,
>   Keep far our foe.

For we have none on whom for help to call,
Save Thee, O God in Heaven, who car'st for all,
And wilt forsake them never, day or night,
>   Who love Thee right.

Father, Thy Name be praised, Thy kingdom come,
Thy will be wrought as in our heavenly home,
Keep us in life, forgive our sins, deliver
>   Us now and ever.

BOHEMIAN BRETHREN.

EVENING.

The Lord preserveth all them that love Him.
Psalm cxlv. 20.

SINK not yet, my soul, to slumber,
   Wake, my heart, go forth and tell
All the mercies without number
   That this by-gone day befell;
Tell how God hath kept afar
All things that against me war,
Hath upheld me and defended,
And His grace my soul befriended.

Father merciful and holy,
   Thee to-night I praise and bless,
Who to labour true and lowly
   Grantest ever meet success.
Many a sin and many a woe,
Many a fierce and subtle foe
Hast Thou checked that once alarmed me,
So that nought to-day has harmed me.

Yes, our wisdom vainly ponders,
   Fathoms not Thy loving thought;
Never tongue can tell the wonders
   That each day for us are wrought.
Thou hast guided me to-day
That no ill hath crossed my way,
There is neither bound nor measure
In Thy love's o'erflowing treasure.

EVENING.

Now the light, that nature gladdens,
    And the pomp of day is gone,
And my heart is tired and saddens
    As the gloomy night comes on:
Ah! then, with Thy changeless light
Warm and cheer my heart to-night,
As the shadows round me gather
Keep me close to Thee, my Father.

Of Thy grace I pray Thee pardon
    All my sins, and heal their smart;
Sore and heavy is their burden,
    Sharp their sting within my heart;
And my foe lays many a snare
But to tempt me to despair;
Only Thou, dear Lord, canst save me,
Let him not prevail to have me.

Have I e'er from Thee departed?
    Now I seek Thy face again,
And Thy Son, the loving-hearted,
    Made our peace through bitter pain.
Yes, far greater than our sin,
Though it still be strong within,
Is the love that fails us never,
Mercy that endures for ever.

Brightness of the eternal city!
    Light of every faithful soul!

EVENING.

Safe beneath Thy sheltering pity
    Let the tempests past me roll:
Now it darkens far and near,
Still, my God, still be Thou here;
Thou canst comfort, and Thou only,
When the night is long and lonely.

E'en the twilight now hath vanished;
    Send Thy blessing on my sleep,
Every sin and terror banished,
    Let my rest be calm and deep.
Soul and body, mind and health,
Wife and children, house and wealth,
Friend and foe, the sick, the stranger,
Keep Thou safe from harm and danger.

Keep me safe till morn is breaking,
    Nightly terrors drive Thou hence,
Let not sickness keep me waking;
    Sudden death and pestilence,
Fire and water, noise of war,
Keep Thou from my house afar;
Let me die not unrepented,
That my soul be not tormented.

O Thou mighty God, now hearken
    To the prayer Thy child hath made;
Jesus, while the night-hours darken,
    Be Thou still my hope, my aid;

EVENING.

Holy Ghost, on Thee I call,
Friend and Comforter of all,
Hear my earnest prayer, O hear me!
Lord, Thou hearest, Thou art near me.

J. RIST.

*The day is Thine, the night also is Thine: Thou
hast made summer and winter.*

Psalm lxxiv. 16, 17.

O LORD, the heaven Thy power displays,
The fruitful earth Thy Word obeys,
The ocean answers to Thy praise,
    And man their lesson learns:
As morning dew in peace distils
Upon the valleys, fields, and hills,
Thy grace the lowly spirit fills,
    When unto Thee it turns.

At Thy command th' untiring sun
Throughout the day his course doth run;
And when at eve his course is done,
    Reposes in the west;
So we throughout our life's increase,
Work on until our day shall cease,
And, at our eve, lie down in peace,
    In Thee to take our rest.

EVENING.

As in the ground the seed we cast,
And wait till Winter's night be past,
In hope, when Spring returns at last,
    Thou wilt the increase give;
So sleep our bodies in the tomb,
Secure, that when Thy day shall come,
Thou wilt revive us from earth's womb,
    In Thee for aye to live.

As Nature works Thy will, O Lord,
As grace Thy mercy doth record,
So we, submissive to Thy Word,
    Thy great behests obey.
For Thy paternal love and power,
For Thy free-giv'n redemption dower,
For Thy all-sanctifying shower,
    To Thee be laud alway.

                              WHITING.

After this manner pray ye.
                          Matthew, vi. 9.

WEARY now I go to bed,
    Close my eyes and rest my head;
    Father, let Thy watchful eye
    Be upon me as I lie.

For the wrong I've done this day,
Look not on it, Lord, I pray;

But forgive the ill I've done,
For the sake of Christ, Thy Son.

For my parents dear I pray;
Father, take them not away;
Let us all in peace awake,
For Thy Son our Saviour's sake.

DR. H. W. DULCKEN.

EVENING.

It shall come to pass that at evening time it shall be light.
Zechariah, xiv. 7.

AT evening time let there be light;
Life's little day draws near its close;
Around us fall the shades of night,
The night of death, the grave's repose.
To crown our joys, to end our woes,
At evening time let there be light!

At evening time let there be light!
Though dull and gloomy wanes the day;
Yet rose the morn divinely bright;
The sunshine's gladness cheered the way.
O for one sweet, one parting ray!
At evening time let there be light!

'T is evening time—let there be light!
For God hath promised—it shall be!
Fear, doubt, and anguish take their flight;
The clouds disperse, the mists they flee;
Our eyes His glory now shall see.
'T is evening time—and there is light.

ANON.

EVENING.

Hear the prayer of Thy servant, which I pray before Thee now, day and night.
Nehemiah, i. 6.

THUS far the Lord has led me on,
Thus far His power prolongs my days,
And every evening shall make known
Some fresh memorial of His grace.

Much of my time has run to waste,
And I perhaps am near my home;
But He forgives my follies past,
He gives me strength for days to come.

I lay my body down to sleep,
Peace is the Pillow for my head;
While well-appointed angels keep
Their watchful stations round my bed.

Faith in His Name forbids my fear:
O may Thy presence ne'er depart!
And in the morning make me hear
The love and kindness of Thy heart.

Thus when the night of death shall come,
My flesh shall rest beneath the ground,
And wait Thy voice to rouse my tomb,
With sweet salvation in the sound.

ISAAC WATTS.

EVENING.

Keep me as the apple of the eye, hide me under the shadow of Thy wings.
Psalm xvii. 8.

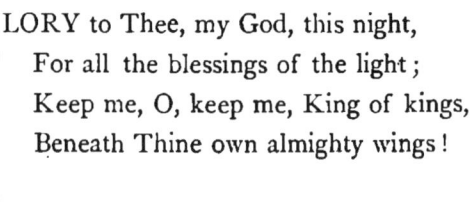

GLORY to Thee, my God, this night,
For all the blessings of the light;
Keep me, O, keep me, King of kings,
Beneath Thine own almighty wings!

Forgive me, Lord, for Thy dear Son,
The ill that I this day have done,
That with the world, myself, and Thee,
I, ere I sleep, at peace may be.

Teach me to live, that I may dread
The grave as little as my bed!
To die, that this vile body may
Rise glorious at the Judgment Day!

O, may my soul on Thee repose,
And may sweet sleep mine eyelids close;
Sleep, that may me more vig'rous make
To serve my God when I awake!

When in the night I sleepless lie,
My soul with heavenly thoughts supply!
Let no ill dreams disturb my rest,
No powers of darkness me molest!

EVENING.

Dull sleep, of sense me to deprive!
I am but half my time alive:
Thy faithful lovers, Lord, are grieved
To lie so long of Thee bereaved.

But though sleep o'er my frailty reigns,
Let it not hold me long in chains!
And now and then let loose my heart,
Till it an hallelujah dart!

The faster sleep the senses binds,
The more unfettered are our minds;
O, may my soul, from matter free,
Thy loveliness unclouded see!

O, when shall I, in endless day,
For ever chase dark sleep away,
And hymns with the supernal choir
Incessant sing, and never tire?

O, may my guardian, while I sleep,
Close to my bed his vigils keep;
His love angelical instil;
Stop all the avenues of ill.

May he celestial joy rehearse,
And thought to thought with me converse;
Or in my stead, all the night long,
Sing to my God a grateful song!

EVENING.

Praise God, from whom all blessings flow;
Praise Him, all creatures here below!
Praise Him above, ye heavenly host;
Praise Father, Son, and Holy Ghost!

BISHOP THOMAS KEN.

NIGHT.

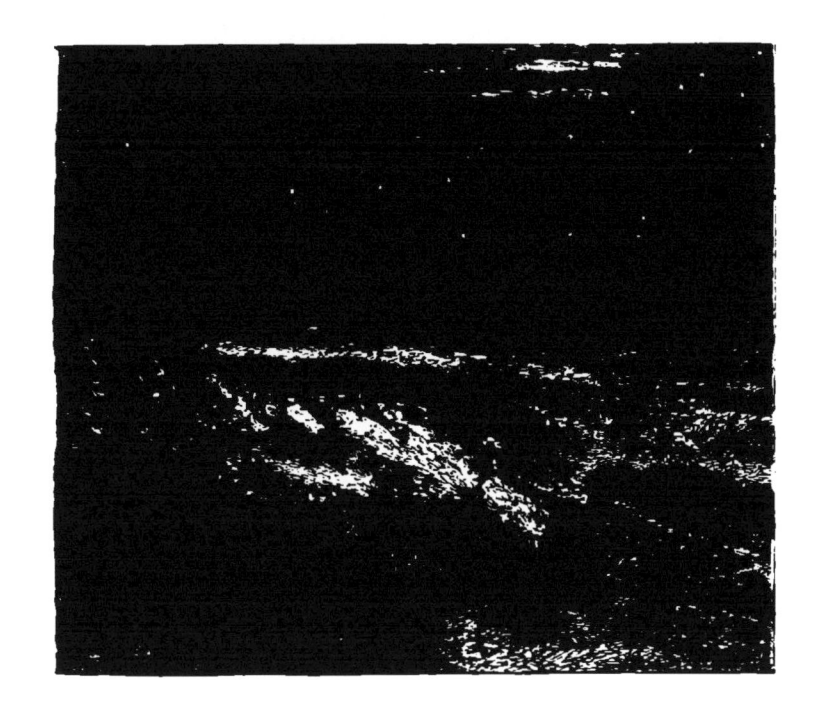

He that keepeth Israel shall neither slumber nor sleep.

Psalm cxxi. 4.

INTERVAL of grateful shade,
   Welcome to my weary head;
   Welcome slumber to mine eyes,
   Tired with glaring vanities.

My great Master still allows
Needful periods of repose;

NIGHT.

By my Heavenly Father blest,
Thus I give my powers to rest.

Heavenly Father! gracious Name!
Night and day His love the same!
Far be each suspicious thought,
Every anxious care forgot.

Thou, my ever-bounteous God,
Crown'st my days with various good,
Thy kind eye, that cannot sleep,
These defenceless hours shall keep.

What though downy slumbers flee,
Strangers to my couch and me?
Sleepless, well I know to rest,
Lodged within my Father's breast.

While the empress of the night
Scatters mild her silver light,
While the vivid planets stray
Various through their mystic way,

While the stars unnumbered roll
Round the ever-constant pole,
Far above these spangled skies
All my soul to God shall rise.

Mid the silence of the night,
Mingling with those angels bright

NIGHT.

Whose harmonious voices raise
Ceaseless love and ceaseless praise,

Through the throng His gentle ear
Shall my tuneless accents hear;
From on high doth He impart
Secret comfort to my heart.

He in these serenest hours
Guides my intellectual powers,
And His Spirit doth diffuse
Sweeter far than midnight dews;

Lifting all my thoughts above
On the wings of faith and love:
Blest alternative to me,
Thus to sleep, or wake with Thee!

What if death my sleep invade?
Should I be of death afraid?
Whilst encircled by Thine arm,
Death may strike, but cannot harm.

What if beams of opening day
Shine around my breathless clay?
Brighter visions from on high
Shall regale my mental eye.

Tender friends awhile may mourn
Me from their embraces torn;

NIGHT.

Dearer, better friends I have
In the realms beyond the grave.

See, the guardian angels nigh
Wait to waft my soul on high!
See the golden gates displayed!
See the crown to grace my head!

See a flood of sacred light,
Which no more shall yield to night!
Transitory world, farewell
Jesus calls, with Him to dwell!

With Thy heavenly presence blest,
Death is life, and labour rest;
Welcome sleep or death to me,
Still secure, for still with Thee!

PHILIP DODDRIDGE.

He that keepeth thee will not slumber.
Psalm cxxi. 3.

THE sun has sunk beneath the wave,
    Another day is done,
Another round upon the stage
    Of this life's course is run.

The evening comes with silent tread,
    All slowly comes the night,

When in the darkened heavens are shown
   A thousand worlds of light.

O grant us, God, Thy guardian care,
   While we lie down to sleep;
Shield us from every evil thing,
   Our souls in safety keep.

Grant that our bodies, all refreshed
   In the new coming day,
May rise to serve Thee with new love,
   With greater fervour pray.

And when our day of life is done,
　When death shall close our eyes,
Grant us to wake in glory bright,
　Hymns singing in the skies!

ANON.

Neither shall any plague come nigh thy dwelling.
Psalm xci. 10.

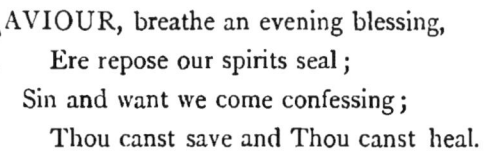

SAVIOUR, breathe an evening blessing,
　Ere repose our spirits seal;
Sin and want we come confessing;
　Thou canst save and Thou canst heal.

Though destruction walk around us,
　Though the arrows past us fly,
Angel guards from Thee surround us;
　We are safe, for Thou art nigh.

Though the night be dark and dreary,
　Darkness cannot hide from Thee:
Thou art He who, never weary,
　Watchest where Thy people be.

Should swift death this night o'ertake us,
　And our couch become our tomb,
May the morn in Heaven awake us,
　Clad in light and deathless bloom.

JAMES EDMESTON.

NIGHT.

> Wait on the Lord, and He shall strengthen
> thine heart: wait, I say, on the Lord.
>
> Psalm xxvii. 14.

NOW darkness over all is spread,
    No sounds the stillness break;
Ah! when shall these sad hours be fled?
    Am I alone awake?

Ah, no! I do not wake alone,
    Alone I do not sleep,
Around me ever watcheth One
    Who wakes with those that weep.

On earth it is so dark and drear,
    With Him so calm and bright,
The stars in solemn radiance clear
    Shine there through all our night.

'T is when the lights of earth are gone
    The heavenly glories shine;
When other comfort I have none,
    Thy comfort, Lord, is mine.

Be still, my throbbing heart, be still,
    Cast off thy weary load,
And make His holy will thy will,
    And rest upon Thy God.

How many a time the night hath come,
  Yet still returned the day;
How many a time thy cross, thy gloom,
  Ere now hath passed away.

And these dark hours of anxious pain
  That now oppress thee sore,
I know will vanish soon again,
  Then I shall fear no more;

For when the night hath lasted long
  We know the morn is near,
And when the trial's sharp and strong
  Our Help shall soon appear.

PASTOR JOSEPHSON.

There shall be no night there.
Revelation, xxii. 5.

MY God, now I from sleep awake,
  The sole possession of me take;
  From midnight terrors me secure,
  And guard my heart from thoughts impure.

Bless'd angels! while we silent lie,
  You hallelujahs sing on high;
You joyful hymn the Ever-blest
Before the throne, and never rest.

NIGHT.

I with your choir celestial join
In offering up a hymn divine;
With you in Heaven I hope to dwell,
And bid the night and world farewell.

My soul, when I shake off this dust,
Lord, in Thy arms I will entrust;
O, make me Thy peculiar care;
Some mansion for my soul prepare!

Give me a place at Thy saints' feet,
Or some fall'n angel's vacant seat!
I'll strive to sing as loud as they
Who sit above in brighter day.

O, may I always ready stand
With my lamp burning in my hand!
May I in sight of Heaven rejoice,
Whene'er I hear the Bridegroom's voice!

All praise to Thee, in light arrayed,
Who light Thy dwelling-place hast made:
A boundless ocean of bright beams
From Thy all-glorious Godhead streams.

The sun in its meridian height
Is very darkness in Thy sight!
My soul, O, lighten and inflame,
With thought and love of Thy great Name!

NIGHT.

Bless'd Jesu, Thou, on Heaven intent,
Whole nights hast in devotion spent;
But I, frail creature, soon am tired,
And all my zeal is soon expired.

My soul, how canst Thou weary grow
Of antedating bliss below,
In sacred hymns and heavenly love,
Which will eternal be above?

Shine on me, Lord,—new life impart!
Fresh ardours kindle in my heart!
One ray of Thy all-quickening light
Dispels the sloth and clouds of night.

Lord, lest the tempter me surprise,
Watch over Thine own sacrifice!
All loose, all idle thoughts cast out,
And make my very dreams devout!

Praise God, from whom all blessings flow;
Praise Him, all creatures here below!
Praise Him above, ye heavenly host;
Praise Father, Son, and Holy Ghost!

BISHOP THOMAS KEN.

Abide with us.
Luke, xxiv. 29.

THROUGH the day Thy love hath spared us;
    Now we lay us down to rest;
Through the silent watches guard us;
    Let no foe our peace molest!
Jesus, Thou our Guardian be!
Sweet it is to trust in Thee.

NIGHT.

Pilgrims here on earth, and strangers,
    Dwelling in the midst of foes:
Us and ours preserve from dangers,
    In Thine arms may we repose!
And, when life's sad day is past,
Rest with Thee in Heaven at last!

THOMAS KELLY.

He shall give His angels charge over thee.
                     Psalm xci. 11.

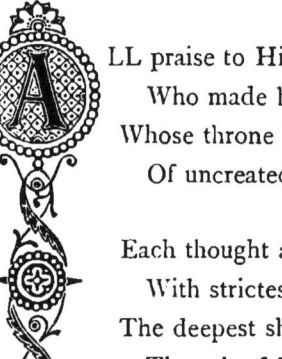

ALL praise to Him who dwells in bliss,
    Who made both day and night,
Whose throne is darkness in th' abyss
    Of uncreated light!

Each thought and deed His piercing eyes
    With strictest search survey;
The deepest shades no more disguise
    Than the full blaze of day.

Whom Thou dost guard, O King of kings
    No evil shall molest:
Under the shadow of Thy wings
    Shall they securely rest.

NIGHT.

Thy angels shall around their beds
  Their constant stations keep;
Thy faith and truth shall shield their heads,
  For Thou dost never sleep.

May we, with calm and sweet repose,
  And heavenly thoughts refreshed,
Our eyelids with the morn unclose,
  And bless the Ever-blessed!

CHARLES WESLEY.

The Lord will bless His people with peace.
Psalm xxix. 11.

FATHER, who didst all things make
  That Heaven and earth might do Thy will,
Bless us this night for Jesu's sake,
  And for Thy work preserve us still.

O Son, who didst redeem mankind,
  And set the captive sinner free,
Keep us this night with peaceful mind,
  That we may safe abide in Thee.

O Holy Ghost, who by Thy power
  The Church elect dost sanctify,
Seal us this night, and hour by hour
  Our hearts and members purify.

NIGHT.

To Father, Son, and Holy Ghost,
The God whom Heaven and earth adore,
From men and from the angel host
Be praise and glory evermore.

ANON.

So Samuel went and lay down.
I. Samuel, iii. 9.

THIS night I lift my heart to Thee,
    Whose dwelling is in Heaven above;
O, deign to hear and answer me,
    My Father—God of love.

Art Thou not, Lord, in every place?
    Is there a thing beneath Thy care?
Though angels only see Thy face,
    Yet Thou art everywhere.

O, give Thine angels charge to keep
    Their wings spread over me this night;
Let them defend me—let me sleep
    Till darkness melts in light.

BARTHOLOMEW.

The day is Thine, the night also is Thine.
Psalm lxxiv. 16.

GOD that madest earth and Heaven,
　　Darkness and light;
Who the day for toil hast given,
　　For rest the night;
May thine angel guards defend us!
Slumber sweet Thy mercy send us!
Holy dreams and hopes attend us,
　　This livelong night!

Guard us waking, guard us sleeping,
　　And, when we die,
May we in Thy mighty keeping
　　All peaceful lie;
When the last dread call shall wake us,
Do not Thou, our God, forsake us,
But to reign in glory take us
　　With Thee on high.　Amen.

BISHOP REGINALD HEBER.

So teach us to number our days, that we may apply our hearts unto wisdom.
Psalm xc. 12.

While the earth remaineth, seedtime and harvest, and cold and heat, and summer and winter, and day and night shall not cease.
Genesis, viii. 22.

Blessed are the dead which die in the Lord: that they may rest from their labours; and their works do follow them.
Revelation, xiv. 13.

We shall all stand before the judgment seat of Christ.
Romans, xiv. 10.

SEEDTIME AND HARVEST.

Seed time and harvest shall not cease.
　　　　　　　　　　　　　　　Genesis, viii. 22.

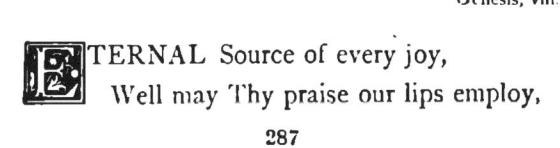

ETERNAL Source of every joy,
　　Well may Thy praise our lips employ,

SEEDTIME AND HARVEST.

While in Thy temple we appear,
Whose goodness crowns the circling year.

The flowery Spring at Thy command
Embalms the air and paints the land;
The summer rays with vigour shine,
To raise the corn and cheer the vine.

Thy hand in Autumn richly pours
Through all our coasts redundant stores,
And Winters softened by Thy care,
No more a face of horror wear.

Seasons and months and weeks and days
Demand successive songs of praise;
Still be the cheerful homage paid
With opening light and evening shade!

O! may our more harmonious tongues
In worlds unknown pursue the songs,
And in those brighter courts adore,
Where days and years revolve no more!

PHILIP DODDRIDGE.

SEEDTIME AND HARVEST.

The pastures are clothed with flocks; the valleys also are covered over with corn.
Psalm lxv. 13.

PRAISE to God, immortal praise,
For the love that crowns our days!
Bounteous Source of every joy,
Let Thy praise our tongues employ.

For the blessings of the field;
For the stores the gardens yield
For the vine's exalted juice;
For the generous olive's use:

Flocks that whiten all the plain;
Yellow sheaves of ripened grain;
Clouds that drop their fattening dews;
Suns that temperate warmth diffuse:

All that Spring with bounteous hand
Scatters o'er the smiling land;
All that liberal Autumn pours
From her rich o'erflowing stores:

These to Thee, my God, we owe,
Source whence all our blessings flow!
And for these my soul shall raise
Grateful vows and solemn praise.

Yet, should rising whirlwinds tear
From its stem the ripening ear,
Should the fig tree's blasted shoot
Drop her green untimely fruit;

Should the vine put forth no more,
Nor the olive yield her store;
Though the sickening flocks should fall,
And the herds desert the stall;

Should Thine altered hand restrain
The early and the latter rain;
Blast each opening bud of joy,
And the rising year destroy;

Yet to Thee my soul shall raise
Grateful vows and solemn praise;
And, when every blessing's flown,
Love Thee for Thyself alone!

ANNA LÆTITIA BARBAULD.

He left not Himself without witness, in that He gave us fruitful seasons.
Acts, xiv. 17.

FOUNTAIN of mercy! God of love,
How rich Thy bounties are!
The rolling seasons as they move
Proclaim Thy constant care.

When in the bosom of the earth
    The sower hid the grain,
Thy goodness marked its secret birth,
    And sent the early rain.

SEEDTIME AND HARVEST.

The Spring's sweet influence was Thine,
  The plants in beauty grew,
Thou gav'st refulgent suns to shine,
  And mild refreshing dew.

These various mercies from above
  Matured the swelling grain;
And yellow harvest crowns Thy love,
  And plenty fills the plain.

Seedtime and harvest, Lord, alone
  Thou dost on man bestow;
Let him not then forget to own
  From whom his blessings flow!

Fountain of love! our praise is Thine;
  To Thee our songs we'll raise,
And all created Nature join
  In sweet harmonious praise!

ANNE FLOWERDEW.

Thou openest Thine hand, and satisfiest the desire of every living thing.
Psalm cxlv. 16.

O LORD of heaven, and earth, and sea,
  To Thee all praise and glory be;
How shall we show our love to Thee,
      Giver of all?

SEEDTIME AND HARVEST.

The golden sunshine, vernal air,
Sweet flowers and fruits Thy love declare:
Where harvests ripen Thou art there,
    Giver of all!

For peaceful homes and healthful days,
For all the blessings earth displays,
We owe Thee thankfulness and praise,
    Giver of all!

Thou didst not spare Thine only Son,
But gav'st Him for a world undone;
And e'en that gift Thou dost outrun,
    And give us all!

Thou giv'st the Spirit's blessed dower,
Spirit of life, and love, and power,
And dost His sevenfold graces shower
    Upon us all!

For souls redeemed, for sins forgiven,
For means of grace and hopes of Heaven,
Father, what can to Thee be given,
    Who givest all?

We lose what on ourselves we spend:
We have as treasures without end
Whatever, Lord, to Thee we lend,
    Who givest all!

SEEDTIME AND HARVEST.

Whatever, Lord, we lend to Thee
Repaid a thousandfold will be;
Then gladly will we give to Thee,
    Giver of all!

To Thee, from whom we all derive—
Our life, our gifts, our power to give,
O may we ever with Thee live,
    Giver of all!

BISHOP OF LINCOLN.

He that ministereth seed to the sower doth minister bread for food.
II. Corinthians, ix. 10.

LORD, in Thy Name Thy servants plead,
    And Thou hast sworn to hear;
Thine is the harvest, Thine the seed,
    The fresh and fading year.

Our hope, when Autumn winds blew wild,
    We trusted, Lord, with Thee,
And now that Spring has on us smiled,
    We wait on Thy decree.

The former and the latter rain,
    The Summer sun and air,
The green ear and the golden grain,
    All Thine, are ours by prayer.

SEEDTIME AND HARVEST.

Thine too by right, and ours by grace,
    The wondrous growth unseen,
The hopes that soothe, the fears that brace,
    The love that shines serene!

So grant the precious things brought forth
    By sun and moon below,
That Thee, in Thy new Heaven and earth,
    We never may forego!

To Father, Son, and Holy Ghost,
    The God whom we adore,
Be glory, as it was, is now,
    And shall be evermore!

JOHN KEBLE.

Pray ye the Lord that He send forth labourers into His harvest.
Matthew, ix. 38.

LORD of the harvest, hear
    Thy needy servants cry;
Answer Thy people's earnest prayer,
    And all our wants supply.

On Thee we humbly wait,
    Our wants are in thy view;
The harvest truly, Lord, is great;
    The labourers are few.

Convert and send forth more
Into Thy Church abroad;
And let them speak Thy Word with power,
Co-workers with their God.

O let them spread Thy Name;
Their mission fully prove;
Thy universal grace proclaim—
Thine all-embracing love.

CHARLES WESLEY.

Because the Lord thy God shall bless thee in all thine increase, therefore thou shalt surely rejoice.

Deuteronomy, xvi. 15.

WE plough the fields, and scatter
The good seed on the land,
But it is fed and watered
By God's almighty hand:
He sends the snow in Winter,
The warmth to swell the grain,
The breezes and the sunshine,
And soft refreshing rain.
All good gifts around us
Are sent from Heaven above,
Then thank the Lord, O thank the Lord,
For all His love.

He only is the Maker
  Of all things near and far;
He paints the wayside flower,
  He lights the evening star;
The winds and waves obey Him,
  By Him the birds are fed;
Much more to us, His children,
  He gives our daily bread.
            All good gifts, &c.

SEEDTIME AND HARVEST.

We thank Thee, then, O Father,
    For all things bright and good
The seedtime and the harvest,
    Our life, our health, our food
Accept the gifts we offer,
    For all Thy love imparts,
And, what Thou most desirest,
    Our humble, thankful hearts.
    All good gifts around us
    Are sent from Heaven above,
Then thank the Lord, O thank the Lord,
    For all His love.

ANON.

*Who giveth food to all flesh: for His mercy
    endureth for ever.*

Psalm cxxxvi. 25.

PRAISE, O praise our God and King,
    Hymns of adoration sing,
        For His mercies still endure,
        Ever faithful, ever sure.

Praise Him that He made the sun
    Day by day his course to run,
        For His mercies still endure,
        Ever faithful, ever sure:

And the silver moon by night,
Shining with her gentle light,
    For His mercies still endure,
    Ever faithful, ever sure.

Praise Him that He gave the rain
To mature the swelling grain,
    For His mercies still endure,
    Ever faithful, ever sure :

And hath bid the fruitful field
Crops of precious increase yield ;
    For His mercies still endure,
    Ever faithful, ever sure.

Praise Him for our harvest store ;
He hath filled the garner floor ;
    For His mercies still endure,
    Ever faithful, ever sure :

And for richer food than this,
Pledge of everlasting bliss ;
    For His mercies still endure,
    Ever faithful, ever sure.

Glory to our bounteous King !
Glory let creation sing !
    Glory to the Father, Son,
    And blest Spirit, Three in One !

SIR HENRY BAKER.

SEEDTIME AND HARVEST.

Thou crownest the year with Thy goodness.
Psalm lxv. 11.

LORD of the harvest! Thee we hail!
Thine ancient promise doth not fail;
The varying seasons haste their round,
With goodness all our years are crowned:
 Our thanks we pay
 This holy day;
O let our hearts in tune be found!

If Spring doth wake the song of mirth,
If Summer warms the fruitful earth;
When winter sweeps the naked plain,
Or Autumn yields its ripened grain;
 Still do we sing
 To Thee, our King;
Through all their changes Thou dost reign.

But chiefly when Thy liberal hand
Scatters new plenty o'er the land,
When sounds of music fill the air,
As homeward all their treasures bear;
 We too will raise
 Our hymn of praise,
For we Thy common bounties share.

Lord of the harvest, all is Thine,—
The rains that fall, the suns that shine,
The seed once hidden in the ground,
The skill that makes our fruits abound!

SEEDTIME AND HARVEST.

New, every year,
Thy gifts appear;
New praises from our lips shall sound!

JOHN HAMPDEN GURNEY.

The Lord is righteous in all His ways, and holy in all His works.
Psalm cxlv. 17.

GOD the Father, whose creation
   Gives to flowers and fruits their birth,
Thou, whose yearly operation
   Brings the hour of harvest mirth,
Here to Thee we make oblation
   Of the August-gold of earth.

God the Word, the sun maturing
   With his blessed ray the corn,
Spake of Thee, O Sun enduring,
   Thee, O everlasting morn,
Thee in whom our woes find curing,
   Thee that liftest up our horn.

God the Holy Ghost, the showers
   That have fattened out the grain,
Types of Thy celestial powers,
   Symbols of baptismal rain,
Shadowed out the grace that dowers
   All the faithful of Thy train.

When the harvest of each nation
  Severs righteousness from sin,
And Archangel proclamation
  Bids to put the sickle in,
And each age and generation
  Sink to woe, or glory win;

Grant that we, or young or hoary,
  Lengthened be our span or brief,
Whatsoe'er the life-long story
  Of our joy or of our grief,
May be garnered up in glory
  As Thine own elected sheaf.

Laud to Him to whom supernal
  Thrones and virtues bend the knee;
Laud to Him from whom infernal
  Powers and dominations flee;
Consubstantial, Co-Eternal,
  Beatific Trinity!

ANON.

The joy in harvest.
Isaiah, ix. 3.

GREAT God, as seasons disappear,
And changes mark the rolling year,
  Thy favour still has crowned our days,
And we would celebrate Thy praise.

The harvest song would we repeat:
Thou givest us the finest wheat;
The joys of harvest we have known:
The praise, O Lord, is all Thine own.

Our tables spread, our garners stored,
O give us hearts to bless Thee, Lord:
Forbid it, Source of light and love,
That hearts and lives should barren prove.

Another harvest comes apace:
Ripen our spirits by Thy grace,
That we may calmly meet the blow
The sickle gives to lay us low.

That so, when angel reapers come
To gather sheaves to Thy blest home,
Our spirits may be borne on high,
To Thy safe garner in the sky.

EDMUND BUTCHER.

The time is come for thee to reap, for the harvest is ripe.
Revelation, xiv. 15.

GREAT Giver of all good, to Thee again
We humbly now present, in joyous strain,
Our Harvest-tide Thanksgiving.

To Thee, in whom we live and move, we come
To praise Thee for the sheaves brought safely home,
    With Harvest-tide Thanksgiving.

Thou dost prepare our corn, and year by year
Before Thine altar, Lord, will we appear
    With Harvest-tide Thanksgiving.

Thine was the former and the latter rain,
Enriching earth, and calling forth again
    The Harvest-tide Thanksgiving.

Thou openest wide, great God, Thy bounteous hand,
And far and wide ascends from all the land
    Glad Harvest-tide Thanksgiving.

SEEDTIME AND HARVEST.

Thou fillest all that live with plenteousness;
They, in return, Thy sacred Name should bless
    In Harvest-tide Thanksgiving.

Thy clouds drop fatness on the teeming earth;
Accept these festal songs of reverent mirth,
    This Harvest-tide Thanksgiving.

The year is crowned with goodness, Lord, by Thee,
Then meet it is that aye should offered be
    The Harvest-tide Thanksgiving.

On every side the little hills rejoice,
On every side sounds forth the grateful voice
    Of Harvest-tide Thanksgiving.

For all Thy blessings, Lord, our thanks we sing,
We all, who sow and reap, together bring
    Our Harvest-tide Thanksgiving.

To Thee, O Trinity in Unity,
All glory, laud, and endless homage be,
    In Harvest-tide Thanksgiving.

                              ANON.

That which thou sowest is not quickened, except it die.
                              I. Corinthians, xv. 36.

LORD of the harvest! once again
   We thank Thee for the ripened grain;
For crops, safe carried, sent to cheer

SEEDTIME AND HARVEST.

Thy servants through another year;
For all sweet holy thoughts supplied
By seedtime and by harvest-tide!

The bare dead grain, in Autumn sown,
Its robe of vernal green puts on;
Glad from its wintry grave it springs,
Fresh garnished by the King of kings:
So, Lord, to those who sleep in Thee
Shall new and glorious bodies be.

Nor vainly of Thy Word we ask
A lesson from the reaper's task:
So shall Thine angels issue forth;
The tares be burnt; the just of earth,
Playthings of sun and storm no more,
Be gathered to their Father's store.

Daily, O Lord, our prayers be said,
As Thou hast taught, for daily bread;
But not alone our bodies feed;
Supply our fainting spirits' need!
O Bread of Life! from day to day
Be Thou their Comfort, Food, and Stay!

JOSEPH ANSTICE.

> *O bless our God, ye people, and make the voice of His praise to be heard.*
>
> Psalm lxvi. 8.

NOW thank we all our God,
 With heart, and hands, and voices,
  Who wondrous things hath done,
 In whom His world rejoices;
  Who from our mothers' arms
   Hath blessed us on our way
  With countless gifts of love,
   And still is ours to-day.

 O may this bounteous God
 Through all our life be near us,
  With ever joyful hearts
 And blessèd peace to cheer us;
  And keep us in His grace,
   And guide us when perplexed,
  And free us from all ills
   In this world and the next.

 All praise and thanks to God,
 The Father, now be given,
  The Son, and Him who reigns
 With Them in highest Heaven,
  The One eternal God,
   Whom earth and Heaven adore,
  For thus it was, is now,
   And shall be evermore.

The harvest is the end of the world, and the reapers are the angels.
Matthew, xiii. 39.

COME, ye thankful people, come,
Raise the song of Harvest-Home!
All is safely gathered in,
Ere the Winter storms begin;
God, our Maker, doth provide
For our wants to be supplied;
Come to God's own temple, come,
Raise the song of Harvest-Home!

We ourselves are God's own field,
Fruit unto His praise to yield;
Wheat and tares together sown,
Unto joy or sorrow grown:
First the blade, and then the ear,
Then the full corn shall appear:
Grant, O harvest Lord, that we
Wholesome grain and pure may be!

For the Lord our God shall come,
And shall take His harvest home!
From His field shall purge away
All that doth offend, that day;
Give His angels charge at last
In the fire the tares to cast,
But the fruitful ears to store
In His garner evermore.

SEEDTIME AND HARVEST.

Then, thou Church triumphant, come,
Raise the song of Harvest-Home!
All are safely gathered in,
Free from sorrow, free from sin;
There for ever purified,
In God's garner to abide:
Come, ten thousand angels, come,
Raise the glorious Harvest-Home!

HENRY ALFORD.

THE OLD AND NEW YEAR

Having obtained help of God.

Acts, xxvi. 22.

GREAT God, we sing that mighty hand
By which supported still we stand;
The opening year Thy mercy shows,
That mercy crowns it till it close.

THE OLD AND NEW YEAR.

By day, by night, at home, abroad,
Still are we guarded by our God ·
By His incessant bounty fed,
By His unerring counsel led.

With grateful hearts the past we own;
The future, all to us unknown,
We to Thy guardian care commit,
Content with what Thou deemest fit.

In scenes exalted or depressed,
Thou art our joy, and Thou our rest;
Thy goodness all our hopes shall raise,
Adored throughout our changing days.

When death shall interrupt these songs,
And seal in silence mortal tongues,
Our Helper, God, in whom we trust,
Shall keep our souls and guard our dust.

PHILIP DODDRIDGE.

In Thee do I put my trust: for Thou art my hope, O Lord God.
Psalm lxxi. 1—5.

THE year is gone beyond recall,
    With all its hopes and fears,
With all its bright and gladdening smiles,
    With all its mourners' tears.

THE OLD AND NEW YEAR.

Thy thankful people praise Thee, Lord,
    For countless gifts received,
And pray for grace to keep the faith
    Which saints of old believed.

To Thee we come, O gracious Lord,
    The new-born year to bless:
Defend our land from pestilence;
    Give peace and plenteousness;

Forgive this nation's many sins,
    The growth of vice restrain,
And help us all with sin to strive,
    And crowns of life to gain.

From evil deeds that stain the past
    We now desire to flee;
And pray that future years may all
    Be spent, good Lord, for Thee.

O Father, let Thy watchful eye
    Still look on us in love,
That we may praise Thee year by year,
    As angels do above.

All glory to the Father be,
    All glory to the Son,
All glory, Holy Ghost, to Thee,
    While endless ages run.

                                ANON.

THE OLD AND NEW YEAR.

Guide me with Thy counsel, and afterward receive me to glory.
Psalm lxxiii. 24

HARP, awake! tell out the story
    Of our love and joy and praise;
Lute, awake! awake our glory!
    Join a thankful song to raise!
Join we, brethren faithful-hearted,
    Lift the solemn voice again
O'er another year departed
    Of our threescore years and ten!

Lo! a theme for deepest sadness,
    In ourselves with sin defiled;
Lo! a theme for holiest gladness,
    In our Father reconciled!
In the dust we bend before Thee,
    Lord of sinless hosts above;
Yet in lowliest joy adore Thee,
    God of mercy, grace, and love!

Gracious Saviour! Thou hast lengthened
    And hast blest our mortal span,
And in our weak hearts hast strengthened
    What Thy grace alone began!
Still, when danger shall betide us,
    Be Thy warning whisper heard;

Keep us at Thy feet, and guide us
By Thy Spirit and Thy Word!

THE OLD AND NEW YEAR.

Let Thy favour and Thy blessing
   Crown the year we now begin;
Let us all, Thy strength possessing,
   Grow in grace, and vanquish sin!
Storms are round us, hearts are quailing,
   Signs in heaven and earth and sea;
But, when heaven and earth are failing,
   Saviour! we will trust in Thee!

HENRY DOWNTON.

---

*Man is of few days and full of trouble: he fleeth also as a shadow,
and continueth not.*
Job, xiv. 1, 2.

ANOTHER year hath fled,—renew,
   Lord, with our days Thy love!
Our days are evil here and few;
   We look to live above.
We will not grieve, though day by day
We pass from earthly joys away;
   Our joy abides in Thee!
   Our joy abides in Thee!

Yet, when our sins we call to mind,
   We cannot fail to grieve;
But Thou art pitiful and kind,
   And wilt our prayer receive.

O Jesu, evermore the same,
Our hope we rest upon Thy Name;
　Our hope abides in Thee!
　Our hope abides in Thee!

For all the future, Lord, prepare
　Our souls with strength Divine;
Help us to cast on Thee our care,
　And on Thy servants shine:
Life without Thee is dark and drear;
Death is not death if Thou art near;
　Our life abides in Thee!
　Our life abides in Thee!

ARTHUR TOZER RUSSELL.

I beseech Thee, shew me Thy glory.
Exodus, xxxiii. 18.

REMARK, my soul, the narrow bounds
　Of the revolving year:
How swift the weeks complete their rounds!
　How short the months appear

So fast eternity comes on,
　And that important day,
When all that mortal life has done
　God's judgment shall survey.

Yet like an idle tale we spend
    The swift-advancing year,
And study artful ways to mend
    The speed of its career.

Waken, O God, my trifling heart,
    Its great concern to see,
That I may act a faithful part,
    And give the year to Thee.

So shall their course more grateful roll,
    If future years arise;
Or this shall bear my happy soul
    To joy that never dies.

PHILIP DODDRIDGE.

Lord, make me to know the measure of my days.
Psalm xxxix. 4.

AWAKE, ye saints, and raise your eyes,
    And raise your voices high;
Awake, and praise that sovereign love
    That shows salvation nigh.

On all the wings of time it flies,
    Each moment brings it near;
Then welcome each declining day,
    Welcome each closing year!

THE OLD AND NEW YEAR.

Not many years their round shall run,
   Nor many mornings rise,
Ere all its glories stand revealed
   To our admiring eyes!

Ye wheels of nature, speed your course!
   Ye mortal powers, decay!
Fast as ye bring the night of death,
   Ye bring eternal day!

PHILIP DODDRIDGE.

Thou carriest them away as with a flood.
Psalm xc. 5.

WHILE with ceaseless course the sun
   Hasted through the former year,
Many souls their race have run,
   Never more to meet us here:

THE OLD AND NEW YEAR.

Fixed in an eternal state,
    They have done with all below;
We a little longer wait,
    But how little, none can know.

As the wingèd arrow flies
    Speedily the mark to find;
As the lightning from the skies
    Darts, and leaves no trace behind;
Swiftly thus our fleeting days
    Bear us down life's rapid stream:
Upward, Lord, our spirits raise!
    All below is but a dream.

Thanks for mercies past receive;
    Pardon of our sins renew;
Teach us, henceforth, how to live
    With eternity in view:
Bless Thy Word to young and old;
    Fill us with a Saviour's love;
And, when life's short tale is told,
    May we dwell with Thee above!

                    JOHN NEWTON.

THE OLD AND NEW YEAR.

I beseech Thee, shew me Thy glory.
Exodus, xxxiii. 18.

NOW, gracious Lord, Thine arm reveal,
    And make Thy glory known;
Now let us all Thy presence feel,
    And soften hearts of stone.

Help us to venture near Thy throne,
    And plead our Saviour's Name;
For all that we can call our own
    Is vanity and shame.

From all the guilt of former sin
    May mercy set us free,
And let the year we now begin
    Begin and end with Thee.

Send down Thy Spirit from above,
    That saints may love Thee more;
And sinners now may learn to love,
    Who never loved before.

And when before Thee we appear
    In our eternal home,
May growing numbers worship here,
    And praise Thee in our room.

JOHN NEWTON.

THE OLD AND NEW YEAR.

Goodness and mercy shall follow me all the days of my life.
Psalm xxiii. 6.

FOR Thy mercy and Thy grace,
Faithful through another year,
Hear our song of thankfulness,
Father and Redeemer, hear!

In our weakness and distress,
Rock of strength! be Thou our stay!
In the pathless wilderness
Be our true and living Way!

Who of us death's awful road
In the coming year shall tread?
With Thy rod and staff, O God,
Comfort Thou his dying head!

Keep us faithful, keep us pure,
Keep us evermore Thine own!
Help, O help us to endure!
Fit us for the promised crown!

So within Thy palace gate
We shall praise, on golden strings,
Thee, the only Potentate,
Lord of lords, and King of kings!

HENRY DOWNTON.

THE OLD AND NEW YEAR.

The Lord that made heaven and earth bless Thee out of Zion.
Psalm cxxxiv. 3.

BLESS, O Lord, the opening year,
    To the souls assembled here:
    Clothe Thy Word with power divine,
    Make us willing to be Thine.

Now may fervent prayer arise,
Winged with faith, and pierce the skies;
Fervent prayer shall bring us down
Gracious answers from Thy throne.

Where Thou hast Thy work begun,
Give new strength the race to run;
Scatter darkness, doubts, and fears;
Wipe away the mourners' tears.

Bless us all, both old and young;
Call forth praise from every tongue:
Let our whole assembly prove
All Thy power and all Thy love.

JOHN NEWTON.

Lord, let it alone this year also.
Luke, xiii. 8.

THE Lord of earth and sky,
    The God of ages, praise,
Who reigns enthroned on high,
    Ancient of endless days;

Who lengthens out our trial here,
And spares us yet another year.

    Barren and withered trees,
    We cumbered long the ground :
    No fruit of holiness
    On our dead souls was found.
Yet mercy stayed our doom severe ;
O ! spare them yet another year.

    Jesus, Thy speaking blood
    For us obtained the grace ;
    O ! since there is bestowed
    On us this longer space,
Let our spared lives Thy praise declare,
And fruit unto perfection bear.

CHARLES WESLEY.

DEATH AND THE GRAVE.

He shall enter into peace.
Isaiah, lvii. 2.

TENDER Shepherd, Thou hast stilled
Now Thy little lamb's brief weeping!

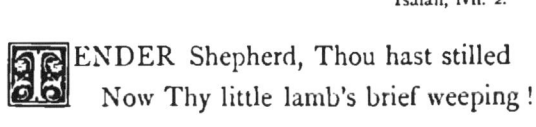

DEATH AND THE GRAVE.

Ah! how peaceful, pale, and mild,
   In its narrow bed 't is sleeping!
     And no sigh of anguish sore
     Heaves that little bosom more.

In this world of care and pain,
   Lord, Thou wouldst no longer leave it;
To the sunny, heavenly plain
   Thou dost now with joy receive it:
     Clothed in robes of spotless white,
     Now it dwells with Thee in light.

Ah, Lord Jesu! grant that we
   Where it lives may soon be living,
And the lovely pastures see
   That its heavenly food are giving:
     Then the gain of death we prove,
     Though Thou take what most we love.

                              ANON

To live is Christ, and to die is gain.
                        Philippians, i. 21

HAPPY soul! thy days are ended,
   All thy mourning days below;
Go, by angel guards attended,
   To the throne of Jesus, go:

Waiting to receive thy spirit,
   Lo! the Saviour stands above;
Shows the purchase of His merit,
   Reaches out the crown of love.

Struggle through thy latest passion,
   To thy dear Redeemer's breast,
To His uttermost salvation,
   To His everlasting rest;

For the joy He sets before thee,
   Bear a momentary pain;
Die, to live a life of glory;
   Suffer, with thy Lord to reign.

CHARLES WESLEY.

Then shall the dust return to the earth, and the spirit shall return unto God who gave it.
Ecclesiastes, xii. 7.

DEATHLESS principle, arise!
   Soar, thou native of the skies!
   Pearl of price, by Jesus bought,
   To His glorious likeness wrought!

   Go, to shine before His throne;
   Deck His mediatorial crown;
   Go, His triumphs to adorn;
   Made for God, to God return!

DEATH AND THE GRAVE.

Lo, He beckons from on high.
Fearless to His presence fly!
Thine the merit of His blood;
Thine the righteousness of God.

Angels, joyful to attend,
Hovering round thy pillow, bend,
Wait to catch the signal given,
And escort thee quick to Heaven.

Is thy earthly house distrest,
Willing to retain her guest?
'T is not thou, but she, must die;
Fly, celestial tenant, fly!

Burst thy shackles, drop thy clay,
Sweetly breathe thyself away;
Singing, to thy crown remove,
Swift of wing, and fired with love.

Shudder not to pass the stream;
Venture all thy care on Him,—
Him whose dying love and power
Stilled its tossing, hushed its roar.

Safe is the expanded wave,
Gentle as a Summer's eve;
Not one object of His care
Ever suffered shipwreck there

DEATH AND THE GRAVE.

See the haven full in view;
Love Divine shall bear thee through;
Trust to that propitious gale;
Weigh thy anchor, spread thy sail.

Saints, in glory perfect made,
Wait thy passage through the shade:
Ardent for thy coming o'er,
See, they throng the blissful shore!

Mount, their transports to improve;
Join the longing choir above;
Swiftly to their wish be given;
Kindle higher joy in Heaven!

Such the prospects that arise
To the dying Christian's eyes;
Such the glorious vista faith
Opens through the shades of death.

AUGUSTUS M. TOPLADY.

Let me die the death of the righteous.
Numbers, xxiii. 10.

HOW blest the righteous when he dies!
   When sinks a weary soul to rest
How mildly beam the closing eyes!
   How gently heaves the expiring breast!

So fades a Summer cloud away;
   So sinks the gale when storms are o'er;
So gently shuts the eye of day;
   So dies a wave along the shore.

A holy quiet reigns around,
   A calm which life nor death destroys;
Nothing disturbs that peace profound
   Which his unfettered soul enjoys.

Farewell, conflicting hopes and fears,
   Where lights and shades alternate dwell!
How bright the unchanging morn appears!
   Farewell, inconstant world, farewell!

Life's labour done, as sinks the clay,
    Light from its load the spirit flies;
While Heaven and earth combine to say,
    How blest the righteous when he dies!

                  ANNA LÆTITIA BARBAULD.

Lo, I am with you alway, even unto the end of the world.
                  Matthew, xxviii. 20.

NOW let our mourning hearts revive,
    And all our tears be dry;
Why should those eyes be drowned in grief
    Which view a Saviour nigh?

What though the arm of conquering death
    Does God's own house invade?
What though the prophet and the priest
    Be numbered with the dead?

Though earthly shepherds dwell in dust,
    The aged and the young;
The watchful eye in darkness closed,
    And mute th' instructive tongue:

Th' Eternal Shepherd still survives,
    New comfort to impart;
His eye still guides us, and His voice
    Still animates our heart.

Lo, I am with you! saith the Lord;
  My Church shall safe abide;
For I will ne'er forsake my own,
  Whose souls in me confide.

Through every scene of life and death
  This promise is our trust;
And this shall be our children's song
  When we are cold in dust.

PHILIP DODDRIDGE.

Sorrow not, even as others which have no hope.
I. Thessalonians, iv. 13.

THOU art gone to the grave; but we will not deplore thee,
  Though sorrows and darkness encompass the tomb:
The Saviour hath passed through its portal before thee,
  And the lamp of His love is Thy guide through the gloom!

Thou art gone to the grave: we no longer behold thee,
  Nor tread the rough path of the world by thy side;
But the wide arms of Mercy are spread to enfold thee,
  And sinners may die, for the Sinless has died!

Thou art gone to the grave; and, its mansion forsaking,
  Perhaps thy weak spirit in fear lingered long;

But the mild rays of Paradise beamed on thy waking,
   And the sound which thou heard'st was the seraphim's song!

DEATH AND THE GRAVE.

Thou art gone to the grave ; but we will not deplore thee,
   Whose God was thy Ransom, thy Guardian, and Guide !
He gave thee, He took thee, and He will restore thee ;
   And death has no sting, for the Saviour has died !

BISHOP REGINALD HEBER.

There shall be a resurrection of the dead, both of the just and unjust.
Acts, xxiv. 15.

EARTH to earth, and dust to dust ;
   Lord, we own the sentence just :
Head and tongue, and hand and heart ;
All in guilt have borne their part :
Righteous is the common doom,
All must moulder in the tomb.

Like the seed in Spring-time sown,
Like the leaves in Autumn strown,
Low these goodly frames must lie,
All our pomp and glory die ;
Soon the Spoiler seeks his prey
Soon he bears us all away.

Yet the seed, upraised again,
Clothes with green the smiling plain ;
Onward as the seasons move,
Leaves and blossoms deck the grove ;

DEATH AND THE GRAVE.

And shall we forgotten lie,
Lost for ever, when we die?

Lord, from Nature's gloomy night
Turn we to the Gospel's light:
Thou didst triumph o'er the grave,
Thou wilt all Thy people save;
Ransomed by Thy blood, the just
Rise immortal from the dust.

JOHN HAMPDEN GURNEY.

Whosoever liveth and believeth in me shall never die.
John, xi. 26.

THERE is a calm for those who weep;
   A rest for weary pilgrims found;
And, while the mouldering ashes sleep,
   Low in the ground,

The soul, of origin Divine,
   God's glorious image, freed from clay,
In Heaven's eternal sphere shall shine,
   A Star of Day.

The sun is but a spark of fire,
   A transient meteor in the sky;
The soul, immortal as its Sire,
   Shall never die!

JAMES MONTGOMERY.

DEATH AND THE GRAVE.

He cometh forth like a flower, and is cut down.
Job, xiv. 2.

WHEN blooming youth is snatched away,
    By death's resistless hand,
Our hearts the mournful tribute pay,
    Which pity must demand.

While pity prompts the rising sigh,
    O may this truth, imprest
With awful power,—I too must die,—
    Sink deep in every breast.

Let this vain world delude no more;
    Behold the gaping tomb:
It bids us seize the present hour,—
    To-morrow death may come

The voice of this alarming scene
    May every heart obey;
Nor be the heavenly warning vain
    Which calls to watch and pray.

O let us now to Jesus fly,
    Whose powerful arm can save,
Then shall our hope ascend on high,
    And triumph o'er the grave.

              ANNE STEELE.

DEATH AND THE GRAVE

The Lord will turn their mourning into joy.
Jeremiah, xxxi. 13.

WHY do we mourn departing friends,
   Or shake at death's alarms?
'T is but the voice that Jesus sends
   To call them to His arms.

Are we not tending upwards, too,
   As fast as time can move?
Nor would we wish the hours more slow,
   To keep us from our Love.

Why should we tremble to convey
   Their bodies to the tomb?
There the Redeemer's body lay,
   And left a long perfume.

The graves of all His saints He blest,
   And softened every bed:
Where should the dying members rest
   But with their dying Head?

Thence He arose, ascending high,
   And showed our feet the way;
Up to the Lord our flesh shall fly,
   At the great rising day.

DEATH AND THE GRAVE.

Then let the last loud trumpet sound,
And bid our kindred rise;
Awake, ye nations underground,
Ye saints, ascend the skies.

ISAAC WATTS.

The dead which die in the Lord.
Revelation, xiv. 13.

THOU God of Love! beneath Thy sheltering wings
We leave our holy dead
To rest in hope! From this world's sufferings
Their souls have fled!

O! when our hearts are burthened with the weight
Of life and all its woes,
Let us remember them, and calmly wait
To our life's close!

ANON.

Your fathers, where are they?
Zechariah, i. 5.

HOW swift the torrent rolls
That bears us to the sea,
The tide that bears our deathless souls
To vast eternity!

Our fathers, where are they,
With all they called their own?

Their joys and griefs have passed away,
  Their wealth and honour gone.

There, where the fathers sleep,
  Must all their children dwell·
Nor other heritage can keep
  Than such a narrow cell.

God of our fathers, be
  Our everlasting Friend;
Lord of the dead and living, we
  Our souls to Thee commend.

Of all the pious dead
  May we the footsteps trace,
Till, gathered round our glorious Head,
  We dwell before Thy face.

PHILIP DODDRIDGE.

There the wicked cease from troubling, and there the weary be at rest.
Job, iii. 17.

BROTHER, thou art gone before us, and thy saintly
  soul is flown
Where tears are wiped from every eye, and sorrow
  is unknown;

From the burden of the flesh, and from care and fear released,
Where the wicked cease from troubling, and the weary are at rest.

The toilsome way thou'st travelled o'er, and borne the heavy load;
But Christ hath taught thy languid feet to reach His blest abode:
Thou 'rt sleeping now, like Lazarus upon his Father's breast,
Where the wicked cease from troubling, and the weary are at rest.

Sin can never taint thee now, nor doubt thy faith assail,
Nor thy meek trust in Jesus Christ and the Holy Spirit fail;
And there thou 'rt sure to meet the good, whom on earth thou lovedst best,
Where the wicked cease from troubling, and the weary are at rest.

Earth to earth and dust to dust, the solemn priest hath said;
So we lay the turf above thee now, and we seal thy narrow bed;
But thy spirit, brother, soars away among the faithful blest,
Where the wicked cease from troubling, and the weary are at rest.

And when the Lord shall summon us, whom thou hast left behind,
May we, untainted by the world, as sure a welcome find!

DEATH AND THE GRAVE.

May each, like thee, depart in peace, to be a glorious guest,
Where the wicked cease from troubling, and the weary are at
    rest!

                       HENRY HART MILMAN.

I will never leave thee, nor forsake thee.
                       Hebrews, xiii. 5.

MUST friends and kindred droop and die,
    And helpers be withdrawn,
While sorrow, with a weeping eye,
    Counts up our comforts gone?

Be Thou our comfort, mighty God!
    Our Helper and our Friend!
Nor leave us in this dangerous road,
    Till all our trials end!

O may our feet pursue the way
    Our pious fathers led;
With love and holy zeal obey
    The counsels of the dead!

Let us be weaned from all below;
    Let hope our grief expel;
While death invites our souls to go
    Where our best kindred dwell.

                       ISAAC WATTS.

DEATH AND THE GRAVE.

Where I am, there ye may be also.
John, xiv. 3.

CHRIST will gather in His own
To the place where He is gone,—
Where their heart and treasure lie,
Where our life is hid on high.

Day by day the Voice saith, "Come,
Enter thine eternal home;"
Asking not if we can spare
This dear soul it summons there.

Had He asked us, well we know
We should cry, O, spare this blow!
Yes, with streaming tears should pray,
"Lord, we love him, let him stay."

But the Lord doth nought amiss,
And, since He hath ordered this,
We have nought to do but still
Rest in silence on His will.

Many a heart no longer here,
Ah! was all too inly dear;
Yet, O Love, 't is Thou dost call,
Thou wilt be our All-in-all.

ANON.

DEATH AND THE GRAVE.

O grave, where is thy victory?
I. Corinthians, xv. 55.

VITAL spark of heavenly flame,
Quit, O quit this mortal frame:
Trembling, hoping, lingering, flying,
O the pain, the bliss of dying!
Cease, fond nature, cease thy strife,
And let me languish into life.

Hark! they whisper; angels say,
"Sister spirit, come away."
What is this absorbs me quite,
Steals my senses, shuts my sight,
Drowns my spirit, draws my breath?
Tell me, my soul, can this be death?

The world recedes: it disappears:
Heaven opens on mine eyes; mine ears
  With sounds seraphic ring!
Lend, lend your wings; I mount, I fly;
O Grave! where is thy victory?
  O Death! where is thy sting?

ALEXANDER POPE.

THE JUDGMENT

The judgment of the great day.
                                        Jude, 6.

LO! He comes, with clouds descending!
Hark! the trump of God is blown,

And th' archangel's voice attending
 Makes the high procession known :
  Sons of Adam !
 Rise, and stand before your God !

Crowns and sceptres fall before Him,
 Kings and conquerors own His sway;
Haughtiest monarchs now adore Him,
 While they see His lightnings play:
  How triumphant
 Is the world's Redeemer now !

Hear His voice, as mighty thunder
 Sounding in eternal roar,
While its echo rends in sunder
 Rocks and mountains, sea and shore :
  Hark ! His accents
 Through th' unfathomed deep resound !

"Come, Lord Jesus ! O, come quickly ! "
 Oft has prayed the mourning Bride :
"Lo !" He answers, "I come quickly !"
 Who Thy coming may abide ?
  All who loved Him,
 All who longed to see His day.

"Come," He saith, "ye heirs of glory;
 Come, ye purchase of my blood ;
Claim the kingdom now before you,
 Rise, and fill the mount of God,

> Fixed for ever
> Where the Lamb on Sion stands."

See! ten thousand burning seraphs
    From their thrones as lightnings fly;
"Take," they cry, "your seats above us,
    Nearest Him that rules the sky!"
        Patient sufferers,
    How rewarded are ye now!

Now their trials all are ended:
    Now the dubious warfare's o'er:
Joy no more with sorrow blended,
    They shall sigh and weep no more;
        God for ever
    Wipes the tear from every eye.

Through His passion all victorious
    Now they drink immortal wine;
In Emanuel's likeness glorious
    As the firmament they shine;
        Shine for ever,
    With the bright and Morning Star.

Shout aloud, ye ethereal choirs!
    Triumph in Jehovah's praise!
Kindle all your heavenly fires,
    All your palms of victory raise
        Shout His conquests,
    Shout salvation to the Lamb '

THE JUDGMENT.

In full triumph see them marching
   Through the gates of massy light,
While the City walls are sparkling
   With meridian glory bright;
     O how lovely
   Are the dwellings of the Lamb!

Hosts angelic all adore Him
   Circling round His orient seat;
Elders cast their crowns before Him,
   Fall and worship at His feet;
     O how holy
   And how reverend is Thy Name!

Hail, Thou Alpha and Omega!
   First and Last, of all alone!
He that is, and was, and shall be,
   And beside whom there is none!
     Take the glory,
   Great eternal Three in One!

               THOMAS OLIVERS.

The day of wrath and revelation of the judgment of God.
               Romans, ii. 5.

DAY of anger, that dread Day
   Shall the sign in Heaven display,
   And the earth in ashes lay.

THE JUDGMENT.

O what trembling shall appear,
When His coming shall be near,
Who shall all things strictly clear!

When the trumpet shall command
Through the tombs of every land
All before the Throne to stand.

Death shall shrink and Nature quake,
When all creatures shall awake,
Answer to their God to make.

See the Book divinely penned,
In which all is found contained,
Whence the world shall be arraigned!

When the judge is on His throne,
All that's hidden shall be shown,
Nought unpublished or unknown!

What shall I before Him say?
How shall I be safe that day,
When the righteous scarcely may?

King of awful majesty,
Saving sinners graciously,
Fount of mercy, save Thou me!

Leave me not, my Saviour, one
For whose soul Thy course was run,
Lest I be that day undone.

THE JUDGMENT.

Thou didst toil my soul to gain;
Didst redeem me with Thy pain:
Be such labour not in vain!

Thou just Judge of wrath severe,
Grant my sins remission here,
Ere Thy reckoning day appear.

My trangressions grievous are;
Scarce look up for shame I dare;
Lord, Thy guilty suppliant spare!

Thou didst heal the sinner's grief,
And didst hear the dying thief:
Even I may hope relief.

All unworthy is my prayer;
Make my soul Thy mercy's care,
And from fire eternal spare!

Place me with Thy sheep, that band
Who shall separated stand
From the goats, at Thy right hand!

When Thy voice in wrath shall say,
"Cursèd ones, depart away!"
Call me with the blest, I pray.

Lord, Thine ear in mercy bow!
Broken is my heart and low:
Guard of my last end be Thou!

In that day, that mournful day,
When to judgment wakes our clay,
Show me mercy, Lord, I pray!

HENRY ALFORD.

Watch, therefore; for ye know neither the day nor the hour wherein the Son of Man cometh.
Matthew, xxv. 13.

THOU Judge of quick and dead,
  Before whose bar severe
With holy joy, or guilty dread,
  We all shall soon appear;
  Our cautioned souls prepare
  For that tremendous day,
And fill us now with watchful care,
  And stir us up to pray.

  To pray and wait the hour,
  The awful hour unknown,
When, robed in majesty and power,
  Thou shalt from Heaven come down,
  The immortal Son of Man,
  To judge the human race,
With all Thy Father's dazzling train,
  With all Thy glorious grace.

THE JUDGMENT.

To damp our earthly joys,
To increase our gracious fears,
For ever let the archangel's voice
Be sounding in our ears;
The solemn midnight cry,
"Ye dead, the Judge is come!
Arise and meet Him in the sky,
And meet your instant doom!"

O may we thus be found,
Obedient to His word,
Attentive to the trumpet's sound,
And looking for our Lord:
O may we thus insure
Our lot among the blest,
And watch a moment, to secure
An everlasting rest!

CHARLES WESLEY.

When the Lord Jesus shall be revealed from Heaven.
II. Thessalonians, i. 7.

THE Lord shall come! the earth shall quake;
The mountains to their centre shake;
And, withering from the vault of night,
The stars withdraw their feeble light.

THE JUDGMENT.

The Lord shall come! but not the same
As once in lowliness He came,—
A silent Lamb before His foes,
A weary Man, and full of woes.

The Lord shall come! a glorious form,
With wreath of flame and robe of storm,
On cherub wings and wings of wind,
Appointed Judge of all mankind.

Can this be He, once wont to stray
A pilgrim on the world's highway,
Oppressed by power and mocked by pride,
The Nazarene, the Crucified?

While sinners, in despair, shall call,
"Rocks, hide us! mountains, on us fall!"
The saints, ascending from the tomb,
Shall joyful sing, "The Lord is come!"

BISHOP REGINALD HEBER.

---

*And I saw a great white throne, and
Him that sat on it.*
Revelation, xx. 11.

GREAT God, what do I see and hear?
　　The end of things created:
Behold the Judge of man appear,
　　On clouds of glory seated!

THE JUDGMENT.

The trumpet sounds, the graves restore
The dead which they contained before;
  Prepare, my soul, to meet Him.

The dead in Christ shall first arise,
  At the last trumpet's sounding;
Caught up to meet Him in the skies,
  With joy their Lord surrounding:
No gloomy fears their souls dismay,
His presence sheds eternal day
  On those prepared to meet Him.

The ungodly, filled with guilty fears,
  Behold His wrath prevailing;
In woe they rise, but all their tears
  And sighs are unavailing:
The day of grace is past and gone;
Trembling they stand before His throne
  All unprepared to meet Him.

Great God, what do I see and hear?
  The end of things created:
Behold the Judge of man appear,
  On clouds of glory seated!
Low at His Cross I view the day
When heaven and earth shall pass away,
  And thus prepare to meet Him.

MARTIN LUTHER.

THE JUDGMENT.

The Son of Man shall come in His glory, and all the holy angels with Him.
Matthew, xxv. 31.

LO! He comes, with clouds descending,
    Once for favoured sinners slain;
Thousand thousand saints attending
    Swell the triumph of His train:
        Hallelujah!
God appears, on earth to reign!

Every eye shall now behold Him,
    Robed in dreadful majesty;
Those who set at nought and sold Him,
    Pierced, and nailed Him to the tree,
        Deeply wailing,
Shall the true Messiah see.

Every island, sea, and mountain,
    Heaven and earth shall flee away;
All who hate Him must, confounded,
    Hear the trump proclaim the day—
        Come to judgment!
Come to judgment, come away!

Now Redemption, long expected,
    See in solemn pomp appear!
All His saints, by man rejected,
    Now shall meet Him in the air:

THE JUDGMENT.

Hallelujah!
See the day of God appear!

Answer Thine own Bride and Spirit;
    Hasten, Lord, the general doom;
The new Heaven and earth t' inherit,
    Take Thy pining exiles home:
        All creation
    Travails, groans, and bids Thee come!

Yea, Amen! let all adore Thee,
    High on Thine eternal throne:
Saviour, take the power and glory;
    Claim the kingdom for Thine own:
        O, come quickly,
    Everlasting God, come down!

VARIATION BY MARTIN MADAN,
FROM CHARLES WESLEY AND JOHN CENNICK.

The judgment of the great day.
            Jude 6.

DAY of Judgment, day of wonders!
    Hark! the trumpet's awful sound,
Louder than a thousand thunders,
    Shakes the vast creation round;
        How the summons
    Will the sinner's heart confound!

THE JUDGMENT.

See the Judge, our nature wearing,
    Clothed in majesty divine;
Ye who long for His appearing,
    Then shall say, This God is mine:
        Gracious Saviour,
    Own me in that day for Thine.

At His call the dead awaken,
    Rise to life from earth and sea;
All the powers of nature, shaken
    By His look, prepare to flee;
        Careless sinner,
    What will then become of Thee?

But to those who have confessèd,
    Loved and served the Lord below,
He will say, Come near, ye blessèd,
    See the kingdom I bestow;
        You for ever
    Shall my love and glory know.

                      JOHN NEWTON.

Glory to God in the highest, and on earth peace, good will toward men.
Luke, ii. 14.

Good tidings of great joy, which shall be to all people. For unto you is born this day a Saviour, which is Christ the Lord.
Luke, ii. 10, 11.

As often as ye eat this bread, and drink this cup, ye do shew the Lord's death till He come.
I. Corinthians, xi. 26.

Go ye and teach all nations, baptizing them in the Name of the Father, and of the Son, and of the Holy Ghost.
Matthew, xxviii. 19.

THE NATIVITY.

Glory to God in the highest, and on earth peace, good will toward men.
Luke, ii. 14.

HARK! the herald angels sing,
"Glory to the new-born King;
Peace on earth and mercy mild;
God and sinners reconciled."

THE NATIVITY.

Joyful, all ye nations, rise;
Join the triumph of the skies:
With the angelic host proclaim,
"Christ is born in Bethlehem."

Christ, by highest Heaven adored,
Christ, the everlasting Lord:
Late in time, behold Him come,
Offspring of a virgin's womb!

Veiled in flesh the Godhead see;
Hail, the Incarnate Deity;
Pleased as Man with men to dwell,
Jesus, our Immanuel.

Hail! the Heaven-born Prince of Peace
Hail! the Sun of Righteousness!
Light and life to all He brings,
Risen with healing in His wings.

Lo! He lays His glory by;
Born that man no more may die;
Born to raise the sons of earth;
Born to give them second birth.

Come, Desire of Nations, come,
Fix in us Thy humble home;
Rise, the woman's conquering Seed:
Bruise in us the serpent's head.

Now display Thy saving power,
Ruined nature now restore;
Now in mystic union join
Thine to ours, and ours to Thine!

Adam's likeness, Lord, efface;
Stamp Thy image in its place;
Second Adam from above,
Reinstate us in Thy love!

Let us Thee, though lost, regain,
Thee, the Life, the Heavenly Man:
O! to all Thyself impart,
Formed in each believing heart!

Sing we, then, with angels sing,
" Glory to the new-born King;
Glory in the highest Heaven,
Peace on earth, and man forgiven."

CHARLES WESLEY.

The Lord hath made known His salvation.
Psalm xcviii. 2.

JOY to the world! the Lord is come;
Let earth receive her King;
Let every heart prepare Him room,
And Heaven and Nature sing.

THE NATIVITY.

Joy to the earth! the Saviour reigns;
    Let men their songs employ;
While fields and floods, rocks, hills, and plains
    Repeat the sounding joy.

No more let sins and sorrows grow,
    Nor thorns infest the ground:
He comes to make His blessings flow
    Far as the curse is found.

He rules the world with truth and grace,
    And makes the nations prove
The glories of His righteousness,
    And wonders of His love.

                        ISAAC WATTS.

Behold the Lamb of God!
                    John, i. 36.

WE 'LL sing, in spite of scorn;
    Our theme is come from Heaven:
To us a Child is born,
    To us a Son is given
The sweetest news that ever came
We 'll sing, though all the world should blame.

    The long expected morn
        Has dawned upon the earth;

THE NATIVITY.

The Saviour Christ is born,
   And angels sing His birth:
We'll join the bright seraphic throng,
We'll share their joys and swell their song.

O! 't is a lofty theme,
   Supplied by angels' tongues!
All other objects seem
   Unworthy of our songs:
This sacred theme has boundless charms;
It fills, it captivates, it warms!

Now sing of peace divine,
   Of grace to guilty man;
No wisdom, Lord, but Thine
   Could form the wondrous plan;
Where peace and righteousness embrace,
And justice goes along with grace.

Give praise to God on high,
   With angels round His throne;
Give praise to God with joy,
   Give praise to God alone!
'T is meet His saints their songs should raise,
And give the Saviour endless praise.

                        THOMAS KELLY.

THE NATIVITY.

When they saw the star, they rejoiced with exceeding great joy
Matthew, ii. 10.

WHEN, marshalled on the mighty plain,
    The glittering host bestuds the sky,
One star alone, of all the train,
    Can fix the sinner's wandering eye.

Hark! hark! to God the chorus breaks,
    From every host, from every gem;
But one alone the Saviour speaks,—
    It is the Star of Bethlehem.

Once on the raging seas I rode;
    The storm was loud, the night was dark,
The ocean yawned, and wildly blowed
    The wind that tossed my foundering bark.

Deep horror then my vitals froze:
    Deathstruck, I ceased the tide to stem,
When suddenly a star arose,—
    It was the Star of Bethlehem.

It was my guide, my light, my all!
    I bade my dark forebodings cease,
And through the storm and danger's thrall
    It led me to the port of peace.

THE NATIVITY.

Now safely moored, my perils o'er,
    I'll sing, first in night's diadem,
For ever and for evermore,
    The Star! the Star of Bethlehem!

                  HENRY KIRKE WHITE.

Unto you is born this day a Saviour, which is Christ the Lord.
                                    Luke, ii. 7.

WHILE shepherds watched their flocks by night
    All seated on the ground,
The angel of the Lord came down,
    And glory shone around.

"Fear not," said he (for mighty dread
    Had seized their troubled mind);
"Glad tidings of great joy I bring
    To you and all mankind.

"To you, in David's town, this day
    Is born of David's line
The Saviour, who is Christ the Lord;
    And this shall be the sign,—

"The heavenly Babe you there shall find
    To human view displayed,
All meanly wrapt in swathing-bands,
    And in a manger laid."

THE NATIVITY.

Thus spake the seraph, and forthwith
  Appeared a shining throng
Of angels, praising God, and thus
  Addressed their joyful song:

"All glory be to God on high,
  And to the earth be peace;
Good will henceforth from Heaven to men
  Begin, and never cease!"

NAHUM TATE.

*There was with the angel a multitude of
the heavenly host praising God.*
Luke, ii. 13.

SONGS of praise the angels sang!
  Joy through the starry heavens rang!
When to the world the Christ was given,
The Prince of Peace, the Lord of Heaven.

O sweet the music was to hear
That filled the slumbering shepherds' ear:
That told of our Creator's plan
Of peace on earth, good will to man.

Quick then was caught the wondrous sound,
  And spread through all the nations round;
And thousands join, their voices raise,
All giving unto God the praise.

THE NATIVITY.

And now this song from shore to shore
Will sound till time shall be no more;
Then shall be heard these words of love
Loud hymning in the Heaven above.

ANON.

*And there was a multitude of the heavenly
host praising God.*
Luke, ii. 13

IT came upon the midnight clear,
    That glorious song of old,
From angels bending near the earth
    To touch their harps of gold:
"Peace to the earth, good will to men
    From Heaven's all-gracious King:"
The world in solemn stillness lay
    To hear the angels sing.

Still through the cloven skies they come
    With peaceful wings unfurled;
And still their heavenly music floats
    O'er all the weary world;
Above its sad and lowly plains
    They bend on heavenly wing,
And ever o'er its Babel sounds
    The blessed angels sing.

Yet with the woes of sin and strife
    The world has suffered long;
Beneath the angel-strain have rolled
    Two thousand years of wrong;
And men, at war with men, hear not
    The love-song which they bring.
O! hush the noise, ye men of strife,
    And hear the angels sing!

And ye, beneath life's crushing load
    Whose forms are bending low,
Who toil along the climbing way
    With painful steps and slow,
Look now! for glad and golden hours
    Come swiftly on the wing:
O! rest beside the weary road,
    And hear the angels sing!

For lo! the days are hastening on,
    By prophet-bards foretold,
When with the ever-circling years
    Comes round the age of gold;
When peace shall over all the earth
    Its ancient splendours fling,
And the whole world send back the song
    Which now the angels sing.

                    EDMUND H. SEARS.

THE NATIVITY.

And His Name shall be called The Prince of Peace.
Isaiah, ix. 6.

THE race that long in darkness pined
    Have seen a glorious Light;
The people dwell in day, who dwelt
    In death's surrounding night.

To hail Thy rise, Thou better Sun,
    The gathering nations come,
Joyous as when the reapers bear
    The harvest treasures home.

For Thou our burden hast removed,
    And quelled th' oppressor's sway,
Quick as the slaughtered squadrons fell
    In Midian's evil day.

To us a Child of Hope is born,
    To us a Son is given;
Him shall the tribes of earth obey,
    Him all the hosts of Heaven.

His Name shall be the Prince of Peace,
    For evermore adored,
The Wonderful, the Counsellor,
    The great and mighty Lord.

His power increasing still shall spread,
   His reign no end shall know;
Justice shall guard His throne above,
   And peace abound below.

       JOHN MORRISON.

Behold, I bring you tidings of great joy.
       Luke, ii. 10.

THE scene around me disappears,
   And, borne to ancient regions,
While time recalls the flight of years,
   I see angelic legions
Descending in an orb of light:
Amidst the dark and silent night
   I hear celestial voices.

Tidings, glad tidings from above
   To every age and nation!
Tidings, glad tidings! God is Love
   To man He sends salvation!
His Son beloved, His only Son,
The work of mercy hath begun:
   Give to His Name the glory!

Through David's city I am led;
   Here all around are sleeping;

THE NATIVITY.

A light directs to yon poor shed;
  There lonely watch is keeping:
I enter; ah! what glories shine!
Is this Immanuel's earthly shrine,
  Messiah's infant Temple?

It is, it is; and I adore
  This Stranger meek and lowly,
As saints and angels bow before
  The throne of God thrice holy!
Faith through the veil of flesh can see
The face of Thy divinity,
  My Lord, my God, my Saviour.

JAMES MONTGOMERY.

Rejoice in the Lord alway; and again I say, rejoice.
Philippians, iv. 4.

HARK, the glad sound! the Saviour comes,
  The Saviour promised long
Let every heart prepare a throne,
  And every voice a song!

He comes, the prisoners to release,
  In Satan's bondage held;
The gates of brass before Him burst,
  The iron fetters yield.

THE NATIVITY.

He comes, from thickest films of vice
    To clear the mental ray,
And on the eyeballs of the blind,
    To pour celestial day.

He comes, the broken heart to bind
    The bleeding soul to cure,
And with the treasures of His grace
    To enrich the humble poor.

Our glad Hosannas, Prince of Prince,
    Thy welcome shall proclaim,
And Heaven's eternal arches ring
    With Thy beloved Name.

PHILIP DODDRIDGE.

I will give thanks unto Thee, O Lord, and sing praises unto Thy Name.
    Psalm xviii. 49.

WHAT sudden blaze of song
    Spreads o'er the expanse of Heaven?
In waves of light it thrills along:
    The angelic signal given—
"Glory to God!" from yonder central fire
Flows out the echoing lay beyond the starry choir;

    Like circles widening round
    Upon a clear blue river,

THE NATIVITY.

Orb after orb, the wondrous sound
    Is echoed on for ever :
" Glory to God on high, on earth be peace,
And love towards men of love—salvation and release."

Yet stay; before thou dare
    To join that festal throng,
Listen and mark that gentle air
    First stirred the tide of song;
'T is not " the Saviour born in David's home
To whom for power and health obedient worlds should
    come ;"

'T is not, " the Christ the Lord :"
    With fixed adoring look
The choir of angels caught the word,
    Nor yet their silence broke ;
But when they heard the sign where Christ should be,
In sudden light they shone and heavenly harmony.

Wrapped in His swaddling bands
    And in His manger laid,
The Hope and Glory of all lands
    Is come to the world's aid :
No peaceful home upon His cradle smiled,
Guests rudely went and came, where slept the royal Child.

But where Thou dwellest, Lord,
    No other thought should be ;

THE NATIVITY.

    Once duly welcomed and adored,
        How should I part from Thee?
Bethlehem must lose Thee soon, but Thou wilt grace
The single heart to be Thy sure abiding-place.

    Thee on the bosom laid
        Of a pure virgin mind,
    In quiet ever, and in shade,
        Shepherd and sage may find;
They who had bowed untaught to Nature's sway,
And they who followed truth along her star-paved way.

    The pastoral spirits first
        Approach Thee, Babe divine,
    For they in lowly thoughts are nursed,
        Meet for Thy lowly shrine;
Sooner than they should miss where Thou dost dwell,
Angels from Heaven will stoop to guide them to Thy cell.

    Still as the day comes round
        For Thee to be revealed,
    By wakeful shepherds Thou art found,
        Abiding in the field;
All through the wintry heaven, and chill night air,
In music and in light Thou dawnest on their prayer.

    O, faint not ye for fear:
        What though your wandering sheep,
    Reckless of what they see and hear,

THE NATIVITY.

Lie lost in wilful sleep?
High Heaven, in mercy to your sad annoy,
Still greets you with glad tidings of immortal joy.

Think on the eternal home
　　The Saviour left for you!
Think on the Lord most holy, come
　　To dwell with hearts untrue:
So shall ye tread untired His pastoral ways,
And in the darkness sing you carol of high praise.

REV. J. KEBLE.

Ye shall find the babe lying in a manger.
Luke, ii. 12.

SING the birth was born to-night,
The Author both of life and light;
　　The angels so did sound it.
And like the ravished shepherds said
Who saw the light, and were afraid,
　　Yet searched, and true they found it.

The Son of God, th' Eternal King,
That did us all salvation bring,
　　And freed the soul from danger,—
He whom the whole world could not take,
The Word which Heaven and earth did make,
　　Was now laid in a manger.

THE NATIVITY.

The Father's wisdom willed it so,
The Son's obedience knew no No,
    Both wills were in one stature;
And as that wisdom had decreed,
The Word was now made flesh indeed,
    And took on Him our nature.

What comfort by Him do we win,
Who made Himself the price of sin,
    To make us heirs of glory!
To see this Babe, all innocence,
A martyr born in our defence,—
    Can man forget this story?

BEN JONSON.

BAPTISM.

Be not thou ashamed of the testimony of our Lord.
II. Timothy, i. 8.

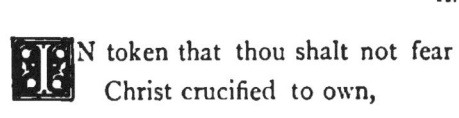

IN token that thou shalt not fear
Christ crucified to own,

BAPTISM.

We print the cross upon thee here,
    And stamp thee His alone.

In token that thou shalt not blush
    To glory in His Name,
We blazon here upon thy front
    His glory and His shame.

In token that thou shalt not flinch
    Christ's quarrel to maintain,
But 'neath His banner manfully
    Firm at thy post remain;

In token that thou too shalt tread
    The path He travelled by,
Endure the cross, despise the shame,
    And sit thee down on high;

Thus outwardly and visibly
    We seal thee for His own;
And may the brow that wears His cross
    Hereafter share His crown.

DEAN ALFORD.

BAPTISM.

He shall baptize you with the Holy Ghost.
Matthew, iii. 11.

COME, Father, Son, and Holy Ghost,
Honour the means ordained by Thee:
Of no mysterious power we boast,
But of the Spirit's ministry.

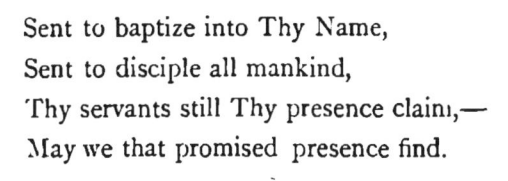

Sent to baptize into Thy Name,
Sent to disciple all mankind,
Thy servants still Thy presence claim,—
May we that promised presence find.

Father! in these reveal Thy Son,—
In these for whom we seek Thy face:
Adopt and seal them as Thine own,
By Thy regenerating grace.

Jesus! with us Thou always art;
Now ratify the sacred sign;
The gift unspeakable impart,
And bless Thine ordinance divine.

Come, Holy Spirit, from on high,
Baptizer of our spirits Thou!
The purifying grace apply,
And witness with the water now.

CHARLES WESLEY.

BAPTISM.

Ask, and it shall be given you; seek, and ye shall find; knock, and it shall be opened unto you.
                                        Matthew, vii. 7.

FATHER, Thou who hast created all
  In wisest love, we pray,
Look on this babe, who at Thy gracious call
  Is entering on life's way,
Bend o'er it now with blessing fraught,
And make Thou something out of nought.
    O Father, hear!

O Son of God, who diedst for us, behold,
  We bring our child to Thee;
Thou tender Shepherd, take it to Thy fold,
  Thine own for aye to be;
Defend it through this earthly strife,
And lead it on the path of life,
    O Son of God!

O Holy Ghost, who broodedst o'er the wave,
  Descend upon this child;
Give it undying life; its spirit lave
  With waters undefiled;
Grant it, while yet a babe, to be
A child of God, a home for Thee,
    O Holy Ghost!

BAPTISM.

O Triune God, what Thou command'st is done;
   We speak, but Thine the might;
This child hath scarce yet seen our earthly sun,
   Yet pour on it Thy light,
In faith and hope, in joy and love,
Thou Sun of all below, above,
   O Triune God! Amen.

ANON.

There shall be one fold and one Shepherd.
John, x. 16.

SHEPHERD of Israel, from above
   Thy feeble flock behold;
And let us never lose Thy love,
   Nor wander from Thy fold.

Thou wilt not cast Thy lambs away;
   Thy hand is ever near,
To guide them lest they go astray,
   And keep them safe from fear.

Thy tender care supports the weak,
   And will not let them fall;
Then teach us, Lord, Thy praise to speak,
   And on Thy Name to call.

We want Thy help, for we are frail;
    Thy light, for we are blind;
Let grace o'er all our doubts prevail,
    To prove that Thou art kind.

Teach us the things we ought to know,
    And may we find them true;
And still, in stature as we grow,
    Increase in wisdom too.

Guide us through life; and when at last
    We enter into rest,
Thy tender arms around us cast,
    And fold us to Thy breast!

WILLIAM HILEY BATHURST.

---

*He shall feed His flock like a shepherd:
He shall gather the lambs with His
arm, and carry them in His bosom.*
Isaiah, xl. 11.

SAVIOUR, who Thy flock art feeding
    With the Shepherd's kindest care,
All the feeble gently leading,
    While the lambs Thy bosom share;

Now, these little ones receiving,
    Fold them in Thy gracious arm;

There, we know, Thy Word believing,
 Only there secure from harm!

Never, from Thy pasture roving,
    Let them be the lion's prey;
Let Thy tenderness so loving
    Keep them all life's dangerous way:

Then within Thy fold eternal
    Let them find a resting-place,
Feed in pastures ever vernal,
    Drink the rivers of Thy grace!

ANON.

Suffer the little children to come.
Mark, x. 14.

SEE, Israel's gentle Shepherd stands,
    With all-engaging charms;
Hark! how He calls the tender lambs,
    And folds them in His arms.

"Permit them to approach," He cries,
    "Nor scorn their humble name;
For 't was to bless such souls as these
    The Lord of angels came."

Invited by the voice Divine,
    We bring them, Lord, to Thee;
Joyful that we ourselves are Thine:
    Thine let our offspring be.

BAPTISM.

If orphans they are left behind,
   Thy guardian care we trust:
That care shall heal our bleeding hearts,
   If weeping o'er their dust.

PHILIP DODDRIDGE.

The angel bless the lads.
Genesis, xlviii. 16.

THE great redeeming Angel, Thee,
   O Jesus, we confess:
Do Thou our great Deliverer be,
   And all our offspring bless.

Early discipled to the Lord,
   May they be taught of Thee,
And, made to know and trust Thy word,
   Wise to salvation be.

Thou who hast borne our sins away,
   Our children's sins remove,
And bring them through their evil day,
   To sing thy praise above.

Partakers of our nature, make
   Partakers of Thy grace;
And then the heirs of glory take
   To dwell before Thy face.

CHARLES WESLEY.

BAPTISM.

And they brought unto Him also infants.
Luke, xviii. 1.

GOD of that glorious gift of grace
By which Thy people seek Thy face,
When in Thy presence we appear,
Vouchsafe us faith to venture near!

Confiding in Thy truth alone,
Here, on the steps of Jesus' throne,
We lay the treasure Thou hast given,
To be received and reared for Heaven.

Lent to us for a season, we
Lend him for ever, Lord, to Thee;
Assured that, if to Thee he live,
We gain in what we seem to give.

Large and abundant blessings shed,
Warm as these prayers upon his head!
And on his soul the dews of grace,
Fresh as these drops upon his face!

Make him and keep him Thine own child,
Meek follower of the Undefiled!
Possessor here of grace and love;
Inheritor of Heaven above!

JOHN S. B. MONSELL.

BAPTISM.

Be ye baptized in the Name of Jesus Christ, and ye shall receive the gift of the Holy Ghost.
                                                          Acts, ii. 38.

WHAT means the water in this font?
What means this simple sacred rite?
Why bring we babes to Zion's mount,
And in this service thus unite?

We claim no power to change the heart,
No mystic grace new life to give;
He must the gift divine impart
By whom our children's spirits live.

This institute of Gospel grace
Proclaims our nature spoiled by sin;
Shadows the change that yet must pass
Upon the living soul within;

Speaks of the Spirit's power to cleanse
The human heart by sin depraved;
And points us to the gracious means
By which alone the soul is saved.

Triune Jehovah! hear our prayer,
As thus we bring our babes to Thee;
Make them in life Thy special care;
Fit them for immortality.

                                        SPENCE.

BAPTISM.

Now, God, we thank Thee and praise Thy glorious Name.
I. Chronicles, xxix. 13.

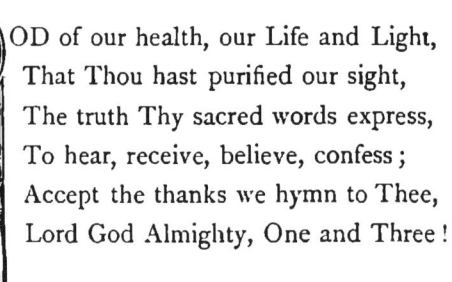

GOD of our health, our Life and Light,
That Thou hast purified our sight,
The truth Thy sacred words express,
To hear, receive, believe, confess;
Accept the thanks we hymn to Thee,
Lord God Almighty, One and Three!

That, washed in Thy thrice holy Name,
A new relation thence we claim,
And, born by nature sons of earth,
Thence share by grace a heavenly birth;
Accept the thanks we hymn to Thee,
Lord God Almighty, One and Three!

That thence we worship Thee alone,
And, whom our vows baptismal own,
To Thee the prayer of faith we bring,
To Thee the song of glory sing:
Accept the thanks we hymn to Thee,
Lord God Almighty, One and Three!

That thence the course we're trained to run
Of goodness at Thy font begun,
Our Saviour's cross to keep in view,
His faith confess, His steps pursue;

Accept the thanks we hymn to Thee,
Lord God Almighty, One and Three!

O Holy, Holy, Holy Thou,
God of our health, preserve us now
Firm in Thy worship, fear, and love,
That we may see Thy face above,
And there our thanks still hymn to Thee,
Lord God Almighty, One and Three!

BISHOP RICHARD MANT.

---

*Baptizing them in the Name of the Father,
and of the Son, and of the Holy Ghost.*
Matthew, xxviii. 19

HEAVENLY Father, may Thy love
  Beam upon us from above:
  Let this infant find a place
  In Thy covenant of grace.

Son of God, be with us here;
  Listen to our humble prayer;
  Let Thy blood on Calvary spilt
  Cleanse this child from nature's guilt.

Holy Ghost, to Thee we cry!
  Thou this infant sanctify;

Thine almighty power display,
Seal him to redemption's day.

Great Jehovah!—Father, Son,
Holy Spirit,—Three in One,
Let the blessing come from Thee;
Thine shall all the glory be.

GUEST.

THE LORD'S SUPPER.

As often as ye eat this bread, and drink this cup, ye do shew the Lord's death till He come.
I. Corinthians, xi. 26.

BREAD of the world in mercy broken,
    Wine of the soul in mercy shed!
By whom the words of life were spoken,
    And in whose death our sins are dead!

Look on the heart by sorrow broken,
    Look on the tears by sinners shed,
And be Thy feast to us the token
    That by Thy grace our souls are fed.

BISHOP REGINALD HEBER.

THE LORD'S SUPPER.

Drink ye all of it.
Matthew, xxvi. 27.

JESUS, Thou Joy of loving hearts!
   Thou Fount of Life! Thou Light of men!
From the best bliss that earth imparts,
   We turn unfilled to Thee again.

Thy truth unchanged hath ever stood;
   Thou savest those that on Thee call;
To them that seek Thee Thou art good,
   To them that find Thee, All in All!

We taste Thee, O Thou Living Bread,
   And long to feast upon Thee still!
We drink of Thee, the Fountain Head,
   And thirst our souls from Thee to fill!

Our restless spirits yearn for Thee,
   Where'er our changeful lot is cast;
Glad, when Thy gracious smile we see,
   Blest, when our faith can hold Thee fast.

O Jesus, ever with us stay!
   Make all our moments calm and bright!
Chase the dark night of sin away!
   Shed o'er the world Thy holy light!

                RAY PALMER.
                FROM ST. BERNARD.

This do in remembrance of me.
Luke, xxii. 19.

ACCORDING to Thy gracious word,
  In meek humility
This will I do, my dying Lord;
  I will remember Thee.

Thy body, broken for my sake,
  My bread from Heaven shall be:
Thy testamental cup I take,
  And thus remember Thee.

Gethsemane can I forget?
  Or there Thy conflict see,
Thine agony and bloody sweat,
  And not remember Thee?

When to the Cross I turn mine eyes,
  And rest on Calvary,
O Lamb of God, my Sacrifice,
  I must remember Thee.

Remember Thee, and all Thy pains,
  And all Thy love to me;
Yea, while a breath, a pulse remains,
  Will I remember Thee.

And when these failing lips grow dumb,
  And mind and memory flee,
When Thou shalt in Thy kingdom come,
  Then, Lord, remember me!

JAMES MONTGOMERY.

And they said, Did not our hearts burn within us as He talked with us by the way?
Luke, xxiv. 32.

THEY talked of Jesus as they went;
  And Jesus, all unknown,
Did at their side Himself present
  With sweetness all his own.
Swift, as he oped the Sacred Word,
  His glory they discerned;
And swift, as His dear voice they heard,
  Their hearts within them burned.

He would have left them, but that they
  With prayers His love assailed:
"Depart not yet! a little stay!"
  They pressed Him, and prevailed.
And Jesus was revealed, as there
  He blessed and brake the bread;
But, while they marked His heavenly air,
  The matchless Guest had fled.

THE LORD'S SUPPER.

And thus at times, as Christians talk
  Of Jesus and His Word,
He joins two friends amidst their walk,
  And makes, unseen, a third.
And O! how sweet their converse flows,
  Their holy theme how clear,
How warm with love each bosom glows,
  If Jesus be but near!

And they that woo His visits sweet
  And will not let Him go,
Oft, while His broken bread they eat,
  His soul-felt presence know:
His gathered friends He loves to meet
  And fill with joy their faith,
When they with melting hearts repeat
  The memory of His death.

But such sweet visits here are brief;
  Dispensed from stage to stage,
(A cheering and a prized relief),
  Of faith's hard pilgrimage.
There is a scene where Jesus ne'er,
  Ne'er leaves His happy guests;
He spreads a ceaseless banquet there
  And love still fires their breasts.

THOMAS GRINFIELD.

THE LORD'S SUPPER.

By whose stripes ye were healed.
I. Peter, ii. 24.

SWEET the moments, rich in blessing,
   Which before the Cross I spend;
Life and health and peace possessing
   From the sinner's dying Friend.

Here I'll sit, with transport viewing
   Mercy's streams, in streams of blood:
Precious drops my soul bedewing,
   Plead and claim my peace with God.

Truly blessed is the station,
   Low before His Cross to lie;
While I see divine compassion
   Floating in His languid eye.

Love and grief my heart dividing,
   With my tears His feet I'll bathe;
Constant still in faith abiding,
   Life deriving from His death.

May I still enjoy this feeling;
   In all need to Jesus go;
Prove His wounds each day more healing,
   And Himself more fully know.

JAMES ALLEN.

THE LORD'S SUPPER.

Take, eat: this is my body, which is broken for you.
I. Corinthians, xi. 24.

WITH all the powers my poor soul hath
Of humble love and loyal faith,
I come, dear Lord, to worship Thee,
Whom too much love bowed low for me.

Down, busy sense; discourses, die;
And all adore faith's mystery!
Faith is my skill—faith can believe
As fast as love new laws shall give.

Faith is my eye; faith strength affords
To keep pace with those gracious words;
And words more sure, more sweet than they,
Love could not think, truth could not say.

O dear memorial of that death
Which still survives and gives us breath!
Live ever, Bread of Life, and be
My food, my joy, my all to me!

Come, glorious Lord! my hopes increase,
And mix my portion with Thy peace!
Come, and for ever dwell in me,
That I may only live to Thee!

THE LORD'S SUPPER.

Come, hidden life, and that long day
For which I languish, come away!
When this dry soul those eyes shall see,
And drink the unsealed Source of Thee;

When Glory's Sun faith's shade shall chase
And, for Thy veil, give me Thy face;
Then shall my praise eternal be
To the eternal Trinity!

    JOHN AUSTIN AND THEOPHILUS DORRINGTON.
        VARIATION FROM RICHARD CRASHAW.

The communion of the body of Christ.
                          I. Corinthians, x 16.

COMMUNION of my Saviour's blood,
    In Him to have my lot and part;
To prove the virtue of that flood
    Which burst on Calvary from His heart;

To feed by faith on Christ, my Bread,
    His body broken on the tree;
To live in Him, my living Head,
    Who died and rose again for me;

This be my joy and comfort here,
    This pledge of future glory mine.

Jesus, in spirit now appear,
And break the bread and pour the wine.

THE LORD'S SUPPER.

From Thy dear hand may I receive
 The tokens of Thy dying love;
And, while I feast on earth, believe
 That I shall feast with Thee above.

Ah! there, though in the lowest place,
 Thee at Thy table could I meet,
And see Thee, know Thee, face to face,
 For such a moment death were sweet!

What then will their fruition be
 Who meet in Heaven with blest accord?
A moment?—No: eternity!
 They are for ever with the Lord.

JAMES MONTGOMERY.

And when they had sung an hymn, they went out.
Mark, xiv. 26.

SITTING around our Father's board,
 We raise our tuneful breath!
Our faith beholds the dying Lord,
 And dooms our sins to death.

We see the blood of Jesus shed,
 Whence all our pardons rise;
The sinner views the atonement made,
 And loves the Sacrifice.

THE LORD'S SUPPER.

Thy cruel thorns, Thy shameful cross,
   Procure us heavenly crowns;
Our highest gain springs from Thy loss,
   Our healing from Thy wounds.

O! 't is impossible that we,
   Who dwell in feeble clay,
Should equal sufferings bear for Thee,
   Or equal thanks should pay.

ISAAC WATTS.

I will go unto the altar of God, unto God my exceeding joy.
                Psalm xliii. 4.

SEND Thy light, Thy truth, my God,
   Thy grace bestow, Thy word fulfil;
And let them lead me in Thy road,
And bring me to Thy holy hill,
Where happy saints, a chosen band,
Exulting in Thy presence stand.

Then to Thine altar will I go,
And pay my destined offerings there,
And freely from my heart shall flow
The fervent, interceding prayer;
A prayer effectual, that shall rise
Accepted through the Sacrifice.

And I will take salvation's cup,
And call upon Thy blessed Name;
My thankful heart to Thee lift up,
Saviour from death and guilt and shame;
Restored in mercy to Thy house,
To render all my grateful vows.

There in Thy truth will I rejoice,
And hymn Thy goodness in my lays;
And mind and heart and soul and voice
Shall join to magnify Thy praise,
And triumph in the best employ,
My God, and mine exceeding joy.

MARCH.

The table of the Lord.
Malachi, i. 12.

MY God, and is Thy table spread?
   And does Thy cup with love o'erflow?
Thither be all Thy children led,
   And let them all its sweetness know.
Hail! sacred feast, which Jesus makes,
   Rich banquet of His flesh and blood;
Thrice happy he who here partakes
   That sacred stream, that heavenly food.

THE LORD'S SUPPER.

Why are these emblems still in vain
   Before unwilling hearts displayed?
Was not for you the Victim slain?
   Are you forbid the children's bread?
O let Thy table honoured be,
   And furnished well with joyful guests;
And may each soul salvation see,
   That here its sacred pledges tastes.

Let crowds approach with hearts prepared,
   With hearts inflamed let all attend;
Nor, when we leave our Father's board,
   The pleasure or the profit end.
Revive Thy dying churches, Lord,
   And bid our drooping graces live;
And more, that energy afford
   A Saviour's blood alone can give.

PHILIP DODDRIDGE.

If I wash thee not, thou hast no part with me.
John, xiii. 8.

OR ever here my rest shall be,
   Close to Thy bleeding side;
This all my hope and all my plea:
   For me the Saviour died.

THE LORD'S SUPPER.

My dying Saviour and my God,
    Fountain for guilt and sin!
Sprinkle me ever with Thy blood,
    And cleanse and keep me clean.

Wash me, and make me thus Thine own;
    Wash me, and mine Thou art;
Wash me, but not my feet alone,—
    My hands, my head, my heart.

The atonement of Thy blood apply,
    Till faith to sight improve;
Till hope in full fruition die,
    And all my soul be love.

                    CHARLES WESLEY.

*The Lamb of God which taketh away the sin
of the world.*
                    John, i. 29.

LAMB of God, whose bleeding love
    We now recall to mind,
Send the answer from above,
    And let us mercy find.
Think on us who think on Thee,
    Every burdened soul release:
O! remember Calvary,
    And bid us go in peace.

THE LORD'S SUPPER.

By Thine agonizing pain
  And bloody sweat, we pray;
By Thy dying love to man,
  Take all our sins away;
Burst our bonds and set us free,
  From iniquity release:
O! remember Calvary,
  And bid us go in peace.

Let Thy blood, by faith applied,
  The sinner's pardon seal;
Speak us freely justified,
  And all our sickness heal;
By Thy passion on the tree,
  Let our griefs and troubles cease:
O! remember Calvary,
  And bid us go in peace.

CHARLES WESLEY.

The bread which we break, is it not the communion of the body of Christ?
    I. Corinthians, x. 16.

LORD, when before Thy throne we meet,
  Thy goodness to adore,
From Heaven, th' eternal mercy-seat,
  On us Thy blessing pour,
And make our inmost souls to be
An habitation meet for Thee!

The Body for our ransom given;
    The Blood in mercy shed;
With this immortal food from Heaven,
    Lord, let our souls be fed!
And, as we round Thy table kneel,
Help us Thy quickening grace to feel!

Be Thou, O Holy Spirit, nigh!
    Accept the humble prayer,
The contrite soul's repentant sigh,
    The sinner's heartfelt tear!
And let our adoration rise,
As fragrant incense, to the skies!

ANON.

The wedding was furnished with guests.
Matthew, xxii. 10.

HOW rich are Thy provisions, Lord!
    Thy table furnished from above:
The fruits of life o'erspread the board,
    The cup o'erflows with heavenly love.

We were the poor, the blind, the lame,
    And help was far, and death was nigh;
But at the Gospel call we came,
    And every want received supply.

THE LORD'S SUPPER.

From the highway that leads to hell,
    From paths of darkness and despair,
Lord, we are come with Thee to dwell,
    Glad to enjoy Thy presence here.

What shall we render to the Son,
    That left the Heaven of His abode,
And to this wretched earth came down,
    To bring us wanderers back to God?

It cost Him death to save our lives;
    To buy our souls it cost His own;
And all the unknown joys He gives
    Were bought with agonies unknown.

Our everlasting love is due
    To Him that ransomed sinners lost,
And pitied rebels when He knew
    The vast expense His love would cost.

ISAAC WATTS.

As He sat at meat with them, He took bread, and blessed it, and brake, and gave to them.
Luke, xxiv. 30.

FOOD that weary pilgrims love,
O Bread of angel hosts above,
    O Manna of the saints,

The hungry soul would feed on Thee;
Ne'er may the heart unsolaced be
   Which for Thy sweetness faints.

O fount of love, O cleansing tide,
Which from the Saviour's piercèd side
   And sacred heart dost flow,
Be ours to drink of Thy pure rill,
Which only can our spirits fill
   And all we need bestow.

Lord Jesu, whom, by power divine
Now hidden 'neath the outward sign,
   We worship and adore,
Grant, when the veil away is rolled,
With open face we may behold
   Thyself for evermore.

ANON.

My flesh is meat indeed, and my blood is drink indeed.
John, vi. 55.

SING, my tongue, the Saviour's glory;
   Of His Cross the mystery sing;
   Lift on high the wondrous trophy,
Tell the triumph of the King:
He, the world's Redeemer, conquers
   Death, through death now vanquishing.

Born for us, and for us given;
   Son of man, like us below,
He, as Man, with men abiding
   Dwells, the seed of life to sow:
He, our heavy griefs partaking,
   Thus fulfils His life of woe.

Word made flesh! His word, life-giving,
   Gives His flesh our meat to be,
Bids us drink His blood, believing
   Through His death we life shall see:
Blessed they who thus receiving
   Are from death and sin set free.

Low in adoration bending,
   Now our hearts our God revere;
Faith her aid to sight is lending;
   Though unseen, the Lord is near:
Ancient types and shadows ending,
   Christ our Paschal Lamb is here.

Praise for ever, thanks and blessing,
   Thine, O gracious Father, be;
Praise be Thine, O Christ, who bringeth
   Life and immortality;
Praise be Thine, Thou quickening Spirit,
   Praise through all eternity!
THOMAS AQUINAS.

THE LORD'S SUPPER.

We will remember Thy love: the upright love Thee.
Solomon's Song, i. 4.

GOD, unseen, yet ever near,
    Thy presence may we feel;
And thus, inspired with holy fear,
    Before Thine altar kneel.

Here may Thy faithful people know
    The blessings of Thy love;
The streams that through the desert flow;
    The manna from above.

We come, obedient to Thy word,
    To feast on heavenly food;
Our meat, the Body of the Lord;
    Our drink, His precious Blood.

Thus would we all Thy words obey;
    For we, O God, are Thine;
And go rejoicing on our way,
    Renewed with strength Divine.

EDWARD OSLER.

THE PASSION OF OUR LORD

A place called Gethsemane.
　　　　　　　　　　Matthew, xxvi. 36.

GO to dark Gethsemane,
　　Ye that feel the tempter's power;
　Your Redeemer's conflict see;
　　Watch with Him one bitter hour;

THE PASSION OF OUR LORD.

Turn not from His griefs away:
Learn of Jesus Christ to pray.

Follow to the judgment-hall;
   View the Lord of life arraigned.
O the wormwood and the gall!
   O the pangs His soul sustained!
Shun not suffering, shame, or loss:
Learn of Him to bear the cross.

Calvary's mournful mountain climb;
   There, adoring at His feet,
Mark that miracle of time,—
   God's own sacrifice complete.
"It is finished!" hear Him cry:
Learn of Jesus Christ to die.

Early hasten to the tomb
   Where they laid His breathless clay;
All is solitude and gloom:
   Who hath taken Him away?
Christ is risen;—He seeks the skies.
Saviour, teach us so to rise.

JAMES MONTGOMERY.

When they had platted a crown of thorns, they put it upon His head.
Matthew, xxvii. 29.

O SACRED head, once wounded,
   With grief and pain weighed down,
How scornfully surrounded
   With thorns, Thine only crown!
How pale Thou art with anguish,
   With sore abuse and scorn!
How does that visage languish
   Which once was bright as morn!

O Lord of life and glory,
   What bliss till now was Thine!
I read the wondrous story,
   I joy to call Thee mine.
Thy grief and Thy compassion
   Were all for sinners' gain;
Mine, mine was the transgression,
   But Thine the deadly pain.

What language shall I borrow
   To praise Thee, heavenly Friend,
For this Thy dying sorrow,
   Thy pity without end?

Lord, make me Thine for ever,
   Nor let me faithless prove;
O let me never, never
   Abuse such dying love!

Be near me, Lord, when dying;
   O! show Thy Cross to me;
And, for my succour flying,
   Come, Lord, to set me free:
These eyes, new faith receiving,
   From Jesus shall not move;
For he who dies believing,
   Dies safely through Thy love.

PAUL GERHARDT.

Surely He hath borne our griefs and carried our sorrows; and with His stripes we are healed.
Isaiah, liii. 4, 5

SING, my tongue, the glorious battle,
   Sing the last, the dread affray;
O'er the cross, the Victor's trophy,
   Sound the glad triumphal lay,
How, the pains of earth enduring,
   Earth's Redeemer won the day.

He, our Maker, deeply grieving
   That the first-made Adam fell,

When he ate the fruit forbidden,
   Whose reward was death and hell,
Marked e'en then this tree the ruin
   Of the first tree to dispel.

Thus the work for our salvation
   He ordainèd to be done,
To the traitor's art opposing
   Art yet deeper than his own;
Thence the remedy procuring
   Whence the fatal wound begun.

Therefore, when at length the fulness
   Of th' appointed time was come,
He was sent, the world's Creator,
   From the Father's heavenly home,
And was found in human fashion,
   Offspring of the Virgin's womb.

Lo, He lies, an infant weeping,
   Where the narrow manger stands,
While the mother-maid His members
   Wraps in mean and lowly bands,
And the swaddling-clothes is winding
   Round His helpless feet and hands.

Part II.

NOW the thirty years accomplished
    Which on earth He willed to see,
Born for this He meets His Passion,
    Gives Himself an offering free;
On the cross the Lamb is lifted,
    There the Sacrifice to be.

There the nails and spear He suffers,
    Vinegar, and gall, and reed;
From His sacred body piercèd
    Blood and water both proceed;
Precious flood, which all creation
    From the stain of sin hath freed.

Faithful cross, above all other,
    One and only noble tree,
None in foliage, none in blossom,
    None in fruit thy peer may be;
Sweetest wood and sweetest iron,
    Sweetest weight is hung on thee.

Bend, O lofty tree, thy branches,
    Thy too rigid sinews bend;
And awhile the stubborn hardness,
    Which thy birth bestowed, suspend;

THE PASSION OF OUR LORD.

And the limbs of Heaven's high Monarch
    Gently on thine arms extend.

Thou alone wast counted worthy
    This world's Ransom to sustain,
That a shipwrecked race for ever
    Might a port of refuge gain,
With the sacred blood anointed
    Of the Lamb for sinners slain.

Praise and honour to the Father,
    Praise and honour to the Son,
Praise and honour to the Spirit,
    Ever three and ever one,
One in might, and one in glory,
    While eternal ages run.

ANON.

Whom they slew, and hanged on a tree.
Acts, x. 39.

LO! on the inglorious tree
    The Lord, the Lord of glory hangs;
    Forsaken now is He,
        And pierced with pangs.

    A shameful death He dies,
Uplifted with transgressors twain;
    A Lamb for sacrifice,
        By sinners slain.

Full is His cup of woe;
In death His drooping head declines;
"'T is done!" He cries; and now
　　His soul resigns.

O come, my soul, and gaze
On that great grief, that crown of thorn;
In deep and dread amaze
　　There look and mourn.

For thee He shed His blood;
Weep, till with woe thine eyes grow dim;
To that accursed wood
　　Thou hast nailed Him.

To Thee, the mighty Lord,
Who washed in blood our sins away,
　　Our boundless gratitude
　　Its thanks would pay.

　　　　　　　　　ANCIENT HYMN.

O our God, hear the prayer of Thy servant.
　　　　　　　　　Daniel ix. 17.

JESUS, who for us didst bear
　　Scorn and sorrow, toil and care,
　　Hearken to our lowly prayer;
　　　　Hear us, holy JESU!

By that hour of agony
Spent while Thine Apostles three
Slumbered in Gethsemane,
    Hear us, holy JESU!

By the prayer Thou thrice didst pray,
That the cup might pass away,
So Thou mightest still obey,
    Hear us, holy JESU!

When temptation sore is rife,
When we faint amidst the strife,
Thou, whose death hath been our life.
    Save us, holy JESU!

While on stormy seas we toss,
Let us count all things as loss,
But Thee only on Thy cross:
    Save us, holy JESU

So, with hope in Thee made fast,
When death's bitterness is past
We may see Thy face at last:
    Save us, holy JESU!

                ABRIDGED FROM
        "THE PEOPLE'S HYMNAL."

He is risen; He is not here: behold the place where they laid Him.
Mark, xvi. 6.

And when they had platted a crown of thorns, they put it upon His head. And they spit upon Him, and took the reed, and smote Him on the head.
Matthew, xxvii. 29, 30.

Jesus cried with a loud voice, and gave up the ghost. And the veil of the temple was rent in twain from the top to the bottom.
Mark, xv. 37, 38.

After the Lord had spoken unto them, He was received up into heaven, and sat on the right hand of God.
Mark, xvi. 19.

THE CRUCIFIXION

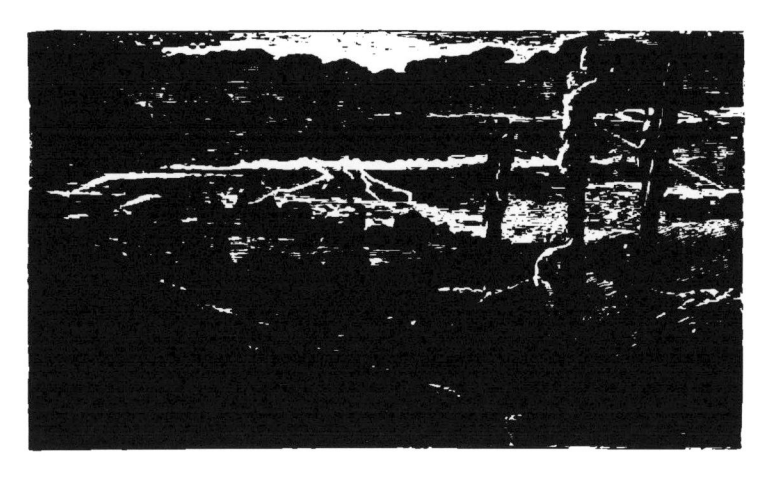

He hath made Him to be sin for us, who knew no sin.
II. Corinthians, v. 21

O WORLD! behold upon the tree
Thy Life is hanging now for thee,
   Thy Saviour yields His dying breath;
The mighty Prince of glory now
For thee doth unresisting bow
   To cruel stripes, to scorn and death.

Draw near, O world, and mark Him well;
Behold the drops of blood that tell
   How sore His conflict with the foe;
And hark! how from that noble heart,
Sigh after sigh doth slowly start
   From depths of yet unfathomed woe.

THE CRUCIFIXION.

I and my sins, that number more
Than yonder sands upon the shore,
   Have brought to pass this agony;
'T is I have caused the floods of woe
That now Thy dying soul o'erflow,
   And those sad hearts that watch by Thee.

'T is I to whom these pains belong,
'T is I should suffer for my wrong,
   Bound hand and foot in heavy chains;
The scourge, the fetters, whatso'er
Thou bearest, 't is my soul should bear,
   For she hath well deserved such pains.

Yet Thou dost even for my sake
On Thee in love the burdens take
   That weighed my spirit to the ground;
Yes, Thou art made a curse for me,
That I might yet be blest through Thee:
   My healing in Thy wounds is found.

From henceforth there is nought of mine
But I would seek to make it Thine,
   Since all myself to Thee I owe.
Whate'er my utmost powers can do,
To thee to render service true,
   Here at Thy feet I lay it low.

Ah! little have I, Lord, to give,
So poor, so base the life I live,

THE CRUCIFIXION.

But yet, till soul and body part,
This one thing I will do for Thee—
The woe, the death endured for me,
   I'll cherish in my inmost heart.

Thy Cross shall be before my sight,
My hope, my joy, by day and night,
   Whate'er I do, where'er I rove;
And, gazing, I will gather thence
The form of spotless innocence,
   The seal of faultless truth and love.

When evil tongues with stinging blame
Would cast dishonour on my name,
   I'll curb the passions that up start,
And take injustice patiently,
And pardon, as Thou pardon'st me,
   With an ungrudging generous heart.

Thy heavy groans, Thy bitter sighs,
The tears that from Thy dying eyes
   Were shed when Thou wast sore oppress'd,
Shall be with me, when at the last
Myself on Thee I wholly cast,
   And enter with Thee into rest.

PAUL GERHARDT.

THE CRUCIFIXION.

Who remembered us in our low estate.
                    Psalm cxxxvi. 23.

PLUNGED in a gulf of dark despair,
    We wretched sinners lay,
Without one cheerful beam of hope,
    Or spark of glimmering day.

With pitying eyes the Prince of Grace
    Beheld our helpless grief :
He saw, and, O amazing love!
    He ran to our relief.

Down from the shining seats above
    With joyful haste He fled ;
Entered the grave in mortal flesh,
    And dwelt among the dead.

O! for this love, let rocks and hills
    Their lasting silence break,
And all harmonious human tongues
    The Saviour's praises speak!

Angels, assist our mighty joys ;
    Strike all your harps of gold!
But, when you raise your highest notes,
    His love can ne'er be told.

                ISAAC WATTS.

THE CRUCIFIXION.

*Behold, and see if there be any sorrow
like unto my sorrow.*
Lamentations, i. 12.

SEE the destined day arise;
  See a willing sacrifice:
  Jesus, to redeem our loss,
  Hangs upon the shameful cross.

Jesus! who but Thou had borne,
Lifted on that tree of scorn,
Every pang and bitter throe,
Finishing Thy life of woe?

Who but Thou had dared to drain,
Steeped in gall, the cup of pain,
And with tender body bear
Thorns and nails and piercing spear?

Thence poured forth the water flowed,
Mingled from Thy side with blood;
Sign to all attesting eyes
Of the finished sacrifice.

Holy Jesus, grant us grace
In that sacrifice to place
All our trust for life renewed,
Pardoned sin and promised good.

                    ANON.

THE CRUCIFIXION.

It is finished.
John, xix. 30.

HARK! the voice of love and mercy
    Sounds aloud from Calvary;
See, it rends the rocks asunder,
    Shakes the earth, and veils the sky!
      "It is finished!"
    Hear the dying Saviour cry.

"It is finished!"—O what pleasure
    Do those gracious words afford!
Heavenly blessings without measure
    Flow to us from Christ the Lord:
      "It is finished!"
    Saints, the dying words record.

Finished, all the types and shadows
    Of the ceremonial law!
Finished, all that God had promised;
    Death and Hell no more shall awe.
      "It is finished!"
    Saints, from hence your comfort draw.

Tune your harps anew, ye seraphs,
    Join to sing the glorious theme;
All in earth and all in Heaven
    Join to praise Immanuel's Name.
      Hallelujah!
    Glory to the bleeding Lamb!

                        EVANS.

THE CRUCIFIXION.

He was wounded for our transgressions.
Isaiah, liii. 5.

"'T IS finished!"—so the Saviour cried,
    And meekly bowed His head, and died.
"'T is finished!" yes! the race is run,
    The battle fought, the victory won.

"'T is finished!"—all that was of old
    Decreed, and prophets had foretold,
Is now fulfilled, as Heaven designed,
    In Thee, the Saviour of mankind.

"'T is finished!"—this Thy dying groan
    Shall sins of every kind atone:
Millions shall be redeemed from death
    By this Thy last expiring breath.

"'T is finished!"—Heaven is reconciled,
    And all the powers of darkness spoiled:
Peace, love, and happiness again
    Return, and dwell with sinful men.

"'T is finished!"—let the joyful sound
    Be heard through all the nations round:
"'T is finished!"—let the echo fly
    Through Heaven and hell, through earth
        and sky.

STENNETT.

THE CRUCIFIXION.

Calvary, there they crucified Him.
Luke, xxiii. 33.

WHEN I survey the wondrous Cross
    On which the Prince of Glory died,
My richest gain I count but loss,
    And pour contempt on all my pride.

Forbid it, Lord, that I should boast
    Save in the death of Christ, my God;
All the vain things that charm me most,
    I sacrifice them to His blood.

See from His head, His hands, His feet,
    Sorrow and love flow mingled down!
Did e'er such love and sorrow meet,
    Or thorns compose so rich a crown?

Were the whole realm of nature mine,
    That were a present far too small;
Love so amazing, so divine,
    Demands my soul, my life, my all!

ISAAC WATTS

THE RESURRECTION AND ASCENSION.

The firstfruits of them that slept.

I. Corinthians, xv. 20.

CHRIST the Lord is risen to-day,
Sons of men and angels say:
Raise your joys and triumphs high,
Sing, ye heavens, and, earth, reply!

THE RESURRECTION AND ASCENSION.

Love's redeeming work is done,
Fought the fight, the battle won:
Lo! our Sun's eclipse is o'er;
Lo! He sets in blood no more.

Vain the stone, the watch, the seal;
Christ hath burst the gates of hell!
Death in vain forbids His rise;
Christ hath opened Paradise!

Lives again our glorious King:
Where, O Death, is now thy sting?
Once He died, our souls to save:
Where thy victory, O Grave?

Soar we now where Christ has led,
Following our exalted Head;
Made like Him, like Him we rise;
Ours the cross, the grave, the skies.

What though once we perished all,
Partners in our parents' fall?
Second life we all receive,
In our heavenly Adam live.

Risen with Him, we upward move;
Still we seek the things above;
Still pursue, and kiss the Son
Seated on His Father's throne.

THE RESURRECTION AND ASCENSION.

Scarce on earth a thought bestow,
Dead to all we leave below;
Heaven our aim and loved abode,
Hid our life with Christ in God:

Hid, till Christ our Life appear
Glorious in His members here;
Joined to Him we then shall shine,
All immortal, all divine.

Hail the Lord of earth and Heaven!
Praise to Thee by both be given!
Thee we greet triumphant now!
Hail, the Resurrection Thou!

King of Glory, Soul of bliss!
Everlasting life is this,—
Thee to know, Thy power to prove,
Thus to sing, and thus to love!

CHARLES WESLEY.

As in Adam all die, even so in Christ shall all be made alive.
I. Corinthians, xv. 22.

ALLELUIA! Alleluia!
Hearts to Heaven and voices raise;
Sing to God a hymn of gladness,
Sing to God a hymn of praise;

He, who on the cross a Victim
  For the world's salvation bled,
Jesus Christ, the King of Glory,
  Now is risen from the dead.

Christ is risen, Christ the first-fruits
  Of the holy harvest field,
Which will all its full abundance
  At His second coming yield;
Then the golden ears of harvest
  Will their heads before Him wave,
Ripened by His glorious sunshine
  From the furrows of the grave.

Christ is risen, we are risen!
  Shed upon us heavenly grace,
Rain, and dew, and gleams of glory
  From the brightness of Thy face;
That we, with our hearts in Heaven,
  Here on earth may fruitful be,
And by angel hands be gathered,
  And be ever, Lord, with Thee.

Alleluia! Alleluia!
  Glory be to God on high;
Alleluia to the Saviour,
  Who has gained the victory;
Alleluia to the Spirit,
  Fount of love and sanctity;
Alleluia! Alleluia!
  To the Triune Majesty.

THE RESURRECTION AND ASCENSION.

When Christ, who is our life, shall appear, then shall ye also appear with Him in glory.
Colossians, iii. 4.

DEAREST of names, our Lord, our King!
Jesus, Thy praise we humbly sing:
In cheerful songs we'll spend our breath,
And in Thee triumph over death.

Death is no more among our foes
Since Christ, the mighty Conqueror, rose;
Both power and sting the Savour broke;
He died, and gave the finished stroke.

Saints die, and we should gently weep;
Sweetly in Jesus' arms they sleep,
Far from this world of sin and woe,
Nor sin, nor pain, nor grief they know.

Death no terrific foe appears;
An angel's lovely form he wears;
A friendly messenger he proves
To every soul whom Jesus loves.

Death is a sleep; and O! how sweet
To souls prepared its stroke to meet!
Their dying beds, their graves are blest,
For all to them is peace and rest.

Their bodies sleep; their souls take wing,
Uprise to Heaven, and there they sing
With joy before the Saviour's face,
Triumphant in victorious grace.

Soon shall the earth's remotest bound
Feel the archangel's trumpet sound;
Then shall the grave's dark caverns shake,
And joyful all the saints shall wake.

Bodies and souls shall then unite,
Arrayed in glory strong and bright;
And all His saints will Jesus bring
His face to see, His love to sing.

O may I live, with Jesus nigh,
And sleep in Jesus when I die!
Then, joyful, when from death I wake,
I shall eternal bliss partake.

SAMUEL MEDLEY.

He laid down His life for us.
I. John, iii. 16.

CHRIST the Lord is risen again!
Christ hath broken every chain!
Hark, the angels shout for joy,
Singing evermore on high,
        Hallelujah.

He who gave for us His life,
Who for us endured the strife,
Is our Paschal Lamb to-day!
We too sing for joy, and say,
    Hallelujah.

He who bore all pains and loss
Comfortless upon the cross,
Lives in glory now on high,
Pleads for us, and hears our cry:
    Hallelujah.

He whose path no records tell,
Who descended into hell,
Who the strong man armed hath bound,
Now in highest Heaven is crowned:
    Hallelujah.

He who slumbered in the grave
Is exalted now to save;
Now through Christendom it rings
That the Lamb is King of kings!
    Hallelujah.

Now He bids us tell abroad
How the lost may be restored,
How the penitent forgiven,
How we too may enter Heaven.
    Hallelujah.

Thou our Paschal Lamb indeed,
Christ, to-day Thy people feed;
Take our sins and guilt away,
That we all may sing for aye,
        Hallelujah.

BOHEMIAN BRETHREN.

*Filled with the Spirit; singing and making melody
in your hearts to the Lord.*
        Ephesians, v. 18, 19.

HOW blest the sacred tie that binds,
  In union sweet, according minds!
How swift the heavenly course they run,
Whose hearts, whose faith, whose hopes are one!

To each the soul of each how dear!
What jealous love, what holy fear!
How doth the generous flame within
Refine from earth, and cleanse from sin!

Their streaming tears together flow
For human guilt and mortal woe;
Their ardent prayers together rise
Like mingling flames in sacrifice.

Together both they seek the place
Where God reveals His awful face;

How high, how strong, their raptures swell,
There's none but kindred souls can tell.

Nor shall the glowing flame expire,
When Nature drops her sickening fire;
Then shall they meet in realms above;
A Heaven of joy, because of love.

ANNA LÆTITIA BARBAULD.

The Lord is risen indeed.
Luke, xxiv. 34.

JESUS Christ is risen to-day,	Hallelujah!
Our triumphant holy day,	Hallelujah!
Who did once upon the cross,	Hallelujah!
Suffer to redeem our loss.	Hallelujah!
Hymns of praise then let us sing,	Hallelujah!
Unto Christ our heavenly King,	Hallelujah!
Who endured the cross and grave,	Hallelujah!
Sinners to redeem and save;	Hallelujah!
But the pain which He endured,	Hallelujah!
Our salvation has procured:	Hallelujah!
Now above the sky He's King,	Hallelujah!
Where the angels ever sing.	Hallelujah!
Sing we to our God above,	Hallelujah!
Praise eternal as His love;	Hallelujah!
Praise Him, all ye heavenly host,	Hallelujah!
Father, Son, and Holy Ghost.	Hallelujah!

ANON.
LAST STANZA BY CHARLES WESLEY.

THE RESURRECTION AND ASCENSION.

Him God raised up the third day.

Acts, x. 40.

AGAIN the Lord of Life and Light
   Awakes the kindling ray,
Unseals the eyelids of the morn,
   And pours increasing day.

O what a night was that which wrapt
   The heathen world in gloom!
O what a Sun, which broke this day
   Triumphant from the tomb!

This day be grateful homage paid,
   And loud hosannas sung;
Let gladness dwell in every heart,
   And praise on every tongue.

Ten thousand differing lips shall join
   To hail this welcome morn,
Which scatters blessings from its wings
   To nations yet unborn.

The powers of darkness leagued in vain
   To bind His soul in death;
He shook their kingdom, when He fell,
   With His expiring breath.

And now His conquering chariot-wheels
    Ascend the lofty skies,
While broke beneath His powerful Cross
    Death's iron sceptre lies.

Exalted high at God's right hand,
    The Lord of all below,
Through Him is pardoning love dispensed,
    And boundless blessings flow.

And still for erring guilty man
    A Brother's pity flows;
And still His bleeding heart is touched
    With memory of our woes.

To Thee, my Saviour and my King,
    Glad homage let me give;
And stand prepared like Thee to die,
    With Thee that I may live!

ANNA LÆTITIA BARBAULD.

Our Lord Jesus Christ, who died for us, that, whether we wake or sleep, we shall live together in Him.
I. Thessalonians, v. 9, 10.

THE foe behind, the deep before,
    Our hosts have dared and passed the sea;
And Pharaoh's warriors strew the shore,
    And Israel's ransomed tribes are free.

THE RESURRECTION AND ASCENSION.

Lift up, lift up your voices now!
The whole wide world rejoices now!
The Lord hath triumphed gloriously!
The Lord shall reign victoriously'
  Happy morrow,
  Turning sorrow
   Into peace and mirth!
 Bondage ending,
 Love descending
  O'er the earth!
 Seals assuring,
 Guards securing,
  Watch His earthly prison:
 Seals are shattered,
 Guards are scattered,
  Christ hath risen!

No longer must the mourners weep,
 Nor call departed Christians dead;
For death is hallowed into sleep,
 And every grave becomes a bed.
  Now once more,
  Eden's door
 Open stands to mortal eyes;
For Christ hath risen, and men shall rise:
  Now at last,
  Old things past,
 Hope and joy and peace begin;
For Christ hath won, and man shall win.

It is not exile, rest on high;
  It is not sadness, peace from strife;
To fall asleep is not to die:
  To dwell with Christ is better life.
    Where our banner leads us
      We may safely go;
    Where our Chief precedes us
      We may face the foe.
    His right arm is o'er us,
      He will guide us through;
    Christ hath gone before us;
      Christians! follow you!

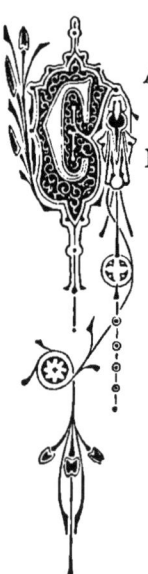

JOHN MASON NEALE.

But now is Christ risen from the dead.
I. Corinthians, xv. 20.

CHRIST the Lord is risen to-day,
  Our triumphant holy day;
He endured the cross and grave,
  Sinners to redeem and save.
Lo! He rises, mighty King!
  Where, O Death! is now thy sting?
Lo! He claims His native sky!
  Grave! where is thy victory?

Sinners! see your ransom paid,
  Peace with God for ever made;

THE RESURRECTION AND ASCENSION.

With your risen Saviour rise,
Claim your mansions in the skies.
Christ the Lord is risen to-day,
Our triumphant holy day;
Loud the song of victory raise;
Shout the great Redeemer's praise!

ANON.

Glory be unto the Lamb for ever.
Revelation, v. 13.

HAIL, Thou once despised Jesus!
   Hail, Thou Galilean King!
Thou didst suffer to release us,
   Thou didst free salvation bring:
Hail, Thou agonizing Saviour,
   Bearer of our sin and shame!
By Thy merits we find favour;
   Life is given through Thy Name.

Paschal Lamb, by God appointed,
   All our sins were on Thee laid;
By Almighty Love anointed,
   Thou hast full atonement made:
All Thy people are forgiven
   Through the virtue of Thy blood;
Opened is the gate of Heaven;
   Peace is made 'twixt man and God.

THE RESURRECTION AND ASCENSION.

Jesus, hail! enthroned in glory,
    There for ever to abide,
All the heavenly hosts adore Thee,
    Seated at Thy Father's side.
There for sinners Thou art pleading;
    There Thou dost our place prepare;
Ever for us interceding
    Till in glory we appear.

Worship, honour, power, and blessing,
    Thou art worthy to receive;
Loudest praises, without ceasing,
    Meet it is for us to give!
Help, ye bright angelic spirits,
    Bring your sweetest, noblest lays;
Help to sing our Saviour's merits,
    Help to chant Immanuel's praise!

Soon we shall, with those in glory,
    His transcendant grace relate;
Gladly sing th' amazing story
    Of His dying love so great:
In that blessed contemplation
    We for evermore shall dwell,
Crowned with bliss and consolation,
    Such as none below can tell.

                    JOHN BAKEWELL.

THE RESURRECTION AND ASCENSION.

God hath highly exalted Him.
Philippians, ii. 9.

COME, all harmonious tongues,
    Your noblest music bring;
'T is Christ the everlasting God,
    And Christ the Man, we sing.

Down to the shades of death
    He bowed His awful head;
Yet He arose to live and reign
    When death itself is dead.

No more the bloody spear,
    The cross and nails no more;
For Hell itself shakes at His Name,
    And all the Heavens adore.

There the Redeemer sits
    High on the Father's throne;
The Father lays His vengeance by,
    And smiles upon His Son.

There His full glories shine
    With uncreated rays,
And bless His saints' and angels' eyes
    To everlasting days.

ISAAC WATTS.

THE RESURRECTION AND ASCENSION.

*Who is this King of glory? The Lord of hosts,
He is the King of glory.*
Psalm xxiv. 10.

GOD is gone up on high
    With a triumphant noise;
The clarions of the sky
    Proclaim the angelic joys.
Join, all on earth, rejoice and sing;
Glory ascribe to glory's King.

God in the flesh below,
    For us He reigns above:
Let all the nations know
    Our Jesus' conquering love.
Join, all on earth, rejoice and sing;
Glory ascribe to glory's King.

All power to our great Lord
    Is by the Father given:
By angel hosts adored,
    He reigns supreme in Heaven.
Join, all on earth, rejoice and sing;
Glory ascribe to glory's King.

High on His holy seat
    He bears the righteous sway
His foes beneath His feet
    Shall sink and die away.

Join, all on earth, rejoice and sing;
Glory ascribe to glory's King.

THE RESURRECTION AND ASCENSION.

His foes and ours are one,
  Satan, the world, and sin;
But He shall tread them down,
  And bring His kingdom in.
Join, all on earth, rejoice and sing;
Glory ascribe to glory's King.

Till all the earth, renewed
  In righteousness divine,
With all the hosts of God
  In one great chorus join.
Join, all on earth, rejoice and sing;
Glory ascribe to glory's King.

CHARLES WESLEY.

---

*Go quickly, and tell His disciples that
He is risen from the dead.*
Matthew, xxviii. 7.

THE Day of Resurrection!
  Earth, tell it out abroad;
The Passover of gladness,
  The Passover of God.
From death to life eternal,
  From earth unto the sky,
Our Christ hath brought us over
  With hymns of victory.

Our hearts be pure from evil,
    That we may see aright
The Lord in rays eternal
    Of resurrection light;
And, listening to His accents,
    May hear so calm and plain
His own "All hail!" and hearing,
    May raise the victor strain.

Now let the heavens be joyful,
    And earth her song begin,
The round world keep high triumph,
    And all that is therein;
Let all things seen and unseen
    Their notes of gladness blend,
For Christ the Lord is risen,
    Our Joy that hath no end.

The trumpet of the jubile.
                      Leviticus, xxv. 9.

BLOW ye the trumpet, blow!
    The gladly solemn sound;
Let all the nations know,
    To earth's remotest bound,
The year of Jubilee is come;
Return, ye ransomed sinners, home.

THE RESURRECTION AND ASCENSION.

Jesus, our great High Priest,
   Hath full atonement made;
Ye weary spirits, rest;
   Ye mournful souls, be glad:.
The year of Jubilee is come
Return, ye ransomed sinners, home.

Extol the Lamb of God,
   The all-atoning Lamb;
Redemption in His blood
   Throughout the world proclaim:
The year of Jubilee is come;
Return, ye ransomed sinners, home.

Ye slaves of sin and hell,
   Your liberty receive,
And safe in Jesus dwell,
   And blest in Jesus live:
The year of Jubilee is come;
Return, ye ransomed sinners, home.

Ye, who have sold for nought
   Your heritage above,
Shall have it back unbought,
   The gift of Jesus' love:
The year of Jubilee is come;
Return, ye ransomed sinners, home.

The Gospel trumpet hear,
   The news of heavenly grace;

And, saved from earth, appear
Before your Saviour's face:
The year of Jubilee is come;
Return, ye ransomed sinners, home.

CHARLES WESLEY.

Whom have I in Heaven but Thee?
Psalm lxxiii. 25.

JESU! behold, the wise from far,
　Led to Thy cradle by a star,
　　Bring gifts to Thee, their God and King!
　O guide us by Thy light, that we
　The way may find, and still to Thee
　　Our hearts, our all, for tribute bring!

Jesu! the pure, the spotless Lamb,
Who to the Temple humbly came,
　Duteous, the legal rites to pay!
O make our proud, our stubborn will
All Thy wise, gracious laws fulfil,
　Whate'er rebellious nature say!

Jesu! who on the fatal wood
Pour'dst out Thy life's last drop of blood,
　Nailed to the accursed shameful cross!

O may we bless Thy love, and be
Ready, dear Lord, to bear for Thee
   All shame, all grief, all pain, and loss!

Jesu! who, by Thine own love slain,
By Thine own power took'st life again,
   And Conqueror from the grave didst rise,
O may Thy death our souls revive,
And e'en on earth a new life give,
   A glorious life, that never dies!

Jesu! who to Thy Heaven again
Return'dst in triumph, there to reign,
   Of men and angels sovereign King!
O may our parting souls take flight
Up to that land of joy and light,
   And there for ever grateful sing!

All glory to the sacred Three,
One undivided Deity!
   All honour, power, and love, and praise!
Still may Thy blessed Name shine bright
In beams of uncreated light,
   Crowned with its own eternal rays!

JOHN WESLEY.
VARIATION FROM JOHN AUSTIN.

It is Christ, who is even at the right hand of God, who also maketh intercession for us.
Romans, viii. 34.

WE sing His love, who once was slain,
Who soon o'er death revived again,
That all His saints through Him might have
Eternal conquests o'er the grave.
    Soon shall the trumpet sound, and we
    Shall rise to immortality.

The saints, who now with Jesus sleep,
His own almighty power shall keep,
Till dawns the bright illustrious day
When death itself shall die away:
    Soon shall the trumpet sound, and we
    Shall rise to immortality.

How loud shall our glad voices sing,
When Christ His risen saints shall bring
From beds of dust and silent clay,
To realms of everlasting day!
    Soon shall the trumpet sound, and we
    Shall rise to immortality.

When Jesus we in glory meet,
Our utmost joys shall be complete;
When landed on that heavenly shore,
Death and the curse will be no more:

THE RESURRECTION AND ASCENSION.

    Soon shall the trumpet sound, and we
    Shall rise to immortality.

Hasten, dear Lord, the glorious day,
And this delightful scene display,
When all Thy saints from death shall rise,
Raptured in bliss beyond the skies!
    Soon shall the trumpet sound, and we
    Shall rise to immortality.

ROWLAND HILL.

It is Christ that died, yea, that is risen again.
Romans, viii. 24.

THE Lord is risen indeed:
    And are the tidings true?
Yes! they beheld the Saviour bleed,
    And saw Him living too.

The Lord is risen indeed:
    Then Justice asks no more;
Mercy and Truth are now agreed,
    Who stood opposed before.

The Lord is risen indeed:
    Then is His work performed;
The captive Surety now is freed,
    And Death, our foe, disarmed.

The Lord is risen indeed:
Then hell has lost its prey;
With Him is risen the ransomed seed,
To reign in endless day.

The Lord is risen indeed:
Attending angels hear,
And to the courts of Heaven with speed
The joyful tidings bear.

While on their golden lyres
They strike each cheerful chord,
We join the bright celestial choirs,
To sing our risen Lord.

THOMAS KELLY.

𝕿he everlasting kingdom of our 𝕷ord and 𝕾aviour 𝕵esus 𝕮hrist.
II. Peter, i. 11.

𝔄nd 𝔊od shall wipe away all tears from their eyes; and there shall be no more death, neither sorrow, nor crying, neither shall there be any more pain; for the former things are passed away.
Revelation, xxi. 4.

𝔄nd 𝕴 heard a voice from heaven, as the voice of many waters; and 𝕴 heard the voice of harpers harping with their harps: and they sung as it were a new song before the throne.
Revelation, xiv. 2, 3.

𝕭ehold, 𝕳e cometh with clouds; and every eye shall see 𝕳im.
Revelation, i. 7.

THE KINGDOM OF CHRIST

Eternal life by Jesus Christ our Lord.
Romans, v. 21.

HARK! hark, my soul, angelic songs are swelling
O'er earth's green fields, and ocean's wave-beat shore:
How sweet the truth those blessed strains are telling
Of that new life, when sin shall be no more.
Angels of Jesus, angels of light,
Singing to welcome the pilgrims of the night.

THE KINGDOM OF CHRIST.

Darker than night life's shadows close around us,
    And, like benighted men, we miss our mark;
God hides Himself, and grace has scarcely found us
    Ere Death finds out his victim in the dark.
Angels of Jesus, angels of light,
Singing to welcome the pilgrims of the night.

Onward we go, for still we hear them singing,
    "Come, weary souls, for Jesus bids you come:"
And, through the dark its echoes sweetly ringing,
    The music of the Gospel leads us home.
Angels of Jesus, angels of light,
Singing to welcome the pilgrims of the night.

Far, far away, like bells at evening pealing,
    The voice of Jesus sounds o'er land and sea,
And laden souls by thousands meekly stealing,
    Kind Shepherd, turn their weary steps to Thee.
Angels of Jesus, angels of light,
Singing to welcome the pilgrims of the night.

Rest comes at length, though life be long and dreary,
    The day must dawn, and darksome night be past;
Faith's journey ends in welcome to the weary,
    And Heaven, the heart's true home, will come at last.
Angels of Jesus, angels of light,
Singing to welcome the pilgrims of the night.

Cheer up, my soul! faith's moonbeams softly glisten
    Upon the breast of life's most troubled sea;

THE KINGDOM OF CHRIST.

And it will cheer the drooping heart to listen
    To those brave songs the angels mean for thee.
Angels of Jesus, angels of light,
Singing to welcome the pilgrims of the night.

Angels, sing on ! your faithful watches keeping ;
    Sing us sweet fragments of the songs above ;
Till morning's joy shall end the night of weeping,
    And life's long shadows break in cloudless love.
Angels of Jesus, angels of light,
Singing to welcome the pilgrims of the night.

                            F. W. FABER, D.D.

They shall speak of the glory of Thy kingdom.
                            Psalm cxlv. 11.

LIFT our voices now in song !
    Sound the organ pealing !
Let each tongue sing forth in praise !
    Let each heart be kneeling !
Let each eye light up with joy—
    The old man and the maiden,
The strong and the richly clad,
    The poor, the heavy laden.

For Jesus, ever blessed,
    Hath promised in His grace

That those who love His dear Name
    Shall see His smiling face;
To all who cry in deep woe
    Will ready succour give,
And those who lie in darkness
    In glory yet shall live.

Dear Christ! the Lord of Glory!
    The Lord of love and peace!
Sits upon His Father's throne—
    His reign shall never cease.
Then let us come with glad voice,
    Each heart rejoice and sing
Praises to the Prince of Peace,
    Loud praises to our King!

GEORGE WOOLER.

Alleluia: for the Lord God omnipotent reigneth.
Revelation, xix. 6.

HARK! the song of Jubilee,
    Loud as mighty thunder's roar,
Or the fulness of the sea
    When it breaks upon the shore:
Hallelujah! for the Lord
God omnipotent shall reign:
Hallelujah! let the word
Echo round the earth and main.

Hallelujah! hark! the sound,
   From the centre to the skies,
Wakes above, beneath, around,
   All creation's harmonies.
See Jehovah's banner furled,
   Sheathed His sword:—He speaks—'tis done:
And the kingdoms of this world
   Are the kingdoms of His Son.

He shall reign from pole to pole
   With illimitable sway;
He shall reign, when like a scroll
   Yonder heavens have passed away
Then the end: beneath His rod
   Man's last enemy shall fall;
Hallelujah! Christ in God,
   God in Christ, is all in all!

JAMES MONTGOMERY.

I know that my Redeemer liveth.
Job, xix. 25.

JESUS lives! no longer now
   Can thy terrors, Death, appal us;
Jesus lives! by this we know
   Thou, O Grave, canst not enthral us
               Alleluia!

Jesus lives! henceforth is death
    But the gate of life immortal;
This shall calm our trembling breath
    When we pass its gloomy portal.
                  Alleluia!

Jesus lives! for us He died;
    Then, alone to Jesus living,
Pure in heart may we abide,
    Glory to our Saviour giving.
                  Alleluia!

Jesus lives! our hearts know well
    Nought from us His love shall sever;
Life, nor death, nor powers of hell
    Tear us from His keeping ever.
                  Alleluia!

Jesus lives! to Him the throne
    Over all the world is given;
May we go where He is gone,
    Rest and reign with Him in Heaven.
                  Alleluia!

FROM THE GERMAN OF
HENRIETTA, ELECTRESS OF BRANDENBURG.

THE KINGDOM OF CHRIST.

And sorrow and sighing shall flee away.

Isaiah, xxxv. 10.

LO! He comes! let all adore Him!
   'T is the God of grace and truth!
Go! prepare the way before Him,
   Make the rugged places smooth!
Lo! He comes, the mighty Lord!
Great His work and His reward.

Let the valleys all be raisèd;
   Go, and make the crooked straight;
Let the mountains be abasèd;
   Let all nature change its state;
Through the desert mark a road,
Make a highway for our God.

Through the desert God is going,
   Through the desert waste and wild,
Where no goodly plant is growing,
   Where no verdure ever smiled;
But the desert shall be glad,
And with verdure soon be clad.

Where the thorn and briar flourished,
   Trees shall there be seen to grow,
Planted by the Lord and nourished,
   Stately, fair, and fruitful too;

They shall rise on every side,
They shall spread their branches wide.

From the hills and lofty mountains
   Rivers shall be seen to flow,
There the Lord will open fountains,
   Thence supply the plains below;
As He passes, every land
Shall confess His powerful hand.

THOMAS KELLY.

The Lord is King for ever and ever.
Psalm x. 16.

THE Lord is King; lift up thy voice,
   O earth, and all ye heavens, rejoice.
From world to world the joy shall ring,
The Lord Omnipotent is King.

The Lord is King; who then shall dare
Resist His will, distrust His care,
Or murmur at His wise decrees,
Or doubt His royal promises?

The Lord is King: child of the dust,
The Judge of all the earth is just:
Holy and true are all His ways;
Let every creature speak His praise.

He reigns! Ye saints, exalt your strains:
Your God is King, your Father reigns;
And He is at the Father's side,
The Man of love, the Crucified.

Come, make your wants, your burdens known:
He will present them at the throne;

THE KINGDOM OF CHRIST.

And angel bands are waiting there,
His messages of love to bear.

O! when His wisdom can mistake,
His might decay, His love forsake,
Then may His children cease to sing,
The Lord Omnipotent is King.

Alike pervaded by His eye,
All parts of His dominion lie,—
This world of ours and worlds unseen,
And the thin boundary between.

One Lord, one empire, all secures;
He reigns,—and life and death are yours.
Through earth and Heaven one song shall ring,
The Lord Omnipotent is King.

JOSIAH CONDER.

Rejoice in the Lord alway: and again I say, Rejoice.
Philippians, iv. 4.

REJOICE, the Lord is King!
   Your Lord and King adore;
   Mortals, give thanks and sing,
   And triumph evermore:
Lift up your heart, lift up your voice;
Rejoice, again I say, rejoice!

THE KINGDOM OF CHRIST.

Jesus the Saviour reigns,
 The God of truth and love;
When He had purged our stains,
 He took His seat above:
Lift up your heart, lift up your voice;
Rejoice, again I say, rejoice!

His kingdom cannot fail;
 He rules o'er earth and Heaven;
The keys of Death and Hell
 Are to our Jesus given:
Lift up your heart, lift up your voice;
Rejoice, again I say, rejoice!

He sits at God's right hand,
 Till all His foes submit,
And bow to His command,
 And fall beneath His feet;
Lift up your heart, lift up your voice;
Rejoice, again I say, rejoice!

He all His foes shall quell,
 Shall all our sins destroy,
And every bosom swell
 With pure seraphic joy:
Lift up your heart, lift up your voice;
Rejoice, again I say, rejoice!

Rejoice in glorious hope:
 Jesus the Judge shall come,

And take His servants up
   To their eternal home:
We soon shall hear th' archangel's voice,
The trump of God shall sound, rejoice!

                             CHARLES WESLEY.

Let the whole earth be filled with His glory.
                             Psalm lxxii. 19.

FROM Greenland's icy mountains,
   From India's coral strand,
Where Afric's sunny fountains
   Roll down their golden sand,
From many an ancient river,
   From many a palmy plain,
They call us to deliver
   Their land from error's chain.

What though the spicy breezes
   Blow soft o'er Ceylon's isle—
Though every prospect pleases,
   And only man is vile;
In vain with lavish kindness
   The gifts of God are strown,
The heathen in his blindness
   Bows down to wood and stone.

Can we whose souls are lighted
   With wisdom from on high,
Can we to men benighted
   The lamp of life deny?
Salvation! O salvation!
   The joyful sound proclaim,
Till each remotest nation
   Has learnt Messiah's Name.

Waft, waft, ye winds, His story,
   And you, ye waters, roll,
Till like a sea of glory
   It spreads from pole to pole;
Till o'er our ransomed nature
   The Lamb for sinners slain,
Redeemer, King, Creator,
   In bliss returns to reign.

              BISHOP REGINALD HEBER.

Thy kingdom is an everlasting kingdom.
                          Psalm cxlv. 13.

I LOVE Thy kingdom, Lord,
   The house of Thine abode,
The Church our blest Redeemer bought
   With His own precious blood.

THE KINGDOM OF CHRIST.

I love Thy Church, O God :
  Her walls before Thee stand,
Dear as the apple of Thine eye,
  And graven on Thy hand.

For her my tears shall fall,
  For her my prayers ascend,
To her my cares and toils be given,
  Till toils and cares shall end.

Beyond my highest joy
  I prize her heavenly ways;
Her sweet communion, solemn vows,
  Her hymns of love and praise.

Jesus, thou Friend divine,
  Our Saviour and our King,
Thy hand from every snare and foe
  Shall great deliverance bring.

Sure as Thy truth shall last,
  To Zion shall be given
The highest glories earth can yield,
  And brighter bliss of Heaven.
DWIGHT.

THE KINGDOM OF CHRIST.

And now, Lord, my hope is in Thee.
Psalm xxxix. 7.

CHRIST, our hope, our heart's desire,
    Redemption's only spring;
Creator of the world art Thou,
    Its Saviour and its King.

How vast the mercy and the love
    Which laid our sins on Thee,
And led Thee to a cruel death,
    To set Thy people free!

But now the bonds of death are burst,
    The ransom has been paid;
And Thou art on Thy Father's throne,
    In glorious robes arrayed.

O may Thy mighty love prevail,
    Our sinful souls to spare;
O may we come before Thy throne,
    And find acceptance there.

O Christ, be Thou our present joy,
    Our future great reward;
Our only glory may it be
    To glory in the Lord.

ANCIENT HYMN.

THE KINGDOM OF CHRIST.

Unto Him that loved us, and washed us from our sins, be glory and dominion for ever and ever.
— Revelation, i. 5, 6.

O LET us raise our voices
   To God, the King of kings,
Our loud hosannas singing,
   Till all the welkin rings;
Let the earth rejoice aloud.

The sea send forth its song;
Let the loud winds sigh and sing
   The forest trees among.

Rejoice! rejoice, ye heavens!
   Your gay attire put on;

THE KINGDOM OF CHRIST.

Sun, and moon, and thousand stars
   With all your beauty shown :
Let all things with life rejoice,
   All tears he wiped away ;
We'll raise our shouts of gladness,
   And joyful music play.

For God, the Lord of Heaven,
   With all His hosts around,
Is coming in His glory !
   O hear the gladsome sound ;
He comes to strike the dark foe,
   To rescue with His might
All those He loves, from darkness
   To joy and endless light.

There in His glory seated,
   Our gracious Lord doth dwell ;
There myriads of angels
   The glad hosannas swell ;
There radiant beams of glory
   Shall ever ceaseless shine,
And flood each heart with gladness,
   In God's own love divine.

                     GEORGE WOOLER.

THE KINGDOM OF CHRIST.

He shall feed His flock like a shepherd.
Isaiah, xl. 11.

IN that book so old and holy
   I would read, and read again,
How our Lord was once so lowly,
   Yet without a spot or stain.

How the little children found Him;
   How He loved them and caressed;
How He called them all around Him,—
   Took them to His loving breast.

How His pity, never failing,
   On the sick was sure to flow;
How the poor, the blind, the ailing,
   Were His brethren here below.

How when each poor wanderer sought Him,
   Guilty, helpless, sorrowing sore,
He received, and helped, and taught him,
   Bade him go and sin no more

With rejoicing hearts and grateful,
   Let us read, and still read on,
How He was so true and faithful,
   How He loved us every one.

How, good Shepherd! He did cherish
   All the flock He came to save,

Watching that not one might perish
   Of the lambs His Father gave.

Let us gladly kneel, and often,
   'Round His feet who loved us best,
Then each stubborn heart He'll soften,
   And in Him shall all be blessed.

     DR. H. W. DULCKEN.

The Son of Man coming in the clouds of Heaven.
     Matthew, xxiv 30.

THE Lord of Might from Sinai's brow
   Gave forth His voice of thunder,
And Israel lay on earth below,
   Outstretched in fear and wonder;
Beneath His feet was pitchy night,
And at His left hand and His right
   The rocks were rent asunder.

The Lord of Love on Calvary,
   A meek and suffering stranger,
Upraised to Heaven His languid eye
   In nature's hour of danger:
For us He bore the weight of woe,
For us He gave His blood to flow,
   And met His Father's anger.

THE KINGDOM OF CHRIST.

The Lord of Love, the Lord of Might,
    The King of all created,
Shall back return to claim His right
    On clouds of glory seated;
With trumpet sound, and angel song,
And hallelujahs loud and long,
    O'er Death and Hell defeated.

BISHOP REGINALD HEBER.

His kingdom ruleth over all.
Psalm ciii. 19.

JESUS shall reign where'er the sun
    Does his successive journeys run;
    His kingdom stretch from shore to shore,
    Till moons shall wax and wane no more.

For Him shall endless prayer be made,
    And praises throng to crown His head;
    His Name, like sweet perfume, shall rise
    With every morning sacrifice.

People and realms of every tongue
    Dwell on His love with sweetest song,
    And infant voices shall proclaim
    Their early blessings on His Name.

Blessings abound where'er He reigns;
The prisoner leaps to lose his chains;

THE KINGDOM OF CHRIST.

The weary find eternal rest,
And all the sons of want are blest.

Where He displays His healing power,
Death and the curse are known no more;
In Him the tribes of Adam boast
More blessings than their father lost.

Let every creature rise, and bring
Peculiar honours to our King;
Angels descend with songs again,
And earth repeat the long Amen!

ISAAC WATTS.

*O praise the Lord, all ye nations: praise Him,
all ye people.*
Psalm cxvii. 1.

FROM all that dwell below the skies
Let the Creator's praise arise;
Let the Redeemer's Name be sung
Through every land, by every tongue!

Eternal are Thy mercies, Lord!
Eternal truth attends Thy word:
Thy praise shall sound from shore to shore,
Till suns shall rise and set no more.

ISAAC WATTS.

He is Lord of lords and King of kings.
Revelation, xvii. 14.

JESUS, King most wonderful,
   Thou Conqueror renowned;
Thou sweetness most ineffable,
   In whom all joys are found,—

When once Thou visitest the heart,
   Then truth begins to shine,
Then earthly vanities depart,
   Then kindles love divine.

O Jesus, light of all below,
   Thou fount of life and fire,
Surpassing all the joys we know,
   All that we can desire,—

May every heart confess Thy name,
   And ever Thee adore;
And, seeking Thee, itself inflame
   To seek Thee more and more.

Thee may our tongues for ever bless;
   Thee may we love alone;
And ever in our lives express
   The image of Thine own.

BERNARD.

HEAVEN.

The Lamb which is in the midst of the throne shall feed them, and shall lead them unto living fountains of waters.

Revelation, vii. 17.

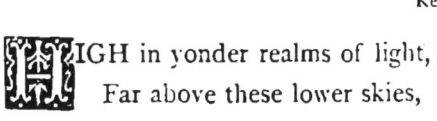

HIGH in yonder realms of light,
Far above these lower skies,

HEAVEN.

Fair and exquisitely bright,
Heaven's unfading mansions rise;
Glad, within their blest abode,
Dwell the raptured saints above,
Where no anxious cares corrode,
Happy in Immanuel's love.

Once the big unbidden tear,
Stealing down the furrowed cheek,
Told, in eloquence sincere,
Tales of woe they could not speak;
But, these days of weeping o'er,
Passed this scene of toil and pain,
They shall feel distress no more,
Never, never weep again.

'Mid the chorus of the skies,
'Mid the angelic lyres above,
Hark! their songs melodious rise,—
Songs of praise to Jesus' love!
Happy spirits, ye are fled
Where no grief can entrance find;
Lulled to rest, the aching head;
Soothed, the anguish of the mind.

All is tranquil and serene,
Calm and undisturbed repose;
There no cloud can intervene,
There no angry tempest blows;

Every tear is wiped away,
Sighs no more shall heave the breast;
Night is lost in endless day,
Sorrow in eternal rest.

RAFFLES.

Now they desire a better country, that is, an heavenly.
Hebrews, xi. 16.

SWEET place, sweet place alone!
  The court of God most High,
The Heaven of heavens, the throne
  Of spotless majesty!
The stranger homeward bends,
  And sigheth for his rest:
Heaven is my home, my friends
  Lodged there in Abraham's breast:
    O happy place!
      When shall I be,
      My God, with Thee,
    To see Thy face?

Earth's but a sorry tent
  Pitched for a few frail days,
A short-leased tenement;
  Heaven's still my song, my praise.
No tears from any eyes
  Drop in that holy choir;
But death itself there dies,
  And sighs themselves expire.

HEAVEN.

O happy place!
  When shall I be,
    My God, with Thee,
  To see Thy face?

There should temptations cease;
  My frailties there should end;
There should I rest in peace
  In the arms of my best Friend.
Jerusalem on high
  My song and city is,
My home whene'er I die,
  The centre of my bliss:
    O happy place!
      When shall I be,
        My God, with Thee,
      To see Thy face?

Thy walls, sweet city, thine,
  With pearls are garnishèd;
Thy gates with praises shine,
  Thy streets with gold are spread;
No sun by day shines there,
  Nor moon by silent night;
O no! these needless are;
  The Lamb's the city's Light:
    O happy place!
      When shall I be,
        My God, with Thee,
      To see Thy face?

HEAVEN.

There dwells my Lord, my King,
   Judged here unfit to live;
There angels to Him sing,
   And lowly homage give:
The Lamb's Apostles there
   I might with joy behold,
The harpers I might hear
   Harping on harps of gold:
     O happy place!
       When shall I be,
       My God, with Thee,
     To see Thy face?

The bleeding martyrs, they
   Within those courts are found,
Clothèd in pure array,
   Their scars with glory crowned!
Ah me! ah me! that I
   In Kedar's tents here stay!
No place like this on high!
   Thither, Lord, guide my way!
     O happy place!
       When shall I be,
       My God, with Thee,
     To see Thy face?

              SAMUEL CROSSMAN.

*These are they which washed their robes, and made them
white in the blood of the Lamb.*

Revelation, vii. 14.

WHO are these like stars appearing,
   These, before God's throne who stand?
Each a golden crown is wearing,—
   Who are all this glorious band?
Alleluia! hark, they sing,
Praising loud their heavenly King.

Who are these in dazzling brightness,
   Clothed in God's own righteousness,
These, whose robes of purest whiteness
   Shall their lustre still possess,
Still untouched by time's rude hand?—
Whence comes all this glorious band?

These are they who have contended
   For their Saviour's honour long,
Wrestling on till life was ended,
   Following not the sinful throng;
These, who well the fight sustained,
Triumph by the Lamb have gained.

These are they whose hearts were riven,
   Sore with woe and anguish tried,

HEAVEN.

Who in prayer full oft have striven
   With the God they glorified;
Now, their painful conflict o'er,
God has bid them weep no more.

These, the Almighty contemplating,
   Did as priests before Him stand,
Soul and body always waiting
   Day and night at His command;
Now in God's most holy place
Blest they stand before His face.

The love of Christ, which passeth knowledge.
Ephesians, iii. 19.

HAPPY saints, who dwell in light,
And walk with Jesus, clothed in white;
Safe landed on that peaceful shore
Where pilgrims meet to part no more.

Released from sin, and toil, and grief,
Death was their gate to endless life;
An opened cage, to let them fly
And build their happy nest on high.

And now they range the heavenly plains,
And sing their hymns in melting strains;

And now their souls begin to prove
The heights and depths of Jesus' love.

He cheers them with eternal smile;
They sing hosannas all the while;
Or, overwhelmed with rapture sweet,
Sink down adoring at His feet.

Ah, Lord! with tardy steps I creep,
And sometimes sing, and sometimes weep;
Yet strip me of this house of clay,
And I will sing as loud as they.

JOHN BERRIDGE.

Glorious things are spoken of thee, O city of God.
Psalm lxxxvii. 3.

GLORIOUS things of thee are spoken,
    Zion, city of our God;
He, whose word cannot be broken,
    Formed thee for His own abode:
On the Rock of Ages founded,
    What can shake thy sure repose?
With salvation's walls surrounded,
    Thou may'st smile at all thy foes.

See, the streams of living waters,
    Springing from eternal love,
Well supply thy sons and daughters,
    And all fear of want remove:

HEAVEN.

Who can faint, while such a river
    Ever flows their thirst to assuage—
Grace, which, like the Lord the giver,
    Never fails from age to age?

Round each habitation hovering,
    See the cloud and fire appear,
For a glory and a covering,
    Showing that the Lord is near:
Thus deriving from their banner
    Light by night and shade by day,
Safe they feed upon the manna
    Which He gives them when they pray.

Saviour, if of Zion's city
    I, through grace, a member am,
Let the world deride or pity,
    I will glory in Thy Name:
Fading is the worldling's pleasure,
    All his boasted pomp and show;
Solid joys and lasting treasure
    None but Zion's children know.

                    JOHN NEWTON.

*Glory, and honour, and power, and might be unto
  our God for ever and ever.*
                                    Revelation, vii. 12.

HARK! the sound of holy voices
    Chanting, at the crystal sea,
Alleluia, Alleluia,
    Alleluia, Lord, to Thee:
Multitude which none can number,
    Like the stars in glory stands,
Clothed in white apparel, holding
    Palms of victory in their hands.

Patriarch and holy prophet,
    Who prepared the way of Christ,
King, Apostle, saint, confessor,
    Martyr, and Evangelist,
Saintly maiden, godly matron,
    Widows who have watched to prayer,
Joined in holy concert, singing
    To the Lord of all, are there.

They have come from tribulation,
    And have washed their robes in blood,
Washed them in the blood of Jesus;
    Tried they were, and firm they stood;
Mocked, imprisoned, stoned, tormented,
    Sawn asunder, slain with sword,

HEAVEN.

They have conquered Death and Satan
 By the might of Christ the Lord.

Marching with Thy cross, their banner,
 They have triumphed following
Thee, the Captain of salvation,
 Thee, their Saviour and their King ;
Gladly, Lord, with Thee they suffered ;
 Gladly, Lord, with Thee they died ;
And by death to life immortal
 They were born and glorified.

Now they reign in heavenly glory,
 Now they walk in golden light,
Now they drink, as from a river,
 Holy bliss and infinite ;
Love and peace they taste for ever,
 And all truth and knowledge see
In the beatific vision
 Of the blessèd Trinity.

God of God, the One-begotten,
 Light of light, Emanuel,
In whose body joined together
 All the saints for ever dwell,
Pour upon us of Thy fulness,
 That we may for evermore
God the Father, God the Son, and
 God the Holy Ghost adore.

The great city, the holy Jerusalem.

Revelation, xxi. 10.

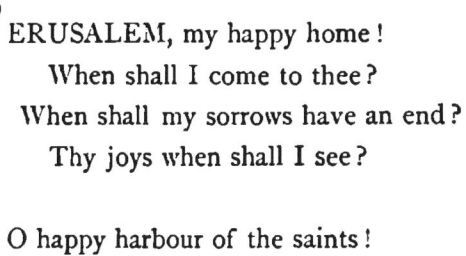

JERUSALEM, my happy home!
　When shall I come to thee?
When shall my sorrows have an end?
　Thy joys when shall I see?

O happy harbour of the saints!
　O sweet and pleasant soil!
In thee no sorrow may be found,
　No grief, no care, no toil!

In thee no sickness may be seen,
　No hurt, no ache, no sore;
There is no death, nor ugly dole,
　But life for evermore.

No dampish mist is seen in thee,
　Nor cold nor darksome night;
There every soul shines as the sun;
　There God Himself gives light.

There lust and lucre cannot dwell;
　There envy bears no sway;
There is no hunger, heat, nor cold,
　But pleasure every way.

HEAVEN.

Jerusalem! Jerusalem!
  God grant I once may see
Thy endless joys, and of the same
  Partaker aye to be!

Thy walls are made of precious stones,
  Thy bulwarks diamonds square,
Thy gates are of right orient pearl,
  Exceeding rich and rare.

Thy turrets and thy pinnacles
  With carbuncles do shine;
Thy very streets are paved with gold,
  Surpassing clear and fine.

Thy houses are of ivory,
  Thy windows crystal clear;
Thy tiles are made of beaten gold:
  —O God, that I were there!

Ah! my sweet home, Jerusalem,
  Would God I were in thee!
Would God my woes were at an end,
  Thy joys that I might see!

We that are here in banishment
  Continually do moan;
We sigh and sob, we weep and wail,
  Perpetually we groan.

HEAVEN.

Our sweet is mixed with bitter gall,
   Our pleasure is but pain;
Our joys scarce last the looking on,
   Our sorrows still remain.

But there they live in such delight,
   Such pleasure and such play,
As that to them a thousand years
   Doth seem as yesterday.

Thy gardens and thy gallant walks
   Continually are green;
There grow such sweet and pleasant flowers
   As nowhere else are seen.

Quite through the streets, with silver sound,
   The Flood of Life doth flow;
Upon whose banks, on every side,
   The Wood of Life doth grow.

There trees for evermore bear fruit,
   And evermore do spring;
There evermore the angels sit,
   And evermore do sing.

Jerusalem! my happy home!
   Would God I were in thee!
Would God my woes were at an end,
   Thy joys that I might see!

ANON.   F. B. P.

HEAVEN.

*I heard a great voice of much people in Heaven,
saying, Alleluia: and again
they said, Alleluia.*
                                        Revelation, xix. 1, 3.

SING Alleluia forth in duteous praise,
O citizens of Heaven, and sweetly raise
      An endless Alleluia.

Ye next, who stand before th' Eternal Light,
In hymning choirs re-echo to the height
      An endless Alleluia.

The Holy City shall take up your strain,
And with glad songs resounding wake again
      An endless Alleluia.

In blissful antiphons ye thus rejoice
To render to the Lord with thankful voice
      An endless Alleluia.

Ye who have gained at length your palms in bliss,
Victorious ones, your chant shall still be this,
      An endless Alleluia.

There, in one grand acclaim, for ever ring
The strains which tell the honour of your King,
      An endless Alleluia.

This is the rest for weary ones brought back,
This is the food and drink which none shall lack,
                An endless Alleluia.

While Thee, by whom were all things made, we praise
For ever, and tell out in sweetest lays
                An endless Alleluia.

Almighty Christ, to Thee our voices sing
Glory for evermore; to Thee we bring
                An endless Alleluia.

---

*And all the angels stood round about the
throne, and worshipped God.*
                Revelation vii. 11.

LO, round the throne, a glorious band,
The saints in countless myriads stand,
Of every tongue redeemed to God,
Arrayed in garments washed in blood.

Through tribulation great they came:
They bore the cross, despised the shame;
From all their labours now they rest,
In God's eternal glory blest.

They see their Saviour face to face,
And sing the triumphs of His grace;

Him day and night they ceaseless praise;
To Him the loud thanksgiving raise:

"Worthy the Lamb, for sinners slain,
Through endless years to live and reign;
Thou hast redeemed us by Thy blood,
And made us kings and priests to God."

O may we tread the sacred road
That holy saints and martyrs trod;
Wage to the end the glorious strife,
And win, like them, a crown of life!

The Lord shewed him all the land.
Deuteronomy, xxxiv. 1.

THERE is a land of pure delight,
Where saints immortal reign;
Infinite day excludes the night,
And pleasures banish pain.

There everlasting Spring abides,
And never-withering flowers:
Death, like a narrow sea, divides
This heavenly land from ours.

Sweet fields beyond the swelling flood
  Stand dressed in living green;
So to the Jews old Canaan stood,
  While Jordan rolled between.

But timorous mortals start and shrink
  To cross this narrow sea.

And linger, shivering on the brink,
    And fear to launch away.

O could we make our doubts remove,
    Those gloomy doubts that rise,
And see the Canaan that we love
    With unbeclouded eyes;

Could we but climb where Moses stood,
    And view the landscape o'er,
Not Jordan's streams, nor death's cold flood,
    Should fright us from the shore.

ISAAC WATTS.

The city had no need of the sun, neither of the moon, for the glory of God did lighten it.
Revelation, xxi. 23.

YE golden lamps of heaven, farewell,
    With all your feeble light;
Farewell, thou ever-changing moon,
    Pale empress of the night.

And thou, refulgent orb of day,
    In brighter flames arrayed,
My soul, that springs beyond thy sphere,
    No more demands thine aid.

HEAVEN.

Ye stars are but the shining dust
   Of my divine abode,
The pavement of those heavenly courts
   Where I shall reign with God.

The Father of eternal light
   Shall there His beams display,
Nor shall one moment's darkness mix
   With that unvaried day.

No more the drops of piercing grief
   Shall swell into mine eyes;
Nor the meridian sun decline
   Amid those brighter skies.

There all the millions of His saints
   Shall in one song unite,
And each the bliss of all shall view
   With infinite delight.

                    PHILIP DODDRIDGE.

These are they which came out of great tribulation.
                            Revelation, vii 14.

HOW bright these glorious spirits shine:
   Whence all their white array?
How came they to the blissful seats
   Of everlasting day?

HEAVEN.

Lo! these are they from sufferings great
   Who came to realms of light,
And in the blood of Christ have washed
   Those robes which shine so bright.

Now with triumphant palms they stand
   Before the throne on high,
And serve the God they love, amidst
   The glories of the sky.

His presence fills each heart with joy,
   Tunes every mouth to sing;
By day, by night, the sacred courts
   With glad hosannas ring.

Hunger and thirst are felt no more,
   Nor suns with scorching ray;
God is their Sun, whose cheering beams
   Diffuse eternal day.

The Lamb, which dwells amidst the throne,
   Shall o'er them still preside,
Feed them with nourishment divine,
   And all their footsteps guide.

'Mong pastures green He'll lead His flock,
   Where living streams appear;
And God the Lord from every eye
   Shall wipe off every tear.

                WILLIAM CAMERON.

HEAVEN.

A great multitude stood before the throne, and before the Lamb, clothed in white.
Revelation, vii. 9.

GIVE me the wings of faith to rise
    Within the veil, and see
The saints above, how great their joys!
    How bright their glories be!

Once they were mourning here below,
    And wet their couch with tears;
They wrestled hard, as we do now,
    With sins and doubts and fears.

I ask them whence their victory came?
    They, with united breath,
Ascribe their conquest to the Lamb,
    Their triumph to His death.

They marked the footsteps that He trod;
    His zeal inspired their breast;
And, following their Incarnate God,
    Possess the promised rest.

Our glorious Leader claims our praise
    For His own pattern given,
While the long cloud of witnesses
    Shows the same path to Heaven.
ISAAC WATTS.

HEAVEN.

They shall hunger no more, neither thirst any more.
Revelation, vii. 16.

THERE is a blessèd home
    Beyond this land of woe,
Where trials never come,
    Nor tears of sorrow flow;
Where faith is lost in sight,
    And patient hope is crowned,
And everlasting light
    Its glory throws around.

There is a land of peace,—
    Good angels know it well;
Glad songs that never cease
    Within its portals swell;
Around its glorious throne
    Ten thousand saints adore
Christ, with the Father One,
    And Spirit, evermore.

O joy all joys beyond,
    To see the Lamb who died,
And count each sacred wound
    In hands, and feet, and side;
To give to Him the praise
    Of every triumph won,
And sing through endless days
    The great things He hath done.

HEAVEN.

Look up, ye saints of God,
   Nor fear to tread below
The path your Saviour trod
   Of daily toil and woe;
Wait but a little while
   In uncomplaining love,
His own most gracious smile
   Shall welcome you above.

SIR HENRY BAKER.

Whence came they?
Revelation, vii. 13.

WHAT are these in bright array,
   This innumerable throng,
Round the altar, night and day,
   Hymning one triumphant song?
"Worthy is the Lamb, once slain,
   Blessing, honour, glory, power,
Wisdom, riches, to obtain,
   New dominion every hour."

These through fiery trials trod;
   These from great affliction came;
Now before the throne of God,
   Sealed with His almighty Name,

Clad in raiment pure and white,
Victor palms in every hand,

Through their dear Redeemer's might,
  More than conquerors they stand.

Hunger, thirst, disease unknown;
  On immortal fruits they feed;
Them the Lamb amidst the throne
  Shall to living fountains lead:
Joy and gladness banish sighs;
  Perfect love dispels all fear;
And for ever from their eyes
  God shall wipe away the tear.

                        JAMES MONTGOMERY.

---

*Open ye the gates, that the righteous
    may enter in.*
                Isaiah, xxvi. 2.

TEN thousand times ten thousand,
  In sparkling raiment bright,
The armies of the ransomed saints
  Throng up the steps of light:
'T is finished—all is finished,
  Their fight with death and sin:
Fling open wide the golden gates,
  And let the victors in!

What rush of hallelujahs
  Fills all the earth and sky!

HEAVEN.

What ringing of a thousand harps
   Bespeaks the triumph nigh!
O day, for which Creation
   And all its tribes were made!
O joy, for all its former woes
   A thousandfold repaid!

O, then what raptured greetings
   On Canaan's happy shore,
What knitting severed friendships up,
   Where partings are no more!
Then eyes with joy shall sparkle
   That brimmed with tears of late:
Orphans no longer fatherless,
   Nor widows desolate.

Bring near Thy great salvation,
   Thou Lamb for sinners slain,
Fill up the roll of Thine elect,
   Then take Thy power, and reign:
Appear, Desire of Nations,—
   Thine exiles long for home;
Show in the heaven Thy promised sign,—
   Thou Prince and Saviour, come!

                              DEAN ALFORD.

*There shall be no more death, neither sorrow,
nor crying, neither shall there
be any more pain.*
                              Revelation, xxi. 4.

THE world is very evil;
    The times are waxing late:
Be sober and keep vigil;
    The Judge is at the gate:

The Judge that comes in mercy,
    The Judge that comes with might,
To terminate the evil,
    To diadem the right.

Arise, arise, good Christian!
    Let right to wrong succeed;
Let penitential sorrow
    To heavenly gladness lead;

To the light that hath no evening,
    That knows nor moon nor sun,
The light so new and golden,
    The light that is but one.

And when the Sole-Begotten
    Shall render up once more
The kingdom to the Father
    Whose own it was before,

Then glory yet unheard of
  Shall shed abroad its ray,
Resolving all enigmas,—
  An endless Sabbath-day.

The peace of all the faithful,
  The calm of all the blest,
Inviolate, unvaried,
  Divinest, sweetest, best.

Yes, peace! for war is needless,—
  Yes, calm! for storm is past,—
And goal from finished labour,
  And anchorage at last.

* * * *

BRIEF life is here our portion;
  Brief sorrow, short-lived care;
The life that knows no ending,
  The tearless life, is *there*.

O happy retribution!
  Short toil, eternal rest!
For mortals and for sinners
  A mansion with the blest!

There grief is turned to pleasure,
  Such pleasure, as below
No human voice can utter,
  No human heart can know.

HEAVEN.

And now we fight the battle,
   But then shall wear the crown
Of full and everlasting
   And passionless renown.

And now we watch and struggle,
   And now we live in hope,
And Sion, in her anguish,
   With Babylon must cope;

But He whom now we trust in
   Shall then be seen and known,
And they that know and see Him
   Shall have Him for their own.

The light that hath no evening,
   The health that hath no sore,
The life that hath no ending,
   But lasteth evermore.

Yes! God, my King and portion,
   In fulness of His grace,
We then shall see for ever,
   And worship face to face.

*   *   *   *

FOR thee, O dear, dear country!
   Mine eyes their vigils keep;
For very love, beholding
   Thy happy name, they weep.

HEAVEN.

The mention of thy glory
   Is unction to the breast,
And medicine in sickness,
   And love, and life, and rest.

O one, O only mansion!
   O Paradise of joy!
Where tears are ever banished,
   And smiles have no alloy!

With jaspers glow thy bulwarks;
   Thy streets with emeralds blaze;
The sardius and the topaz
   Unite in thee their rays:

Thine ageless walls are bonded
   With amethyst unpriced:
Thy saints build up its fabric,
   And the corner-stone is Christ.

The Cross is all thy splendour,
   The Crucified thy praise:
His laud and benediction
   Thy ransomed people raise.

Thou hast no shore, fair ocean!
   Thou hast no time, bright day!
Dear fountain of refreshment
   To pilgrims far away!

Upon the Rock of Ages
    They raise thy holy tower:
Thine is the victor's laurel,
    And thine the golden dower.

    *   *   *   *

JERUSALEM the golden,
    With milk and honey blest,
Beneath thy contemplation
    Sink heart and voice oppressed.

I know not, O I know not
    What joys await us there,
What radiancy of glory,
    What light beyond compare!

They stand, those halls of Sion,
    Conjubilant with song,
And bright with many an angel,
    And all the martyr throng.

The Prince is ever in them;
    The daylight is serene;
The pastures of the blessed
    Are decked in glorious sheen.

There is the throne of David,
    And there, from care released,
The song of them that triumph,
    The shout of them that feast.

And they who, with their Leader,
   Have conquered in the fight,
For ever and for ever
   Are clad in robes of white.

ST. BERNARD.
TRANSLATED BY DR. J. M. NEALE.

We know we have a building of God, an house not made with hands.
II. Corinthians, v. 1.

AS when the weary traveller gains
   The height of some o'erlooking hill,
His heart revives, if 'cross the plains
   He eyes his home, though distant still;

Thus when the Christian pilgrim views,
   By faith, his mansion in the skies,
The sight his fainting strength renews,
   And wings his speed to reach the prize.

The thought of home his spirit cheers;
   No more he grieves for trouble past,
Nor any future trial fears,
   So he may safe arrive at last.

" 'T is there," he says, " I am to dwell
   With Jesus in the realms of day;

Then I shall bid my cares farewell,
   And He shall wipe my tears away."

Jesus, on Thee our hope depends,
   To lead us on to Thine abode;
Assured our home will make amends
   For all our toil while on the road.

JOHN NEWTON.

The things which are seen are temporal; but the things which are not seen are eternal.
              II. Corinthians, iv. 18.

THE roseate hues of early dawn,
   The brightness of the day,
The crimson of the sunset sky,
   How fast they fade away!
O! for the pearly gates of Heaven!
   O! for the golden floor!
O! for the Sun of Righteousness
   That setteth nevermore!

The highest hopes we cherish here,
   How fast they tire and faint!
How many a spot defiles the robe
   That wraps an earthly saint!
O! for a heart that never sins!
   O! for a soul wash'd white!

O! for a voice to praise our King,
  Nor weary day or night!

Here faith is ours, and heavenly hope,
  And grace to lead us higher:
But there are perfectness and peace
  Beyond our best desire.
O! by Thy love and anguish, Lord!
  O! by Thy life laid down!
O! that we fall not from Thy grace,
  Nor cast away our crown!

CECIL FRANCIS ALEXANDER.

They go from strength to strength, every one appeareth before God.
Psalm lxxxiv. 7.

COME ye, whose willing feet
  Pursue the heavenly road,
Thus let us often meet
  To bless our King and God,
And seek the grace to travel on,
Till all appear before His throne.

Nearer and nearer still,
  We to our country come,
To the celestial hill
  Where we shall be at home,—
The new Jerusalem above,
The seat of everlasting love.

HEAVEN.

The ransomed sons of God,
   Earth's idols let us scorn,
As to our high abode
   We joyfully return,
And still with growing strength proceed,
Where God the Spirit deigns to lead.

Our Saviour, Prince, and Head,
   Our all in all is He,
'Tis in His steps we tread,
   His face we soon shall see.
Glory to God! then pain is done,
For earth is passed, and Heaven is won.

HON. BAPTIST NOEL.

So shall we ever be with the Lord.
I. Thessalonians, iv. 17.

FOR ever to behold Him shine,
For evermore to call Him mine,
   And see Him still before me;
For ever on His face to gaze,
And meet His full assembled rays,
While all the Father He displays
   To all the saints in glory!

Not all things else are half so dear
As His delightful presence here—

HEAVEN.

What must it be in Heaven!
'T is Heaven on earth to hear Him say,
As now I journey day by day,
" Poor sinner, cast thy fears away,
   Thy sins are all forgiven."

But how must His celestial voice
Make my enraptured heart rejoice,
   When I in glory hear Him!
While I before the heavenly gate
For everlasting entrance wait,
And Jesus on His throne of state
   Invites me to come near Him.

" Come in, thou blessed, sit by me;
With my own life I ransomed thee;
   Come, taste my perfect favour:
Come in, thou happy spirit, come;
Thou now shalt dwell with me at home;
Ye blissful mansions, make him room,
   For he must stay for ever."

JOSEPH SWAIN.

GENERAL HYMNS

Let the children of Zion be joyful in their King.
Psalm cxlix. 2.

PRAISE ye the Lord, prepare your glad voice
　　His praise in the great assembly to sing;
In our great Creator let Israel rejoice,
　And children of Zion be glad in their King.

GENERAL HYMNS.

Let all who adore Jehovah, our Lord,
   With heart and with tongue His praises express,
Who always takes pleasure His saints to reward
   And with His salvation the humble to bless.

With glory adorned His people shall sing
   To God, who their heads with safety doth shield;
Such honour and triumph His favour shall bring;
   O therefore, for ever, all praise to Him yield.

TATE AND BRADY.

O Lord, attend unto my cry, give ear unto my prayer.
Psalm xvii. 1.

GOD, who made the earth and sea,
Hear us when we cry to Thee;
O hear us when we pray for peace:
Let the war of nations cease;
   Cause angry hearts to melt with love,
   That peace through all the world be wove.

O Jesus! blessed, holy Name!
Thou to earth all lowly came,
To succour those who wept in woe,
For each grief dear pity show;
   O let Thy Name, o'er sea and land,
   A beacon-light for ever stand.

Great, holy Spirit, hear us now,
Fill our hearts as low we bow;
O guide us by Thy star of light,
Through this sinful world's dark night:
   Be with us in the battle fight,
   And help us through the wrong to right.

Mysterious Godhead, three in one,
Let Thy will on earth be done;
And, if it please Thee in our day,
That we stumble on the way,
   O grant we yet may gain the prize,
   And live with Thee beyond the skies.

ANON.

The gift of God is eternal life.
Romans, vi. 23

ETERNITY, eternity,
   How long art thou, eternity!
Yet hasteth on toward thee our life,
E'en as the war steed to the strife,
The messenger toward home, doth go,
Or ship to shore, or bolt from bow.

   Eternity, eternity,
   How long art thou, eternity!

As in a globe, so smooth and round,
Beginning ne'er and end are found,
Eternity, not more can we
Beginning find, or end, in thee.

    Eternity, eternity,
      How long art thou, eternity!
Thou art a ring of awful mould,
"For ever" is thy centre called,
And "Never" thy circumf'rence wide,
For unto thee no end can tide.

    Eternity, eternity,
      How long art thou, eternity!
And if a little bird bore forth
One single sand-corn from the earth,
And took in thousand years but one,
Ere thou wert past, the world were gone.

    Eternity, eternity,
      How long art thou, eternity!
In thee, if every thousandth year,
An eye should drop one little tear,
To hold the water thence would grow
Nor heaven nor earth were wide enow.

    Eternity, eternity,
      How long art thou, eternity!
The sand and water in the sea
But portions of thy whole can be;

No reck'ning long can e'er suffice
To give the measure of thy size.

 Eternity, eternity,
  How long art thou, eternity!
Hear, man! So long as God shall reign,
So long continue Hell and pain;
So long last Heaven and joy also.—
O, lengthened joy! O, lengthened woe!

TRANSLATED BY DR. H. W. DULCKEN,
FROM AN OLD GERMAN HYMN.

Fight the good fight of faith
I. Timothy, vi. 12.

MUCH in sorrow, oft in woe,
 Onward, Christians, onward go;
Fight the fight, and worn with strife,
Steep with tears the Bread of Life.

Onward, Christians, onward go;
Join the war and face the foe,
Faint not! much doth yet remain;
Dreary is the long campaign.

Shrink not, Christians! will ye yield?
Will ye quit the painful field?

GENERAL HYMNS.

Will ye flee in danger's hour?
Know ye not your Captain's power?

Let your drooping hearts be glad;
March, in heavenly armour clad;
Fight, nor think the battle long;
Victory soon shall tune your song.

Let not sorrow dim your eye,
Soon shall every tear be dry;
Let not woe your course impede;
Great your strength, if great your need.

Onward, then, to battle move;
More than conquerors ye shall prove;
Though opposed by many a foe,
Christian soldiers, onward go!

FRAGMENT BY HENRY KIRKE WHITE,
COMPLETED BY FANNY FULLER MAITLAND.

Unto Him that loved us be glory for ever.
Revelation, i. 5, 6.

FOR a thousand tongues to sing
  My dear Redeemer's praise,
The glories of my God and King,
  The triumphs of His grace!

My gracious Master and my God,
    Assist me to proclaim,
To spread, through all the earth abroad,
    The honours of Thy Name.

Jesus! the Name that charms our fears,
    That bids our sorrows cease;
'T is music in the sinner's ears,
    'T is life, and health, and peace!

He breaks the power of cancelled sin,
    He sets the prisoners free;
His blood can make the foulest clean;
    His blood avails for me.

He speaks, and, listening to His voice,
    New life the dead receive;
The mournful, broken hearts rejoice,
    The humble poor believe.

Hear Him, ye deaf; His praise, ye dumb,
    Your loosened tongues employ;
Ye blind, behold your Saviour come,
    And leap, ye lame, for joy!

CHARLES WESLEY.

*I will say of the Lord, He is my refuge; my God:
in Him will I trust.*
Psalm xci. 2.

MY trust is in the Lord;
What foe can injure me?
Why bid me like a bird
Before the fowler flee?
The Lord is on His heavenly throne,
Omnipotent to save His own.

The wicked may assail
The tempter sorely try,
All earth's foundations fail,
All nature's springs be dry;
Yet God is in His holy shrine,
And I am strong while He is mine.

His flock to Him is dear,
He watches them from high;
He sends them trials here,
To fit them for the sky;
But safely will He tend and keep
The humblest, feeblest of His sheep.

His foes a season here
May triumph and prevail;
But, ah! the hour is near
When all their hopes must fail;
While like the sun His saints shall rise,
And shine with Him above the skies.

HENRY FRANCIS LYTE.

Here we have no continuing city, but we seek one to come.
Hebrews, xiii. 14.

FRIEND after friend departs;
  Who hath not lost a friend?
There is no union here of hearts
  That finds not here an end:
Were this frail world our only rest,
Living or dying, none were blest.

Beyond the flight of time,
  Beyond this vale of death,

There surely is some blessed clime,
  Where life is not a breath,
Nor life's affections transient fire,
Whose sparks fly upwards to expire.

There is a world above,
  Where parting is unknown;
A whole eternity of love,
  Formed for the good alone;
And faith beholds the dying here
Translated to that happier sphere.

Thus star by star declines
  Till all are passed away,
As morning high and higher shines
  To pure and perfect day;
Nor sink those stars in empty night;
They hide themselves in Heaven's own light.

JAMES MONTGOMERY.

---

*Except the Lord keep the city, the watchman
waketh but in vain.*
Psalm cxxvii. 1.

THE Lord is Lord, and King of kings,
  Our safe defence and true;
To Him, with all our heart of love,
  Allegiance is due.

In vain the watchman watcheth o'er
    The city in the night,
Unless the Lord be watching too,
    And helping in the fight.

In vain the sinner battles with
    His close-besetting sin;
Unless the Lord is helping him,
    The fight he cannot win.

Then help us, Lord, to keep the watch;
    Thy armour to put on;
Shield us with Thy mighty shield,
    Life's battle-field upon.

                    GEORGE WOOLER.

Take good heed unto yourselves, that ye love the Lord your God.
                                  Joshua, xxiii. 11.

WHOM should we love like Thee,
    Our God, our Guide, our King,
The Tower to which we flee,
    The Rock to which we cling?
O for a thousand tongues to show
The debt that we to mercy owe!

The storm upon us fell,
    The floods around us rose,

The depths of death and hell
Seemed on our souls to close :
To God we cried in strong despair,
And God was nigh to help our prayer.

He came, the King of kings,
He bowed the sable sky,
And on the tempest's wings
Rode glorious from on high.
The earth before her Maker shook,
The mountains quaked at His rebuke.

Above the storm He stood,
And awed it to repose;
He drew us from the flood,
And scattered all our foes.
He sets us in a spacious place,
And there upholds us by His grace.

Whom should we love like Thee,
Our God, our Guide, our King,
The Tower to which we flee,
The Rock to which we cling?
O for a thousand tongues to show
The debt that we to mercy owe!

HENRY FRANCIS LYTE.

It shall be said in that day, Lo, this is our God; we will be glad and rejoice in His salvation.
                                    Isaiah, xxv. 9.

REJOICE to-day with one accord,
  Sing out with exultation;
Rejoice and praise our mighty Lord,
  Whose arm hath brought salvation;
    His works of love proclaim
    The greatness of His Name;
    For He is God alone
    Who hath His mercy shown:
Let all His saints adore Him!

When in distress to Him we cried,
  He heard our sad complaining;
O, trust in Him whate'er betide,
  His love is all-sustaining;
    Triumphant songs of praise
    To Him our hearts shall raise;
    Now every voice shall say,
    "O praise our God alway:"
Let all His saints adore Him!

Rejoice to-day with one accord,
  Sing out with exultation;
Rejoice and praise our mighty Lord,
  Whose arm hath brought salvation;

His works of love proclaim
The greatness of His Name;
For He is God alone
Who hath His mercy shown:
Let all His saints adore Him!

ANON.

*Now we see through a glass, darkly; but then
face to face.*
I. Corinthians, xiii. 12.

GOD, when darkness round us reigns,
   When puzzling doubts arise,
When we in vain do strive to guess
   The mystery of the skies:

The mystery of Thy Godhead, Lord,
   The mystery of Thy love,
Why man should fall, and Thou shouldst leave
   Thy glorious home above;

Why wretchedness should e'er be born;
   Why poverty and sin;
Why some should weep, and some should toil,
   Their scanty bread to win;

Why Thy great providence is hid;
   Nor can we see the end,
When our poor thoughts go stumbling on,
   And know not where they tend;

Then, Lord, be Thou our guiding light,
    The lamp of faith to give,
To lead us from the darksome cave,
    Where darkened doubts do live.

Though blind our eyes, we cannot see,
    Let Hope stretch out her hand;
And, led by Faith, in faith go on,
    On to the "happy land."

Shield us, Lord, from sin and doubt,
    Let our weak hearts adore;
With Thee to help, to guide, to love,
    O we shall doubt no more.

The holy light of Thy dear love
    Will make each mystery plain;
Each trembling fear shall fly away,
    Nor shall we doubt again.
GEORGE WOTTON.

My yoke is easy, and my burden is light.
Matthew, xi. 30.

COME, take my yoke, the Saviour said;
    To follow me be not afraid;
For I in heart am lowly, meek,
    And offer you the rest you seek.

GENERAL HYMNS.

The yoke of Pleasure may allure,
And promise bliss that will endure;
But, when it has thy youth despoiled,
'T will cast thee off as garment soiled.

Take not on thee the yoke of Wealth;
'T will eat thy soul, destroy thy health,
And make thee feel how cheap the cost,
If worlds could buy the peace it lost.

Ambition, too, its yoke displays,
And hangs out its perennial bays;
Be not, poor soul, by it misled;
I offer thee a crown instead.

Then take my yoke, 't is soft and light,
'T will ne'er disturb thy rest at night,
But guide thee to that world above,
Where no restraint is known but love.

ROBERT SMITH.

He maketh the storm a calm, so that the waves thereof are still.
Psalm cvii. 29.

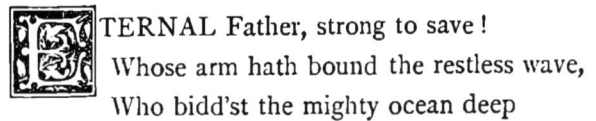

ETERNAL Father, strong to save!
Whose arm hath bound the restless wave,
Who bidd'st the mighty ocean deep
Its own appointed limits keep;
O hear us when we cry to Thee
For those in peril on the sea.

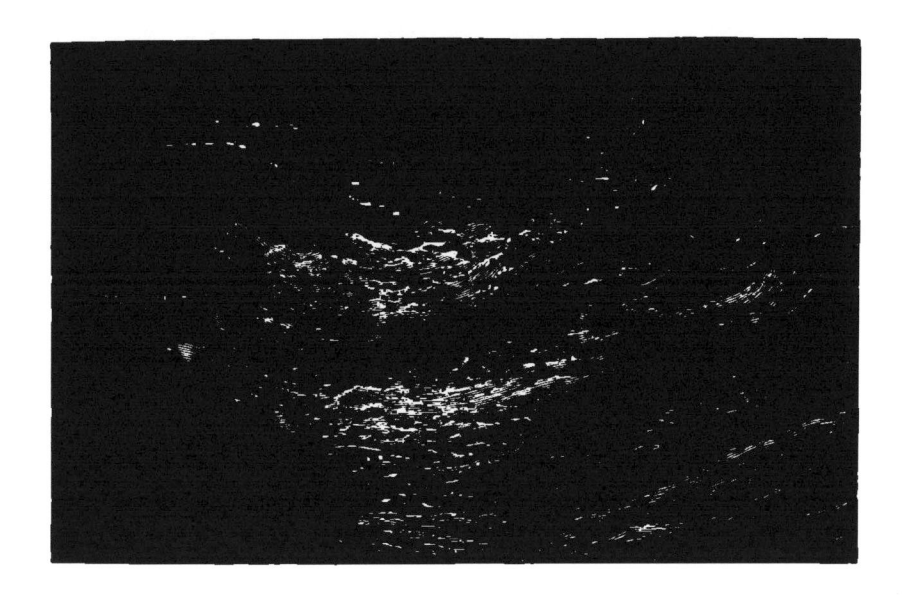

O Christ! whose voice the waters heard,
And hushed their raging at Thy word,
Who walkedst on the foaming deep,
And calm amidst its rage didst sleep;
 O hear us when we cry to Thee
 For those in peril on the sea.

Most Holy Spirit! who didst brood
Upon the chaos dark and rude,
And bid its angry tumult cease,
And give, for wild confusion, peace;
 O hear us when we cry to Thee
 For those in peril on the sea.

O Trinity of love and power!
Our brethren shield in danger's hour;

From rock and tempest, fire and foe,
Protect them wheresoe'er they go;
 Thus evermore shall rise to Thee
 Glad hymns of praise from land and sea.

ANON.

Behold, I stand at the door, and knock.
Revelation, iii. 20.

BEHOLD! a Stranger's at the door!
 He gently knocks, has knocked before,
 Has waited long, is waiting still:
 You treat no other friend so ill.

But will He prove a Friend indeed?
 He will! the very Friend you need!
 The Man of Nazareth, 'tis He,
 With garments dyed at Calvary.

O lovely attitude! He stands,
 With melting heart, and laden hands!
 O matchless kindness! and He shows
 This matchless kindness to His foes.

Rise, touched with gratitude divine;
 Turn out His enemy and thine,
 That hateful, hell-born monster, Sin,
 And let the Heavenly Stranger in.

If thou art poor (and poor thou art),
Lo! He has riches to impart;
Not wealth in which mean av'rice rolls;
O better far—the wealth of souls!

Thou'rt blind; He'll takes the scales away,
And let in everlasting day:
Naked thou art; but He shall dress
Thy blushing soul in righteousness.

Art thou a weeper? Grief shall fly,
For who can weep with Jesus by?
No terror shall thy hopes annoy;
No tear, except the tear of joy.

Admit Him, for the human breast
Ne'er entertained so kind a Guest:
Admit Him, for you can't expel;
Where'er He comes, He comes to dwell.

Admit Him ere His anger burn;
His feet, departed, ne'er return!
Admit Him, or the hour's at hand
When at His door denied you'll stand.

Yet know (nor of the terms complain)
If Jesus comes, He comes to reign;
To reign, and with no partial sway;
Thoughts must be slain that disobey!

Sovereign of souls! Thou Prince of Peace!
O may Thy gentle reign increase!
Throw wide the door, each willing mind!
And be His empire all mankind!

       JOSEPH GRIGG

Hear thou, therefore, the word of the Lord.
       I. Kings, xxii. 19.

THE winds were howling o'er the deep,
 Each wave a watery hill;
The Saviour wakened from His sleep;
 He spake, and all was still.

The madman in a tomb had made
 His mansion of despair:
Woe to the traveller who strayed
 With heedless footstep there!

The chains hung broken from his arm,
 Such strength can hell supply;
And fiendish hate, and fierce alarm,
 Flashed from his hollow eye.

He met that glance, so thrilling sweet;
 He heard those accents mild;
And, melting at Messiah's feet,
 Wept like a weanèd child.

O! madder than the raving man!
   O! deafer than the sea!
How long the time since Christ began
   To call in vain on me!

He called me when my thoughtless prime
   Was early ripe to ill;
I passed from folly on to crime,
   And yet He called me still.

He called me in the time of dread,
   When death was full in view;
I trembled on my feverish bed,
   And rose to sin anew.

Yet, could I hear Him once again,
   As I have heard of old,
Methinks He should not call in vain
   His wanderer to the fold.

O Thou that every thought canst know,
   And answer every prayer,
O! give me sickness, want, or woe,
   But snatch me from despair!

My struggling will by grace control!
   Renew my broken vow!
What blessed light breaks on my soul?
   My God! I hear Thee now!

             BISHOP REGINALD HEBER.

I will not let thee go except thou bless me.
Genesis, xxxii. 26.

COME, O thou Traveller unknown,
   Whom still I hold, but cannot see,
My company before is gone,
   And I am left alone with Thee;
With Thee all night I mean to stay,
And wrestle till the break of day.

I need not tell Thee who I am,
   My misery or sin declare;
Thyself hast called me by my name:
   Look on Thy hands, and read it there!
But who, I ask Thee, who art Thou?
Tell me Thy Name, and tell me now.

In vain Thou strugglest to get free,
   I never will unloose my hold;
Art Thou the Man that died for me?
   The secret of Thy love unfold.
Wrestling, I will not let Thee go
Till I Thy Name, Thy nature know.

Wilt Thou not yet to me reveal
   Thy new, unutterable Name?
Tell me, I still beseech Thee, tell:
   To know it now resolved I am:

Wrestling, I will not let Thee go
Till I Thy Name, Thy nature know.

'T is all in vain to hold Thy tongue,
   Or touch the hollow of my thigh;
Though every sinew be unstrung,
   Out of my arms Thou shalt not fly:
Wrestling, I will not let Thee go
Till I Thy Name, Thy nature know.

What though my shrinking flesh complain,
   And murmur to contend so long?
I rise superior to my pain;
   When I am weak, then I am strong:
And when my all of strength shall fail,
I shall with the God-Man prevail.

My strength is gone; my nature dies;
   I sink beneath Thy weighty hand,
Faint to revive, and fall to rise;
   I fall, and yet by faith I stand:
I stand, and will not let Thee go,
Till I Thy Name, Thy Nature know.

Yield to me now, for I am weak,
   But confident in self-despair;
Speak to my heart, in blessings speak,
   Be conquered by my instant prayer!
Speak, or Thou never hence shalt move,
And tell me if Thy Name is Love?

'T is Love! 't is Love! Thou diedst for me!
    I hear Thy whisper in my heart!
The morning breaks, the shadows flee;
    Pure universal Love Thou art!
To me, to all, Thy bowels move;
Thy nature, and Thy Name, is Love!

My prayer hath power with God; the grace
    Unspeakable I now receive;
Through faith I see Thee face to face,
    I see Thee face to face, and live:
In vain I have not wept and strove;
Thy nature, and Thy Name, is Love.

I know Thee, Saviour, who Thou art,—
    Jesus, the feeble sinner's Friend!
Nor wilt Thou with the night depart,
    But stay, and love me to the end!
Thy mercies never shall remove;
Thy nature, and Thy Name, is Love!

The Sun of Righteousness on me
    Hath rose, with healing in His wings;
Withered my nature's strength, from Thee
    My soul its life and succour brings;
My help is all laid up above;
Thy nature, and Thy Name, is Love.

Contented now upon my thigh
    I halt, till life's short journey end;

GENERAL HYMNS.

All helplessness, all weakness, I
  On Thee alone for strength depend;
Nor have I power from Thee to move;
Thy nature, and Thy Name, is Love.

Lame as I am, I take the prey,
  Hell, earth, and sin, with ease o'ercome;
I leap for joy, pursue my way,
  And as a bounding hart fly home!
Through all eternity to prove
  Thy nature, and Thy Name, is Love!

CHARLES WESLEY.

I would seek unto God, and unto God would I commit my cause.
Job, v. 8.

JESUS! lead us with Thy power
  Safe unto the promised rest;
Hide our souls within Thy bosom;
  Let us slumber on Thy breast;
Feed us with the heavenly manna,
  Bread that angels eat above;
Let us drink from the holy fountain
  Draughts of everlasting love!

Throughout the desert wild conduct us
  With a glorious pillar bright,

In the day a cooling comfort,
    And a cheering fire by night ;
Be our Guide in every peril,
    Watch us hourly night and day ;
Otherwise we'll err and wander
    From Thy Spirit far away.

In Thy presence we are happy ;
    In Thy presence we're secure ;
In Thy presence all afflictions
    We will easily endure ;
In Thy presence we can conquer,
    We can suffer, we can die ;
Far from Thee, we faint and languish :
    Lord, our Saviour, keep us nigh !

WILLIAM WILLIAMS.

Sing praises unto our King, sing praises ; for
    God is the King of all the earth.
Psalm xlvii. 6, 7.

LORD, fill my heart with joyful song,
    O let my tongue tell forth Thy praise,
Now, and all my whole life long,
    Thou God of everlasting days !

Lord Jesus, teach me now to know
    There is no home but Heaven above ;

GENERAL HYMNS.

There is no lasting joy can flow,
But from Thine everlasting love.

As soars the eagle in the sky,
Then seeks its high-up rocky nest,
Lord Jesus, so my soul would fly,
And find a home upon Thy breast.

All laud and glory, Lord, be Thine;
    Dear Jesus, Saviour, Prince of Peace!
Fill every heart with love divine,
    Let angry warfare ever cease.

Let it be ours to sing Thy praise,
    Let every tongue proclaim Thy Name;
Now, and to the end of days,
    Our shouts of song be still the same.

                        ANON

I delight to do Thy will, O my God.
                      Psalm xl. 8.

FATHER, whate'er of earthly bliss
    Thy sovereign will denies,
Accepted at Thy throne of grace
    Let this petition rise:

Give me a calm and thankful heart,
    From every murmur free;
The blessings of Thy grace impart,
    And make me live to Thee.

Let the bless'd hope that Thou art mine
    My life and death attend;
Thy presence through my journey shine,
    And crown my journey's end.

                    ANNE STEELE.

Press toward the mark for the prize of the high calling of God in Christ Jesus.
Philippians, iii. 14.

ONWARD, Christian soldiers,
    Marching as to war,
With the Cross of Jesus
    Going on before.
Christ the Royal Master
    Leads against the foe,
Forward into battle,
    See, His banners go.
        Onward, Christian soldiers,
            Marching as to war,
        With the Cross of Jesus
            Going on before.

At the sign of triumph
    Satan's host doth flee;
On, then, Christian soldiers,
    On to victory!
Hell's foundations quiver
    At the shout of praise;
Brothers, lift your voices,
    Loud your anthems raise.
        Onward, Christian soldiers,
            Marching as to war,
        With the Cross of Jesus
            Going on before.

Like a mighty army
  Moves the Church of God;
Brothers, we are treading
  Where the saints have trod,
We are not divided,
  All one body we,
One in hope and doctrine,
  One in charity.
    Onward, Christian soldiers,
      Marching as to war,
    With the Cross of Jesus
      Going on before.

Crowns and thrones may perish,
  Kingdoms rise and wane,
But the Church of Jesus
  Constant will remain;
Gates of hell can never
  'Gainst that Church prevail;
We have Christ's own promise,
  And that cannot fail.
    Onward, Christian soldiers,
      Marching as to war,
    With the Cross of Jesus
      Going on before.

Onward, then, ye people,
  Join our happy throng,
Blend with ours your voices
  In the triumph song;

Glory, laud, and honour,
　Unto Christ the King,
This through countless ages
　Men and angels sing.
　　Onward, Christian soldiers,
　　　Marching as to war,
　　With the Cross of Jesus
　　　Going on before.

　　　　　　　　　ANON.

Be of good comfort, rise; He calleth Thee.
　　　　　　　　　Mark, x. 49.

A THOUSAND years have fleeted,
　And, Saviour! still we see
Thy deed of love repeated
　On all who come to Thee.
As He who sat benighted,
　Afflicted, poor, and blind;
So now (Thy word is plighted)
　Joy, light, and peace I find.

Dark gloom my spirit filling,
　Beside the way I sat;
Desire my heart was thrilling;
　But anguish more than that.
To me no ray was granted,
　Although I heard the psalms

The faithful sweetly chanted,
   And felt the waving palms.

With grief my heart was aching;
   O'erwhelming were my woes,
Till, heaven-born courage taking,
   To Thee my cry arose:
"O David's Son, relieve me;
   My bitter anguish quell;
Thy promised succour give me,
   And this dark night dispel!"

With tears that fast were flowing
   I sought Thee through the crowd,
My heart more tender growing,
   Until I wept aloud:
O! then my grief diminished;
   For then they cried to me,
"Blind man, thy woe is finished;
   Arise, He calleth thee!"

I came with steps that faltered;
   Thy course I felt Thee check;
Then straight my mind was altered,
   And bowed my stubborn neck:
Thou saidst, "What art thou seeking?"
   "O Lord! that I might see!"
O! then I heard Thee speaking:
   "Believe, and it shall be."

Our hope, Lord, faileth never,
   When Thou Thy word dost plight:
My fears then ceased for ever,
   And all my soul was light.
Thou gavest me Thy blessing;
   From former guilt set free,
Now heavenly joy possessing,
   O Lord! I follow Thee!

FRANCES ELIZABETH COX.
FROM FREDERIC DE LA MOTTE FOUQUÉ.

Hosanna to the Son of David: blessed is He that cometh in the Name of the Lord.
Matthew, xxi. 9.

HOSANNA to the Living Lord!
   Hosanna to the Incarnate Word!
   To Christ, Creator, Saviour, King,
   Let earth, let Heaven, Hosanna sing.
      Hosanna! Lord! Hosanna in the highest!

"Hosanna," Lord, Thine angels cry;
"Hosanna," Lord, Thy saints reply:
   Above, beneath us, and around,
   The dead and living swell the sound.
      Hosanna! Lord! Hosanna in the highest!

O Saviour, with protecting care
Return to this Thy house of prayer,
Assembled in Thy sacred Name,
Where we Thy parting promise claim.
    Hosanna! Lord! Hosanna in the highest!

But, chiefest, in our cleansèd breast,
Eternal, bid Thy Spirit rest;
And make our secret soul to be
A temple pure, and worthy Thee.
    Hosanna! Lord! Hosanna in the highest!

So, in the last and dreadful day,
When earth and Heaven shall melt away,
Thy flock, redeemed from sinful stain,
Shall swell the sound of praise again.
    Hosanna! Lord! Hosanna in the highest!

BISHOP REGINALD HEBER.

Preserve my soul, O Thou my God; save Thy servant that trusteth in Thee.
Psalm lxxxvi. 2.

WHEN angels swell the heavenly choir,
  And tune their harps of gold,
And, in their sweetest songs of praise,
  Their holy love unfold;

When angels all are fluttering round,
    Thy love-looks, God, to share,
And each will see Thee as Thou art,
    Great God! shall I be there?

When all the cloud of witnesses
    Are thronging round Thy throne,
Where ne'er is seen the tear to fall,
    Where never heard the groan;
But all are radiant in Thy love,
    Each head the crown doth wear,
Each hand doth bear the palm of life:
    O God! shall I be there?

When all the ransomed of the world
    Come, Jesus Lord, to Thee,
Who through the fire of life hath gone,
    Through grief and misery;
There, sheltering in Thy bosom, stand,
    In all Thy love and care;
To hear the joyous sound, "Well done!"
    God, grant that I be there!

When all the toils of life are done,
    The dusty road is past;
When all the sands of life are run,
    I come to die at last;
When all the light of earth has gone,
    And death stands cold and bare;

Then, while I pass the valley through,
   O Christ, be with me there!

Be with me there, to bear me on,
   On to the land of light,
Where all the holy good are gone,
   The blessèd and the bright;
To sing the glad new song of love,
   And Thy dear smile to share;
In joy, Lord Jesus, Father, God,
   Let me be with Thee there.

GEORGE WOOLER.

God is the strength of my heart, and my portion for ever.
Psalm lxxiii. 26.

LORD, I would delight in Thee,
   And on Thy care depend;
To Thee in every trouble flee,
   My best, my only Friend.

When all created streams are dried,
   Thy fulness is the same;
May I with this be satisfied,
   And glory in Thy Name!

Why should the soul a drop bemoan,
   Who has a fountain near?

GENERAL HYMNS.

A fountain which will ever run
With waters sweet and clear.

No good in creatures can be found,
  But may be found in Thee;
I must have all things, and abound,
  While God is God to me.

O that I had a stronger faith,
  To look within the veil!
To credit what my Saviour saith,
  Whose word can never fail!

He that has made my Heaven secure,
  Will here all good provide;

GENERAL HYMNS.

While Christ is rich, can I be poor?
What can I want beside?

O Lord, I cast my care on Thee;
I triumph and adore:
Henceforth my great concern shall be
To love and please Thee more.

JOHN RYLAND.

Restore unto me the joy of Thy salvation.
Psalm li. 12.

WEARY of wandering from my God,
And now made willing to return,
I hear, and bow me to the rod;
For Him, not without hope, I mourn:
I have an Advocate above,
A Friend before the throne of love.

O Jesu, full of pardoning grace,
More full of grace than I of sin;
Yet once again I seek Thy face,
Open Thine arms and take me in,
And freely my backslidings heal,
And love the faithless sinner still!

Thou know'st the way to bring me back,
My fallen spirit to restore;

O, for Thy truth and mercy's sake,
   Forgive, and bid me sin no more!
The ruins of my soul repair,
   And make my heart a house of prayer!

The stone to flesh again convert,
   The veil of sin once more remove;
Drop Thy warm blood upon my heart,
   And melt it with Thy dying love:
This rebel heart by love subdue,
And make it soft and make it new!

Give to mine eyes refreshing tears,
   And kindle my relentings now;
Fill all my soul with filial fears,
   To Thy sweet yoke my spirit bow;
Bend by Thy grace, O! bend, or break
The iron sinew in my neck!

Ah! give me, Lord, the tender heart,
   'That trembles at th' approach of sin;
A godly fear of sin impart,
   Implant, and root it deep within;
That I may dread Thy gracious power,
And never dare offend Thee more!

CHARLES WESLEY.

The Lord Jehovah is my strength; He also is my salvation.
                              Isaiah, xii. 2.

ON bended knee I seek Thee, Lord:
    Blessed Saviour! holy Name!
O kindle now within my heart
    A pure and righteous flame,
That I may fight the battle well,
    And never turn away nor flee,
But, strengthened by Thy ready arm,
    Lord Jesus! let me cling to Thee.

Though care and suffering be my lot,
    Though friends depart and leave me;
Though unkind words from those I love
    Should deeply wound and grieve me;
Though darkness gather o'er my path,
    And thunders roar around me,
That I can see nor light nor love:
    Lord Jesus! I would cling to Thee.

There is no other Name but Thine,
    'Mong the glorious names above,
Which fills the sinner's aching heart
    With our heavenly Father's love.
There is no other way to life
    That our beclouded sense can see,

But Thou alone, King, Saviour, God!
   Lord Jesus! I would cling to Thee.

Dear Saviour! by Thy holy love,
   By Thy tears, Thine agony!
O by Thy groans and bloody sweat!
   By the cross on Calvary!
By Thy resurrection power!
   By Thy ascension mystery!
O hear my cry, Redeemer, Lord:
   Lord Jesus! let me cling to Thee.

GEORGE WOOLER.

*The Lord Most High, He is a great
King over all the earth.*
Psalm xlvii. 2.

GLORY to God on high!
   Let earth to Heaven reply;
     Praise ye His Name;
   His love and grace adore,
   Who all our sorrows bore;
   And praise Him evermore:
     Worthy the Lamb!

Jesus, our Lord and God,
   Bore sin's tremendous load;
     Praise ye His Name:

Tell what His arm hath done,
What spoils from death He won;
  Sing His great Name alone:
    Worthy the Lamb!

While they around the throne
Join cheerfully in one,
  Praising His Name;
We who have felt His blood
Sealing our peace with God,
Sound His high praise abroad:
    Worthy the Lamb!

Join, all the ransomed race,
Our Lord and God to bless;
  Praise ye His Name;
In Him we will rejoice,
Making a joyful noise,
Shouting with heart and voice,
    Worthy the Lamb!

Though we must change our place,
Yet shall we never cease
  Praising His Name;
To Him our tribute bring,
Hail Him our gracious King,
And without ceasing sing,
    Worthy the Lamb!

Now let the hosts above,
In realms of endless love,
  Praise His great Name;
To Him ascribèd be,
Honour and majesty,
Through all eternity:
  Worthy the Lamb!

JAMES ALLEN.

*Thus saith the Lord, I have made the earth and created man,
  and all the host have I commanded.*
Isaiah, xlv. 11, 12.

CREATOR Spirit! by whose aid
  The world's foundations first were laid,
  Come, visit every humble mind;
  Come, pour Thy joys on all mankind;
  From sin and sorrow set us free,
  And make us temples worthy Thee.

Thou Strength of His almighty hand,
Whose power does Heaven and earth command,
Thrice holy Fount, thrice holy Fire,
Our hearts with heavenly love inspire;
Come, and Thy sacred unction bring,
To sanctify us while we sing.

Plenteous of grace, descend from high,
Rich in Thy sevenfold energy;

Give us Thyself, that we may see
The Father and the Son by Thee;
Make us eternal truths receive,
And practise all that we believe.

Immortal honour, endless fame
Attend the Almighty Father's Name;
Let God the Son be glorified,
Who for lost man's redemption died;
And equal adoration be,
Eternal Comforter, to Thee.

CHARLEMAGNE.
PARAPHRASED BY JOHN DRYDEN.

Strengthened with all might, according to His glorious power.
Colossians, i. 11.

WHAT care the saints of God, if they
'Mid pain and wounds are called away
    To their reward?
What matters one short day of tears,
Which ushers in the countless years
    With their dear Lord?

To all the saints of God saith He—
Take up your cross and follow me;
    I lead mine own;
I go your mansion to prepare,
And you in bliss shall meet me there
    Before the throne.

The lot of God's elect below
Was ever thus, and must be so
    While earth shall last;
Trials must lie about our feet
Till in the courts of God we meet,
    All troubles past.

But there the Lord in that bright day
For His own saints shall wipe away
    Tears from all eyes;

And no more sorrow shall be there,
No tears, no weeping, no more care
    Beyond the skies.

In trembling here we strive to find
The path to bliss, nor look behind
    In doubt and fear;
While, sometimes faint and sometimes loud,
The murmur of the tempest-cloud
    Falls on our ear.

But all the saints of Jesus know
That when the storms of trouble blow,
    They see in faith
Their Saviour walking on the wave,
And He is ever strong to save
    Their souls from death.

ANON.

I reckon that the sufferings of this present time are not worthy to be compared with the glory which shall be revealed in us.
Romans, viii. 18.

LET our choir new anthems raise,
    Wake the morn with gladness:
God Himself to joy and praise
    Turns the martyrs' sadness:
This the day that won their crown,
    Opened Heaven's bright portal,

GENERAL HYMNS.

As they laid the mortal down;
    And put on the immortal.

Never flinched they from the flame,
    From the torture, never;
Vain the foeman's sharpest aim,
    Satan's last endeavour:
For by faith they saw the land
    Decked in all its glory,
Where triumphant now they stand
    With the victor's story.

Up and follow, Christian men!
    Press through toil and sorrow!
Spurn the night of fear, and then,—
    O, the glorious morrow!
Who will venture on the strife?
    Who will first begin it?
Who will seize the land of life?
    Warriors, up and win it!

ANON.

Sing ye to the Lord, for He hath triumphed gloriously.
Exodus, xv. 21.

SOUND the loud timbrel o'er Egypt's dark sea,
Jehovah hath triumphed, His people are free!
Sing, for the pride of the tyrant is broken:
His chariots and horsemen, all splendid and brave,

GENERAL HYMNS.

How vain was their boasting! the Lord hath but spoken,
And chariots and horsemen are sunk in the wave.
Sound the loud timbrel, o'er Egypt's dark sea,
Jehovah hath triumphed, His people are free!

Praise to the Conqueror, praise to the Lord;
His word was our arrow, His breath was our sword:
Who shall return to tell Egypt the story
Of those she sent forth in the hour of her pride?
The Lord hath looked out from His pillar of glory,
And all her brave thousands are dashed in the tide.
Sound the loud timbrel o'er Egypt's dark sea,
Jehovah hath triumphed, His people are free!

THOMAS MOORE.

*Ye shall receive a crown of glory that fadeth
not away.*
I. Peter, v. 4.

ART thou weary, art thou languid,
 Art thou sore distrest?
"Come to me," saith One, "and coming
     Be at rest!"

Hath He marks to lead me to Him,
 If He be my guide?
"In His feet and hands are wound-prints,
     And His side."

Hath He diadem as Monarch
   That His brow adorns?
"Yea, a crown, in very surety,
                        But of thorns.'

If I find Him, if I follow,
   What His guerdon here?
"Many a sorrow, many a labour,
                        Many a tear."

If I still hold closely to Him,
   What hath He at last?
"Sorrow vanquished, labour ended,
                        Jordan past."

If I ask Him to receive me,
   Will He say me nay?
"Not till earth, and not till heaven
                        Pass away."

Finding, following, keeping, struggling,
   Is He sure to bless?
"Angels, martyrs, prophets, virgins,
                        Answer, 'Yes!'"

He was bruised for our iniquities.
Isaiah, liii. 5.

THERE is a green hill far away
    Without a city wall,
Where the dear Lord was crucified
    Who died to save us all.

We may not know, we cannot tell
    What pains He had to bear,
But we believe it was for us
    He hung and suffered there.

He died that we might be forgiven,
    He died to make us good,
That we might go at last to Heaven,
    Saved by His precious blood.

There was no other good enough
    To pay the price of sin,
He only could unlock the gate
    Of Heaven, and let us in.

O, dearly, dearly has He loved,
    And we must love Him too,
And trust in His redeeming blood,
    And try His works to do.

ANON.

Watch ye, and pray always, that ye may be accounted worthy.
Luke, xxi. 36.

"CHRISTIAN! seek not yet repose,"
Hear thy guardian angel say;
Thou art in the midst of foes,
　　"Watch and pray."

Principalities and powers,
Mustering their unseen array,
Wait for thy unguarded hours:
　　"Watch and pray."

Gird thy heavenly armour on,
Wear it ever night and day;
Ambushed lies the evil one:
　　"Watch and pray."

Hear the victors who o'ercame;
Still they mark each warrior's way;
All with one sweet voice exclaim
　　"Watch and pray."

Hear, above all, hear thy Lord,
Him thou lovest to obey;
Hide within thy heart His word,
　　"Watch and pray."

Watch, as if on that alone
Hung the issue of the day;
Pray, that help may be sent down:
"Watch and pray."

ANON.

---

*The day of the Lord so cometh as a thief
in the night.*
I. Thessalonians, v. 2.

HASTE, traveller, haste! the night comes on,
And many a shining hour is gone;
The storm is gathering in the west,
And thou art far from home and rest;
   Haste, traveller, haste!

O far from home thy footsteps stray;
Christ is the Life, and Christ the Way;
And Christ the Light, thy setting Sun,
Sinks ere thy morning is begun;
   Haste, traveller, haste!

Awake, awake! pursue thy way
With steady course, while yet 't is day;
While thou art sleeping on the ground,
Danger and darkness gather round;
   Haste, traveller, haste!

The rising tempest sweeps the sky;
The rains descend, the winds are high;
The waters swell, and death and fear
Beset thy path, nor refuge near;
                Haste, traveller, haste!

O yes! a shelter you may gain,
A covert from the wind and rain,

A hiding-place, a rest, a home,
A refuge from the wrath to come;
   Haste, traveller, haste!

Then linger not in all the plain,
Flee for thy life, the mountain gain;
Look not behind, make no delay,
O speed thee, speed thee on thy way;
   Haste, traveller, haste!

Poor, lost, benighted soul! art thou
Willing to find salvation now?
There yet is hope; hear mercy's call;
Truth! Life! Light! Way! in Christ is all!
   Haste to Him, haste!

      WILLIAM BENGO COLLYER.

*Looking unto Jesus, the author and finisher
of our faith.*
      Hebrews, xii. 2.

GRACIOUS Spirit, dwell with me!
 I myself would gracious be,
  And with words that help and heal,
  Would Thy life in mine reveal,
And with actions bold and meek,
Would for Christ my Saviour speak.

Truthful Spirit, dwell with me!
I myself would truthful be:
By Thy wisdom kind and clear,
Let Thy life in mine appear,
And with actions brotherly
Speak my Lord's sincerity.

Tender Spirit, dwell with me!
I myself would tender be:
Shut my heart up like a flower
At temptation's darksome hour,
Open it when shines the Sun,
And His love by fragrance own.

Mighty Spirit, dwell with me!
I myself would mighty be:
Mighty so as to prevail
Where unaided man must fail,
Ever by a mighty hope
Pressing on, and bearing up.

Holy Spirit, dwell with me!
I myself would holy be:
Separate from sin, I would
Choose and cherish all things good,
And whatever I can be
Give to Him who gave me Thee!

THOMAS T. LYNCH.

GENERAL HYMNS.

I know whom I have believed, and am persuaded that He is able to keep that which I have committed unto Him.
II. Timothy, i. 12.

I WEEP, but not rebellious tears;
I mourn, but not in hopeless woe;
I droop, but not with doubtful fears;
For whom I 've trusted, Him I know:
Lord, I believe,—assuage my grief,
And help, O help my unbelief!

My days of youth and health are o'er,
My early friends are dead and gone;
And there are times it tries me sore
To think I 'm left on earth alone:
But then faith whispers, "'T is not so;
He will not leave nor let thee go."

Blind eyes! fond heart! that vainly sought
Enduring bliss in things of earth!
Remembering, but with transient thought,
My heavenly home, my second birth,
Till God in mercy broke at last
The bonds that held me down so fast.

As link by link was rent away,
My heart wept blood, so sharp the pain;
But I have lived to count this day,
That temporal loss, eternal gain:

For all that once detained me here
Now draws me to a holier sphere,—

A holier sphere, a happier place,
Where I shall know as I am known,
And see my Saviour face to face;
And meet, rejoicing, round His throne
The faithful few, made perfect there,
From earthly stain and mortal care.

CAROLINE SOUTHEY.

Go ye into all the world, and preach the Gospel to every creature.
Mark, xvi. 15.

THE heathen perish day by day,
Thousands on thousands pass away:
O Christians, to their rescue fly;
Preach Jesus to them ere they die.

Wealth, labour, talents freely give,
Yea, life itself, that they may live.
What hath your Saviour done for you?
And what for Him will ye not do?

Thou Spirit of the Lord, go forth;
Call in the south, wake up the north;
Of every clime, from sun to sun,
Gather God's children into one.

JAMES MONTGOMERY.

*Stand up and bless the Lord your God
for ever and ever.*
                        Nehemiah, ix. 5.

STAND up! stand up for Jesus,
  Ye soldiers of the Cross!
Lift high His royal banner,
  It must not suffer loss;
From vict'ry unto vict'ry
  His army shall He lead,
Till every foe is vanquished,
  And Christ is Lord indeed.

Stand up! stand up for Jesus!
  The trumpet-call obey;
Forth to the mighty conflict,
  In this His glorious day:
Ye that are men, now serve Him
  Against unnumbered foes;
Your courage rise with danger,
  And strength to strength oppose.

Stand up! stand up for Jesus!
  Stand in His strength alone;
The arm of flesh will fail you;
  Ye dare not trust your own;
Put on the Gospel armour,
  And, watching unto prayer,
Where duty calls, or danger,
  Be never wanting there.

Stand up! stand up for Jesus!
  The strife will not be long;
This day the noise of battle,
  The next the victor's song;
To him that overcometh,
  A crown of life shall be;
He with the King of Glory
  Shall reign eternally.

DUFFIELD.

We have turned every one to his own way.
Isaiah, liii. 6.

ALL we like sheep have gone astray,
  And left our Shepherd-guide;
We've wandered from the valley fair,
  To the bare mountain-side.
O, bring us back, Almighty God!
  Back to the flowery plain,
Where the clear, ever-living stream
  Of water flows again.

All we like sheep have gone astray,
  Have wandered far and wide
Into the world of care and cold,
  And cast our God aside.

O Shepherd, gather up Thy sheep!
  O, give the weary rest!
And grant that all our little lambs
  May nestle on Thy breast.

O, cleanse our souls from every sin,
  From each dull earthly stain!
That we may, through Thy holy love,
  To life be born again.
Then shall we sing with holy joy
  All glory to the Lamb,
And enter, free, with victor palms,
  The New Jerusalem.

G. W.

For I know that my Redeemer liveth.
Job, xix. 25.

AH! I shall soon be dying,
    Time swiftly glides away;
But on my Lord relying,
    I hail the happy day,—

The day when I must enter
    Upon a world unknown;
My helpless soul I venture
    On Jesus Christ alone.

He once a spotless victim,
    Upon Mount Calvary bled:
Jehovah did afflict Him,
    And bruise Him in my stead.

Hence all my hope arises,
    Unworthy as I am;
My soul most surely prizes
    The sin-atoning Lamb.

To Him by grace united,
    I joy in Him alone;
And now, by faith, delighted
    Behold Him on His throne.

GENERAL HYMNS.

There He is interceding
  For all who on Him rest;
The grace from Him proceeding
  Shall lead me to His breast.

Then with the saints in glory
  The grateful song I'll raise,
And chant my blissful story
  In high seraphic lays.

JOHN RYLAND.

Lord, make me to know the measure of my days, that I may know how frail I am.
Psalm xxxix. 4.

I HOPED that with the brave and strong
  My portioned task might lie;
To toil amid the busy throng
  With purpose pure and high;
But God has fixed another part,
  And He has fixed it well;
I said so with my breaking heart
  When first this trouble fell.

These weary hours will not be lost,
  These days of misery,
These nights of darkness, tempest-tost,—
  Can I but turn to Thee;

With secret labour to sustain
  In patience every blow,
To gather fortitude from pain,
  And holiness from woe.

If Thou shouldst bring me back to life,
  More humble I should be,
More wise, more strengthened for the strife,
  More apt to lean on Thee :
Should death be standing at the gate,
  Thus should I keep my vow :
But, Lord ! whatever be my fate,
  O let me serve Thee now !

ANNE BRONTË.

He giveth His beloved sleep.

Psalm cxxvii. 2.

CALM on the bosom of thy God,
  Fair spirit, rest thee now !
E'en while with us thy footsteps trod,
  His seal was on thy brow.

Dust to its narrow house beneath !
  Soul to its home on high !
They that have seen thy look in death,
  No more need fear to die.

FELICIA D. HEMANS.

GENERAL HYMNS.

I live by the faith of the Son of God, who loved me, and gave Himself for me.
Galatians, ii. 20.

I LAY my sins on Jesus,
    The spotless Lamb of God;
He bears them all, and frees us
    From the accursèd load.
I bring my guilt to Jesus,
    To wash my crimson stains
White in His blood most precious,
    Till not a spot remains.

I tell my wants to Jesus;
    All fulness dwells in Him:
He heals all my diseases;
    He doth my soul redeem.
I lay my griefs on Jesus,
    My burdens and my cares;
He from them all releases;
    He all my sorrows shares.

I rest my soul on Jesus,
    This weary soul of mine;
His right hand me embraces;
    I on His breast recline.
I love the Name of Jesus,
    Immanuel, Christ, the Lord;

Like fragrance on the breezes
   His goodness forth is poured.

I long to be like Jesus,
   Meek, loving, lowly, mild;
I long to be like Jesus,
   The Father's holy child.
I long to be with Jesus
   Amid the heavenly throng,
To sing, with saints, His praises,
   And learn the angels' song.

HORATIUS BONAR.

God is able to make all grace abound toward you.
II. Corinthians, ix. 8.

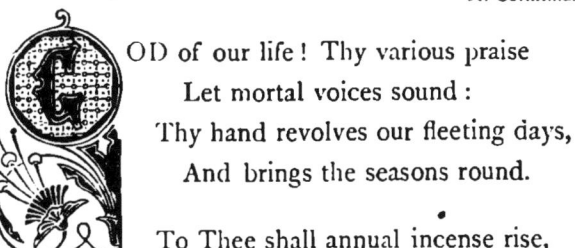

GOD of our life! Thy various praise
   Let mortal voices sound:
Thy hand revolves our fleeting days,
   And brings the seasons round.

To Thee shall annual incense rise,
   Our Father and our Friend;
While annual mercies from the skies
   In genial streams descend.

In every scene of life, Thy care
   In every age we see;

And constant as Thy favours are,
  So let our praises be.

Still may Thy love, in every scene,
  In every age appear;
And let the same compassion deign
  To bless the opening year.

O keep this foolish heart of mine
  From anxious passion free;
Each comfort teach me to resign,
  And trust my all to Thee.

If mercy smile, let mercy bring
  My wandering soul to God;
And in affliction I will sing
  If Thou wilt bless the rod.

OTTIWELL HEGINBOTHAM.

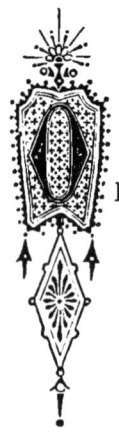

Give us day by day our daily bread.
Luke, xi. 3.

O KING of earth, and air, and sea!
  The hungry ravens cry to Thee;
  To Thee the scaly tribes, that sweep
  The bosom of the boundless deep:
  To Thee the lions roaring call;
  The common Father, kind to all:

Then grant Thy servants, Lord, we pray,
Our daily bread from day to day.

The fishes may for food complain,
The ravens spread their wings in vain,

The roaring lions lack and pine;
But, God, Thou carest still for Thine:
Thy bounteous hand with food can bless
The bleak and lonely wilderness;
And Thou hast taught us, Lord, to pray
For daily bread from day to day.

And O! when through the wilds we roam
That part us from our heavenly home;
When, lost in danger, want, and woe,
Our faithless tears begin to flow;
Do Thou the gracious comfort give,
By which alone the soul may live,
And grant Thy servants, Lord, we pray,
The bread of life from day to day!

BISHOP REGINALD HEBER.

Behold the works of the Lord. He maketh wars to cease.
Psalm xlvi. 8, 9.

O GOD of love, O King of peace,
  Make wars throughout the world to cease;
The wrath of sinful man restrain:
Give peace, O God, give peace again.

Remember, Lord, Thy works of old,
The wonders that our fathers told,

Remember not our sins' dark stain :
Give peace, O God, give peace again.

Whom shall we trust but Thee, O Lord?
Where rest but on Thy faithful Word?
None ever called on Thee in vain :
Give peace, O God, give peace again.

Where saints and angels dwell above,
All hearts are knit in holy love ;
O bind us in that heavenly chain :
Give peace, O God, give peace again.

ANON.

Surely He hath borne our griefs, and carried our sorrows.
Isaiah, liii. 4.

FROM the cross uplifted high,
Where the Saviour deigns to die,
What melodious sounds I hear,
Bursting on my ravished ear !—
"Love's redeeming work is done ;
Come and welcome, sinner, come.

"Sprinkled now with blood the throne :
Why beneath thy burdens groan?
On my piercèd body laid,
Justice owns the ransom paid ;

GENERAL HYMNS.

Bow the knee, and kiss the Son;
Come and welcome, sinner, come.

"Spread for thee the festal board,
See, with richest dainties stored;
To thy Father's bosom pressed,
Yet again a child confessed,
Never from His house to roam—
Come and welcome, sinner, come.

"Soon the days of life shall end;
Lo! I come, your Saviour, Friend,
Safe your spirit to convey
To the realms of endless day;
Up to my eternal home,
Come and welcome, sinner, come."

THOMAS HAWEIS.

Guide me with Thy counsel, and afterward receive me to glory.
Psalm lxxiii. 24.

GUIDE me, O Thou great Jehovah!
    Pilgrim through this barren land;
    I am weak, but Thou art mighty;
Hold me with Thy powerful hand!
    Bread of Heaven! Bread of Heaven!
Feed me now and evermore!

Open now the crystal fountain,
   Whence the healing streams do flow;
Let the fiery cloudy pillar
   Lead me all my journey through;
      Strong Deliverer! Strong Deliverer!
Be Thou still my Strength and Shield!

When I tread the verge of Jordan,
   Bid my anxious fears subside;
Death of death, and hell's destruction,
   Land me safe on Canaan's side.
      Songs of praises, songs of praises,
I will ever give to Thee!

                              WILLIAM WILLIAMS.

*The Lord of Hosts is with us; the God of Jacob
is our refuge.*
                              Psalm xlvi. 11.

GOD is our refuge in distress,
   Our shield of hope through every care,
   Our Shepherd watching us to bless,
   And therefore will we not despair;
      Although the mountains shake,
      And hills their place forsake,
      And billows o'er them break,
         Yet still will we not fear,—
   For Thou, O God, art ever near.

God is our hope and strength in woe,
Through earth He maketh wars to cease,
His power breaketh spear and bow,
His mercy sendeth endless peace;

Then though the earth remove,
And storms rage high above,
And seas tempestuous prove,
Yet still will we not fear,—
The Lord of Hosts is ever near.

MARTIN LUTHER.

Pray unto the Lord for it, for in the peace thereof shall ye have peace.
Jeremiah, xxix. 7.

LORD, while for all mankind we pray,
Of every clime and coast,
O hear us for our native land,—
The land we love the most.

Our fathers' sepulchres are here,
   And here our kindred dwell;
Our children too: how should we love
   Another land so well?

O guard our shores from every foe,
   With peace our borders bless;
With prosperous times our cities crown,
   Our fields with plenteousness.

Unite us in the sacred love
   Of knowledge, truth, and Thee;
And let our hills and valleys shout
   The songs of liberty.

Here may religion, pure and mild,
   Upon our Sabbaths smile,
And piety and virtue reign,
   And bless our native isle.

Lord of the nations, thus to Thee
   Our country we commend;
Be Thou her refuge and her trust,
   Her everlasting Friend.

                       J. REYNELL WREFORD.

*He shall cover thee with His feathers, and
under His wings shalt thou trust.*
                               Psalm xci. 4.

GOD of Bethel, by whose hand
  Thy people still are fed,
Who through this weary pilgrimage
  Hast all our fathers led;

Our vows, our prayers, we now present
  Before Thy throne of grace;
God of our fathers! be the God
  Of their succeeding race.

Through each perplexing path of life
  Our wandering footsteps guide;
Give us each day our daily bread,
  And raiment fit provide.

O spread Thy covering wings around
  Till all our wanderings cease,
And at our Father's loved abode
  Our souls arrive in peace!

Such blessings from Thy gracious hand
  Our humble prayers implore;
And Thou shalt be our chosen God,
  And portion evermore.

VARIATION BY JOHN LOGAN,
FROM PHILIP DODDRIDGE.

Who is like unto the Lord our God, who dwelleth on high!
Psalm cxiii. 5.

COME, Thou fount of every blessing,
   Tune my heart to sing Thy grace;
Streams of mercy never-ceasing
   Call for songs of loudest praise.
Teach me some celestial measure,
   Sung by ransomed hosts above;
O! the vast, the boundless treasure
   Of my Lord's unchanging love.

Here I raise my Ebenezer;
   Hither by Thy help I'm come;
And I hope, by Thy good pleasure,
   Safely to arrive at home.
Jesus sought me when a stranger,
   Wandering from the fold of God;
He, to rescue me from danger,
   Interposed His precious blood.

O! to grace how great a debtor
   Daily I'm constrained to be!
Let that grace, Lord, like a fetter,
   Bind my wandering heart to Thee.
Prone to wander; Lord, I feel it;
   Prone to leave the God I love;
Take my heart, O take and seal it,
   Seal it from Thy courts above.

ROBERT ROBINSON.

Lead me, O Lord, in Thy righteousness; make Thy way straight before my face.
Psalm v. 8.

JESUS, still lead on,
   Till our rest be won;
And although the way be cheerless,
We will follow, calm and fearless:
   Guide us by Thy hand
   To our Fatherland.

If the way be drear,
   If the foe be near,
Let not faithless fears o'ertake us,
Let not faith and hope forsake us;
   For, through many a foe,
   To our home we go.

When we seek relief
   From a long-felt grief;
When oppressed by new temptations,
Lord, increase and perfect patience;
   Show us that bright shore
   Where we weep no more.

Jesus, still lead on
   Till our rest be won:

Heavenly Leader, still direct us,
Still support, console, protect us,
　　Till we safely stand
　　In our Fatherland.

ZINZENDORF.

Thou hast created all things, and for Thy pleasure they are and were created.

Revelation, iv. 11.

HOLY, holy, holy, Lord
　God of Hosts, when heaven and earth,
　Out of darkness, at Thy word,
　Issued into glorious birth,
All Thy works before Thee stood,
And Thine eye beheld them good;
While they sang, with sweet accord,
Holy, holy, holy Lord.

Holy, holy, holy Three,
One Jehovah evermore,
Father, Son, and Spirit, we,
Dust and ashes, would adore:
Lightly by the world esteemed,
From that world by Thee redeemed,
Sing we here, with glad accord,
Holy holy, holy Lord.

Holy, holy, holy, all
Heaven's triumphant choir shall sing;
When the ransomed nations fall
At the footstool of their King,
Then shall saints and seraphim,
Harps and voices swell one hymn,
Round the throne with full accord,
Holy, holy, holy Lord.

JAMES MONTGOMERY.

My grace is sufficient for thee.
II. Corinthians, xii. 9.

O LORD, how happy should we be
If we could cast our care on Thee,
  If we from self could rest;
And feel at heart that One above
In perfect wisdom, perfect love,
  Is working for the best.

How far from this our daily life,
How oft disturbed by anxious strife,
  By sudden wild alarms;
O, could we but relinquish all
Our earthly props, and simply fall
  On Thine almighty arms!

Could we but kneel and cast our load,
E'en while we pray, upon our God,
  Then rise with lightened cheer;
Sure that the Father, who is nigh
To still the famished ravens' cry,
  Will hear in that we fear.

We cannot trust Him as we should,
So chafes weak nature's restless mood

To cast its peace away;
But birds and flowerets round us preach,
All, all the present evil teach
Sufficient for the day.

Lord, make these faithless hearts of ours
Such lessons learn from birds and flowers;
Make them from self to cease;
Leave all things to a Father's will,
And taste, before Him lying still,
E'en in affliction, peace.

JOSEPH ANSTICE.

---

*Trust ye in the Lord for ever, for in the Lord
Jehovah is everlasting strength.*
Isaiah, xxvi. 4.

KING of kings, before whose throne
　　The angels bow, no gift can we
Present that is indeed our own,
　　Since heaven and earth belong to Thee:
Yet this our souls through grace impart,
The offering of a thankful heart.

O Jesu, set at God's right hand,
　　With Thine eternal Father plead
For all Thy loyal-hearted band,
　　Who still on earth Thy succour need;

For them in weakness strength provide,
And through the world their footsteps guide.

O Holy Spirit, Fount of breath,
  Whose comforts never fail nor fade,
Vouchsafe the life that knows no death,
  Vouchsafe the light that knows no shade;
And grant that we through all our days
May share Thy gifts, and sing Thy praise.

VARIATION BY THOMAS DARLING,
FROM JOHN QUARLES.

Shew us Thy mercy, O Lord, and grant us Thy salvation.
Psalm lxxxv. 7.

O LORD, turn not Thy face away
  From them that lowly lie,
Lamenting sore their sinful life
  With tears and bitter cry;
Thy mercy-gates are open wide
  To them that mourn their sin;
O shut them not against us, Lord,
  But let us enter in.

We need not to confess our fault,
  For surely Thou canst tell;
What we have done, and what we are
  Thou knowest very well;

GENERAL HYMNS.

Wherefore, to beg and to entreat,
  With tears we come to Thee,
As children that have done amiss
  Fall at their father's knee.

And need we then, O Lord, repeat
  The blessing which we crave,
When Thou dost know, before we speak,
  The thing that we would have?
Mercy, O Lord, mercy we ask,
  This is the total sum;
For mercy, Lord, is all our prayer;
  O let Thy mercy come!

VARIATION BY BISHOP REGINALD HEBER,
FROM JOHN MARDLEY.

---

*Thanks unto the Father, which hath made us meet to be partakers
of the inheritance of the saints in light.*
Colossians, i. 12.

ON wings of faith, mount up, my soul, and rise;
View thine inheritance beyond the skies;
Nor heart can think, nor mortal tongue can tell
What endless pleasures in those mansions dwell:
There our Redeemer lives, all bright and glorious,
O'er sin, and death, and hell He reigns victorious.

No gnawing grief, no sad heart-rending pain,
In that blest country can admission gain;

No sorrow there, no soul-tormenting fear,
  For God's own hand shall wipe the falling tear:
There our Redeemer lives all bright and glorious,
O'er sin, and death, and hell He reigns victorious.

Before the throne a crystal river glides,
  Immortal verdure decks its cheerful sides;
There the fair tree of life majestic rears
  Its blooming head, and sovereign virtue bears:
There our Redeemer lives, all bright and glorious,
O'er sin, and death, and hell He reigns victorious.

No rising sun his needless beams displays,
  No sickly moon emits her feeble rays;
The Godhead there celestial glory sheds,
  The exalted Lamb eternal radiance spreads:
There our Redeemer lives, all bright and glorious,
O'er sin, and death, and hell He reigns victorious.

One distant glimpse my eager passion fires!—
  Jesus! to Thee my longing soul aspires!
When shall I at my heavenly home arrive,—
  When leave this earth, and when begin to live?
For there my Saviour lives, all bright and glorious,
O'er sin, and death, and hell He reigns victorious.

JOSEPH STRAPHAN.

GENERAL HYMNS.

Let us offer the sacrifice of praise to God continually.
Hebrews, xiii. 15.

JESUS, with all Thy saints above
My tongue would bear her part,
Would sound aloud Thy saving love,
And sing Thy bleeding heart.

All glory to the dying Lamb,
And never-ceasing praise,
While angels live to know His Name,
Or saints to feel His grace.

ISAAC WATTS.

*Remember me, O Lord, with the favour that Thou bearest
unto Thy people.*
Psalm cvi. 4.

O THOU from whom all goodness flows,
   I lift my heart to Thee;
In all my sorrows, conflicts, woes,
   Dear Lord, remember me!

When groaning on my burdened heart
   My sins lie heavily,
My pardon speak, new peace impart,
   In love remember me!

Temptations sore obstruct my way,
   And ills I cannot flee:
Oh, give me strength, Lord, as my day;
   For good remember me!

Distrest in pain, disease, and grief,
   This feeble body see:
Grant patience, rest, and kind relief;
   Hear, and remember me!

If on my face, for Thy dear Name,
   Shame and reproaches be;
All hail reproach, and welcome shame,
   If Thou remember me!

The hour is near; consigned to death
   I own the just decree:
"Saviour!" with my last parting breath
   I'll cry, "remember me!"

                     THOMAS HAWEIS.

Our Lord Jesus Christ, by whom we have access by faith into this grace.
                 Romans, v. 1, 2.

LORD of the vast creation,
   Support of worlds unknown,
Desire of every nation,
   Behold us at Thy throne.
We come, for mercy crying,
   Through Thine atoning blood;
And, on Thy grace relying,
   We seek each promised good.

We bless that condescension
   Which brought Thee down to earth,
Of which the seers made mention
   Who prophesied Thy birth.
We celebrate the glory
   That marked Thy wondrous way,
And own the joyful story
   Which claims this hallowed day.

O! when shall Thy salvation
Be known through every land,
And men in every station
Obey Thy great command?
In God's own Son believing,
From sin may they be free;
And Gospel grace receiving,
Find life and peace in Thee.

BULMER.

---

*Let Thine hand help me, for I have
chosen Thy precepts.*
Psalm cxix. 173.

HELP us, Lord, each hour of need,
　Thy heavenly succour give;
Help us in thought and word and deed,
　Each hour on earth we live.

O help us, when our spirits bleed
　With contrite anguish sore;
And when our hearts are cold and dead,
　O help us, Lord, the more.

O help us, through the prayer of faith,
　More firmly to believe;
For still the more Thy servant hath,
　The more shall he receive.

O help us, Saviour, from on high,—
We know no help but Thee;
O help us so to live and die,
As Thine in Heaven to be.

HENRY HART MILMAN.

*The Lord shall be unto Thee an everlasting
light, and thy God thy glory.*

Isaiah, lx. 19.

THE leaves around me falling,
    Are preaching of decay;
The hollow winds are calling,
    "Come, pilgrim, come away."
The day in night declining,
    Says I too must decline;
The year is life resigning—
    Its lot foreshadows mine.

The light my path surrounding,
    The love to which I cling,
The hopes within me bounding,
    The joys that round me sing,
All melt like stars of even
    Before the morning's ray,
Pass upward into Heaven,
    And chide at my delay.

The friends, gone there before me,
   Are calling from on high,
And joyous angels o'er me
   Tempt sweetly to the sky.
"Why wait," they say, "and wither,
   'Mid scenes of death and sin?
O rise to glory hither
   And find true life begin!"

I hear the invitation,
   And fain would rise and come,
A sinner, to salvation;
   An exile, to his home.

GENERAL HYMNS.

But while I here must linger,
Thus, thus let all I see
Point out with faithful finger,
To Heaven, O Lord, and Thee.

HENRY FRANCIS LYTE.

Yea, Lord, Thou knowest that I love Thee.
John, xxi. 16.

MY God, I love Thee, not because
I hope for Heaven thereby;
Nor because they who love Thee not
Are lost eternally.

Thou, O my Jesus, Thou didst me
Upon the cross embrace;
For me didst bear the nails and spear,
And manifold disgrace;

And griefs, and torments numberless,
And sweat of agony;
E'en death itself,—and all for one
Who was Thine enemy.

Then why, O blessed Jesus Christ,
Should I not love Thee well?
Not for the sake of winning Heaven,
Or of escaping hell.

Not with the hope of gaining aught,
　　Nor seeking a reward;
But as Thyself has lovèd me,
　　O ever-loving Lord.

E'en so I love Thee, and will love,
　　And in Thy praise will sing,
Because Thou art my loving God,
　　And my redeeming King.

FRANCIS XAVIER.
TRANSLATED BY E. CASWELL.

Whatsoever ye do, do it heartily, as to the Lord, knowing that of the Lord ye shall receive the reward.
Colossians, iii. 23, 24.

TEACH me, my God and King,
　　In all things Thee to see;
And what I do in anything,
　　To do it as for Thee.

To scorn the senses' sway,
　　While still to Thee I tend:
In all I do be Thou the Way,
　　In all be Thou the End.

All may of Thee partake:
　　Nothing so small can be,
But draws, when acted for Thy sake,
　　Greatness and worth from Thee.

GENERAL HYMNS.

If done beneath Thy laws,
E'en servile labours shine :
Hallowed is toil, if this the cause,
The meanest work divine.

GEORGE HERBERT.

Ho, every one that thirsteth, come ye to the waters : without money and without price.
Isaiah, lv. 1.

I HEARD the voice of Jesus say,
"Come unto me and rest;
Lay down, thou weary one, lay down
Thy head upon my breast!"
I came to Jesus as I was,
Weary, and worn, and sad;
I found in Him a resting-place,
And He has made me glad.

I heard the voice of Jesus say,
"Behold! I freely give
The living water; thirsty one,
Stoop down, and drink, and live!"
I came to Jesus, and I drank
Of that life-giving stream;
My thirst was quenched, my soul revived,
And now I live in Him.

I heard the voice of Jesus say,
  "I am this dark world's light;
Look unto me, thy morn shall rise
  And all thy day be bright."
I looked to Jesus, and I found
  In Him my Star, my Sun;
And in that light of life I'll walk
  Till travelling days are done.

HORATIUS BONAR.

God knoweth your hearts.
Luke, xvi. 15.

GOD is a Spirit, just and wise,
  He sees our inmost mind;
In vain to Heaven we raise our cries,
And leave our souls behind.

Nothing but truth before His throne
   With honour can appear;
The painted hypocrites are known
   Through the disguise they wear.

Their lifted eyes salute the skies,
   Their bending knees the ground;
But God abhors the sacrifice,
   Where not the heart is found.

Lord, search my thoughts and try my ways,
   And make my soul sincere;
Then shall I stand before Thy face,
   And find acceptance there.

ISAAC WATTS.

All Thy works shall praise Thee, O Lord.
Psalm cxlv. 10.

THE strain upraise of joy and praise,	Alleluia!
To the glory of their King	
Shall the ransomed people sing	Alleluia!
And the choirs that dwell on high	
Shall re-echo through the sky	Alleluia!
They in the rest of Paradise who dwell,	
The blessèd ones, with joy the chorus swell,	Alleluia!

The planets beaming on their heavenly way,
The shining constellations join, and say,   Alleluia!

    Ye clouds that onward sweep,
        Ye winds on pinions light,
    Ye thunders echoing loud and deep,
        Ye lightnings, wildly bright,
    In sweet consent unite your   Alleluia!

    Ye floods and ocean billows,
        Ye storms and winter snow,
    Ye days of cloudless beauty,
        Hoar frost and Summer glow,
    Ye groves that wave in Spring,
    And glorious forests, sing,   Alleluia!

First let the birds, with painted plumage gay,
Exalt their great Creator's praise, and say,   Alleluia!

Then let the beasts of earth, with varying strain,
Join in creation's hymn, and cry again,   Alleluia!

Here let the mountains thunder forth sonorous,   Alleluia!
There let the valleys sing in gentler chorus,   Alleluia!

Thou jubilant abyss of ocean, cry,   Alleluia!
Ye tracts of earth and continents, reply,   Alleluia!
To God, who all creation made,
The frequent hymn be duly paid: Alleluia!

This is the strain, the eternal strain, the Lord
    Almighty loves :   Alleluia!
This is the song, the heavenly song, that Christ
    the King approves :   Alleluia!

Wherefore we sing, both heart and voice awaking, Alleluia!
And children's voices echo, answer making,   Alleluia!

      Now from all men be outpoured
      Alleluia to the Lord;
      With Alleluia evermore
      The Son and Spirit we adore.

Praise be done to the Three in One,
      Alleluia! Alleluia! Alleluia! Amen.

                                        REV. J. M. NEALE, D.D.

INDEX

	Author.	Page
Abide with me! fast falls the eventide	Henry Francis Lyte	250
Accept, my God, my evening song	Simon Browne (Variation from Isaac Watts.)	249
According to Thy gracious Word	James Montgomery	393
Again returns the day of holy rest	John Mason	91
Again the Lord of Life and Light	Anna Lætitia Barbauld	439
Ah! I shall soon be dying	John Ryland	577
Alleluia! alleluia!	Anon	431
All people that on earth do dwell	John Hopkins	29
All praise to Him who dwells in bliss	Charles Wesley	282
All we like sheep have gone astray	G. W.	575
And can it be that I should gain	Charles Wesley	129
Another year hath fled, renew	Arthur Tozer Russell	316
Approach, my soul, the mercy-seat	John Newton	54
Art thou weary, art thou languid	Anon	564
As when the weary traveller gains	John Newton	512
At evening time let there be light	Anon	266
A thousand years have fleeted	Frances Elizabeth Cox (From Frederic de la Motte Fouqué.)	547
Awake, and sing the song	Martin Madan (Variation from William Hammond.)	212
Awake, my soul, and with the sun	Bishop Thomas Ken	236
Awake, my soul, in joyful lays	Samuel Medley	211
Awake, ye saints, and raise your eyes	Philip Doddridge	318
Awake, ye saints, awake!	Henry Francis Lyte	94
Before Jehovah's awful throne	Isaac Watts	3
Behold, a Stranger's at the door	Joseph Grigg	534
Behold! how glorious is yon sky	Nicolai	148
Behold, the sun, that seemed but now	George Wither	247
Behold the throne of grace	John Newton	45
Blessed Jesus, at Thy Word	Catherine Winkworth (From the German of Clausnitzer.)	57

INDEX.

	Author.	Page
Bless, O Lord, the opening year	John Newton	323
Blest are the humble souls that see	Isaac Watts	187
Blest be Thy love, dear Lord	John Austin	132
Blow ye the trumpet, blow!	Charles Wesley	449
Bread of the world, in mercy broken	Bishop Reginald Heber	391
Brightest and best of the sons of the morning	Bishop Reginald Heber	161
Brother, thou art gone before us, and thy saintly soul is flown	Henry Hart Milman	340

Calm on the bosom of Thy God	Felicia D. Hemans	579
Christian, seek not yet repose	Anon	567
Christ, my hidden life, appear	Charles Wesley	164
Christ the Lord is risen again	Bohemian Brethren	434
Christ the Lord is risen to-day	Charles Wesley	429
Christ the Lord is risen to-day	Anon	442
Christ, whose glory fills the skies	Charles Wesley	227
Christ will gather in His own	Anon	343
Come, all harmonious tongues	Isaac Watts	445
Come, Father, Son, and Holy Ghost	Charles Wesley	379
Come, my soul, thy suit prepare	John Newton	41
Come, O come! in pious lays	George Wither	8
Come, O thou Traveller unknown	Charles Wesley	538
Come, take my yoke, the Saviour said	Robert Smith	531
Come, Thou almighty King	Martin Madan	79
Come, Thou fount of every blessing	Robert Robinson	591
Come, we that love the Lord	Isaac Watts	200
Come, ye thankful people, come	Henry Alford	309
Come ye, whose willing feet	Hon. Baptist Noel	514
Commit thou all thy griefs (From Paul Gerhardt.)	John Wesley	218
Communion of my Saviour's blood	James Montgomery	398
Compared with Christ, in all beside	Augustus M. Toplady	191
Creator Spirit! by whose aid (Paraphrased by John Dryden.)	Charlemagne	559

Day of anger, that dread Day	Henry Alford	348
Day of Judgment, day of wonders!	John Newton	356
Dearest of names, our Lord, our King!	Samuel Medley	433
Deathless principle, arise!	Augustus M. Toplady	327
Do not I love Thee, O my Lord?	Philip Doddridge	171

Earth to earth, and dust to dust	John Hampden Gurney	334
Ere another Sabbath's close	Gerard Thomas Noel	89
Eternal Father, strong to save	Anon	532
Eternal Source of every joy	Philip Doddridge	287
Eternity, eternity (From an old German Hymn.)	Dr. H. W. Dulcken	519

INDEX.

	Author.	Page
Fain would my thoughts fly up to Thee	JOHN AUSTIN	144
Faith! 't is a precious grace	BENJAMIN BEDDOME	110
Far from my heavenly home	HENRY FRANCIS LYTE	162
Far from the world, O Lord, I flee	WILLIAM COWPER	193
Father of life and light	S. FLETCHER	244
Father, whate'er of earthly bliss	ANNE STEELE	544
Father, when we bend the knee	ANON	56
Fierce passions discompose the mind	WILLIAM COWPER	139
For ever here my rest shall be	CHARLES WESLEY	403
For ever to behold Him shine	JOSEPH SWAIN	515
For ever with the Lord!	JAMES MONTGOMERY	222
Forth in Thy Name, O Lord, I go	CHARLES WESLEY	243
For Thy mercy and Thy grace	HENRY DOWNTON	322
Fountain of mercy! God of love	ANNE FLOWERDEW	290
Friend after friend departs	JAMES MONTGOMERY	525
From all that dwell below the skies	ISAAC WATTS	477
From Egypt's bondage come	THOMAS KELLY	137
From Greenland's icy mountains	Bishop REGINALD HEBER	463
From the cross uplifted high	THOMAS HAWEIS	585
Give me the wings of faith to rise	ISAAC WATTS	501
Glorious things of Thee are spoken	JOHN NEWTON	486
Glory to God on high	JAMES ALLEN	557
Glory to Thee, my God, this night	Bishop THOMAS KEN	268
God is a Spirit, just and wise	ISAAC WATTS	609
God is gone up on high	CHARLES WESLEY	446
God is our refuge in distress	MARTIN LUTHER	587
God moves in a mysterious way	WILLIAM COWPER	19
God of my life, to Thee I call	WILLIAM COWPER	45
God of our health, our Life, our Light	Bishop RICHARD MANT	388
God of our life! Thy various praise	OTTIWELL HEGINBOTHAM	581
God of that glorious gift of grace	JOHN S. B. MONSELL	386
God of the morning, at whose voice	ISAAC WATTS	235
God that madest earth and Heaven	Bishop REGINALD HEBER	285
God the Father, whose creation	ANON	302
Go to dark Gethsemane	JAMES MONTGOMERY	411
Go up, go up, my heart	HORATIUS BONAR	146
Go, worship at Immanuel's feet	ISAAC WATTS	175
Gracious Spirit, dwell with me	THOMAS T. LYNCH	570
Great Father of mankind	PHILIP DODDRIDGE	95
Great Giver of all good, to Thee again	ANON	304
Great God, as seasons disappear	EDMUND BUTCHER	303
Great God, we sing that mighty hand	PHILIP DODDRIDGE	311
Great God, what do I see and hear?	MARTIN LUTHER	353
Guide me, O Thou great Jehovah!	WILLIAM WILLIAMS	567
Hail, morning known among the blest	Dr. WARDLAW	65
Hail, Thou once despised Jesus!	JOHN BAKEWELL	443

INDEX.

	Author.	Page
Hallelujah! song of gladness	*Thirteenth Century*	141
Happy soul, thy days are ended	CHARLES WESLEY	326
Happy the home, when God is there	ANON	47
Hark! hark, my soul, angelic songs are swelling...	F. W. FABER, D.D.	457
Hark, my soul, how everything	JOHN AUSTIN	26
Hark, my soul! it is the Lord	WILLIAM COWPER	99
Hark, the glad sound! the Saviour comes	PHILIP DODDRIDGE	371
Hark, the herald angels sing	CHARLES WESLEY	359
Hark! the song of Jubilee	JAMES MONTGOMERY	460
Hark! the sound of holy voices	ANON	489
Hark! the voice of love and mercy	JONATHAN EVANS	426
Harp, awake! tell out the story	HENRY DOWNTON	314
Haste, traveller, haste! the night comes on	WILLIAM BENGO COLLYER	568
Hear, gracious God! a sinner's cry	SAMUEL MEDLEY	147
Hear my prayer, O heavenly Father	HARRIETT PARR	252
Heavenly Father, may Thy love	GUEST	389
Here behold me as I cast me	CATHERINE WINKWORTH	133
High in yonder realms of light	RAFFLES	479
Holy, holy, holy Lord	JAMES MONTGOMERY	593
Holy, Holy, Holy! Lord God Almighty	Bishop REGINALD HEBER	31
Hosanna to the living Lord	Bishop REGINALD HEBER	549
How blest the righteous when he dies!	ANNA LÆTITIA BARBAULD	330
How blest the sacred tie that binds	ANNA LÆTITIA BARBAULD	436
How bright these glorious spirits shine	WILLIAM CAMERON	499
How rich are thy provisions, Lord!	ISAAC WATTS	406
How sweet, how heavenly is the sight	JOSEPH SWAIN	189
How sweet the Name of Jesus sounds	JOHN NEWTON	166
How swift the torrent rolls	PHILIP DODDRIDGE	358
How vast the treasure we possess	ISAAC WATTS	203
How welcome to the saints, when pressed	JOHN NEWTON	86

I heard the voice of Jesus say	HORATIUS BONAR	608
I hoped that with the brave and strong	ANNE BRÖNTE	578
I lay my sins on Jesus	HORATIUS BONAR	580
I love Thy kingdom, Lord	DWIGHT	469
I need Thee, precious Jesu	ANON	153
Interval of grateful shade	PHILIP DODDRIDGE	271
In that book so old and holy	Dr. H. W. DULCKEN	474
In Thy Name, O Lord, assembling	THOMAS KELLY	90
In token that thou shalt not fear	Dean ALFORD	377
I praise the earth, in beauty seen	Bishop REGINALD HEBER	142
I sing th' almighty power of God	ISAAC WATTS	21
I sing the birth was born to-night	BEN JONSON	375
It came upon the midnight clear	EDMUND H. SEARS	367
It is the Sabbath morning now	ANON	73
I weep, but not rebellious tears	CAROLINE SOUTHEY	572
I will praise Thee every day	WILLIAM COWPER	210

INDEX

Title	Author	Page
Jehovah reigns, His throne is high	ISAAC WATTS	16
Jerusalem, my happy home!	ANON. F. B. P.	491
Jesu! behold, the wise from far	JOHN WESLEY (Variation from John Austin.)	451
Jesu, lover of my soul	CHARLES WESLEY	102
Jesu, my strength, my hope	CHARLES WESLEY	123
Jesus, cast a look on me	JOHN BERRIDGE	59
Jesus Christ is risen to-day, Hallelujah!	ANON (Last stanza by Charles Wesley.)	438
Jesus, I my cross have taken	HENRY FRANCIS LYTE	111
Jesus! lead us with Thy power	WILLIAM WILLIAMS	541
Jesus lives! no longer now	ELECTRESS OF BRANDNBRG	461
Jesus, Lord, we look to Thee	CHARLES WESLEY	163
Jesus, my all, to Heaven is gone	JOHN CENNICK	168
Jesus shall reign where'er the sun	ISAAC WATTS	476
Jesus, still lead on	ZINZENDORF	592
Jesus, the very thought of Thee	ST. BERNARD	199
Jesus, Thou Joy of loving hearts	RAY PALMER (From St. Bernard.)	392
Jesus, Thy boundless love to me	PAUL GERHARDT	182
Jesus, where'er Thy people meet	WILLIAM COWPER	81
Jesus, who for us didst bear	"People's Hymnal"	418
Jesus, with all Thy saints above	ISAAC WATTS	600
Joy is a fruit that will not grow	JOHN NEWTON	208
Joy to the world! the Lord is come	ISAAC WATTS	361
Just as I am—without one plea	CHARLOTTE ELLIOTT	118
Lamb of God, whose bleeding love	CHARLES WESLEY	404
Leave all to God	CATHERINE WINKWORTH (Translated from Anton Ulrich, Duke of Brunswick.)	107
Let all the world in every corner sing	GEORGE HERBERT	29
Let me be with Thee where Thou art	CHARLOTTE ELLIOTT	152
Let our choir new anthems raise	ANON	562
Lift our voices now in song	GEORGE WOOLER	459
Lo! God is here! let us adore	JOHN WESLEY (From Gerhard Tersteegen.)	87
Lo! He comes! let all adore Him!	THOMAS KELLY	463
Lo! He comes, with clouds descending	MARTIN MADAN (From Charles Wesley and John Cennick.)	355
Lo! He comes, with clouds descending	THOMAS OLIVERS	345
Lo! on the inglorious tree	Ancient Hymn	417
Lord, fill my heart with joyful song	ANON	542
Lord, from my bed again I rise	BARTHOLOMEW	242
Lord God of morning and of night	FRANCIS TURNER PALGRAVE	234
Lord, have mercy when we pray	HENRY HART MILMAN	48
Lord, in the day Thou art about	JOHN HAMPDEN GURNEY (From John Mason.)	183
Lord, in the morning Thou shalt hear	ISAAC WATTS	245
Lord, in Thy Name Thy servants plead	JOHN KEBLE	294
Lord of my life, whose tender care	ANON	53

INDEX.

	Author.	Page
Lord of the harvest, hear	Charles Wesley	295
Lord of the harvest! once again	Joseph Anstice	306
Lord of the harvest! Thee we hail!	John Hampden Gurney	300
Lord of the Sabbath, hear our vows	Philip Doddridge	69
Lord of the vast creation	Rev. John Bulmer	602
Lord, teach us how to pray aright	James Montgomery	63
Lord, we come before Thee now	William Hammond	35
Lord, when before Thy throne we meet	Anon	405
Lord, when I lift my voice to Thee	William Hiley Bathurst	52
Lord, when we bend before Thy throne	Joseph D. Carlisle	46
Lord, while for all mankind we pray	J. Reynell Wreford	588
Lo, round the throne	Anon	495
Lo! the storms of life are breaking	Dean Alford	116
Love divine, all love excelling	Charles Wesley	188
Much in sorrow, oft in woe	H. Kirke White	521
Must friends and kindred droop and die	Isaac Watts	342
My faith looks up to Thee	Ray Palmer	125
My God and Father, while I stray	Charlotte Elliott	127
My God, and is Thy table spread?	Philip Doddridge	402
My God, I love Thee, not because	Francis Xavier (Translated by E. Caswell.)	606
My God, now I from sleep awake	Bishop Thomas Ken	278
My God, the spring of all my joys	Isaac Watts	204
My Lord, my love was crucified	John Mason	78
My thoughts surmount these lower skies	Isaac Watts	159
My trust is in the Lord	Henry Francis Lyte	524
Nearer, my God, to Thee	Sarah Flower Adams	217
Now darkness over all is spread	Pastor Josephson	277
Now, gracious Lord, Thine arm reveal	John Newton	321
Now I have found the ground wherein	John Wesley (From Zinzendorf.)	130
Now it belongs not to my care	Richard Baxter	122
Now let our mourning hearts revive	Philip Doddridge	331
Now thank we all our God	Anon	308
Now the thirty years accomplished	Anon	416
Object of my first desire	Augustus M. Toplady	198
O Christ, our hope, our heart's desire	*Ancient Hymn*	471
O day most calm, most bright!	George Herbert	70
O Father, Thou who hast created all	Anon	380
O Father, who didst all things make	Anon	283
O food that weary pilgrims love	Anon	407
O for a closer walk with God!	William Cowper	170
O for a thousand tongues to sing	Charles Wesley	522
Of Thy love some gracious token	Thomas Kelly	97

INDEX.

	Author.	Page
O God, my Strength and Fortitude	Thomas Sternhold	25
O God of Bethel, by whose hand	John Logan (From Philip Doddridge.)	590
O God of love, O King of peace	Anon	584
O God of mercy, God of might	John Keble	62
O God! Thou knowest all our wants	Anon	28
O God, unseen, but ever near	Edward Osler	410
O God, we thank Thee for the love	Anon	240
O God, when darkness round us reigns	George Wooler	530
O God, who made the earth and sea	Anon	518
O happy saints, who dwell in light	John Berridge	485
O help us, Lord, each hour of need	Henry Hart Milman	603
O holy Saviour, Friend unseen	Charlotte Elliott	117
O how blest the congregation	Henry Francis Lyte	92
O Israel, blest beyond compare!	Philip Doddridge	207
O Jesu, Lord of heavenly grace	John Chandler (From St. Ambrose.)	239
O Jesus, King most wonderful	St. Bernard	478
O King of earth, and air, and sea!	Bishop Reginald Heber	582
O King of kings, before whose throne	Thomas Darling (Variation from John Quarles.)	596
O let us raise our voices	George Wooler	472
O light, whose beams illumine all	Anon	257
O Lord, another day is flown	H. Kirke White	50
O Lord, how happy should we be	Joseph Anstice	594
O Lord, I would delight in Thee	John Ryland	552
O Lord of heaven, and earth, and sea	Bishop of Lincoln	292
O Lord, the heaven Thy power displays	Whiting	263
O Lord, turn not Thy face away	Bishop Reginald Heber (Variation from John Mardley.)	597
On bended knee I seek Thee, Lord	George Wooler	556
Once more, my soul, the rising day	Isaac Watts	244
On silent wings an angel	Dr. H. W. Dulcken	224
Onward, Christian soldiers	Anon	545
On wings of faith, mount up, my soul, and rise	Joseph Straphan	598
O praise ye the Lord, prepare your glad voice	Tate and Brady	517
O sacred head, once wounded	Paul Gerhardt	413
O send Thy light, Thy truth, my God	Rev. Henry March	401
O Thou from whom all goodness flows	Thomas Haweis	601
O Thou, the contrite sinner's Friend	Charlotte Elliott	109
O Thou to whom, in ancient time	John Pierpoint	85
O timely happy, timely wise	John Keble	228
O where shall rest be found?	James Montgomery	156
O world! behold upon the tree	Paul Gerhardt	421
O worship the King	Sir Robert Grant	17
Plunged in a gulf of dark despair	Isaac Watts	424
Praise, O praise our God and King	Sir Henry Baker	298
Praise the Lord, His glories show	Henry Francis Lyte	6

INDEX.

	Author.	Page
Praise to God, immortal praise	Anna Lætitia Barbauld	289
Prayer is not heard through noisy sound	Anon	51
Prayer is the soul's sincere desire	James Montgomery	33
Rejoice, the Lord is King!	Charles Wesley	466
Rejoice, though storms assail thee	Anon	215
Rejoice to-day with one accord	Anon	529
Remark, my soul, the narrow bounds	Philip Doddridge	317
Rise, my soul, and stretch thy wings	Martin Madan	157
Rock of ages, cleft for me	Augustus M. Toplady	135
Saviour, breathe an evening blessing	James Edmiston	276
Saviour, when in dust to Thee	Sir Robert Grant	36
Saviour, who Thy flock art feeding	Anon	382
See how great a flame aspires	Charles Wesley	179
See Israel's gentle Shepherd stands	Philip Doddridge	384
See the destined day arise	Anon	425
Servants of God, in joyful lays	James Montgomery	30
Shepherd of Israel, from above	William Hiley Bathurst	381
Since Thou hast added now, O God	George Wither	230
Sing Alleluia forth in duteous praise	Anon	494
Sing, my tongue, the glorious battle	Anon	414
Sing, my tongue, the Saviour's glory	Thomas Aquinas	408
Sink not yet, my soul, to slumber	J. Rist	260
Sitting around our Father's board	Isaac Watts	400
Sometimes a light surprises	William Cowper	195
Songs of praise the angels sang!	G. W.	366
Sound the loud timbrel o'er Egypt's dark sea	Thomas Moore	563
Source of good, whose power controls	Richard Massie (From John Frank.)	184
Sovereign Ruler of the skies	John Ryland	172
Stand up and bless the Lord	James Montgomery	68
Stand up! stand up for Jesus	Duffield	574
Sun of my soul, Thou Saviour dear	John Keble	253
Sweet is the solemn voice that calls	Henry Francis Lyte	83
Sweet place, sweet place alone!	Samuel Crossman	481
Sweet the moments, rich in blessing	James Allen	396
Teach me, my God and King	George Herbert	607
Tender Shepherd, Thou hast stilled	Anon	325
Ten thousand times ten thousand	Dean Alford	505
The child leans on its mother's breast	Isaac Williams	196
The Day of Resurrection!	Anon	448
The day of rest once more comes round	Thomas Kelly	84
The festal morn, my God, is come	James Merrick	74
The foe behind, the deep before	John Mason Neale	440
The great redeeming Angel, Thee	Charles Wesley	385

INDEX.

	Author.	Page
The heathen perish day by day	JAMES MONTGOMERY	573
The hour of my departure's come	MICHAEL BRUCE	160
The leaves around me falling	HENRY FRANCIS LYTE	604
The Lord is King; lift up Thy voice	JOSIAH CONDER	464
The Lord is Lord, and King of kings	GEORGE WOOLER	526
The Lord is risen indeed	THOMAS KELLY	454
The Lord my pasture shall prepare	JOSEPH ADDISON	23
The Lord of earth and sky	CHARLES WESLEY	323
The Lord of Might from Sinai's brow	Bishop REGINALD HEBER	475
The Lord shall come! the earth shall quake	Bishop REGINALD HEBER	352
The night is come, wherein at last we rest	BOHEMIAN BRETHREN	258
The race that long in darkness pined	JOHN MORRISON	369
There is a blessèd home	Sir HENRY BAKER	502
There is a calm for those who weep	JAMES MONTGOMERY	335
There is a dwelling-place above	Bishop RICHARD MANT	181
There is a fountain filled with blood	WILLIAM COWPER	101
There is a green hill far away	ANON	566
There is a land of pure delight	ISAAC WATTS	496
There is a pure and tranquil wave	WILLIAM BALL	154
There's not a bird with lonely nest	Baptist WRIOTHESLEY NOEL	205
The roseate hues of early dawn	CECIL FRANCIS ALEXANDER	513
The scene around me disappears	JAMES MONTGOMERY	370
The spacious firmament on high	ANDREW MARVEL	1
The strain upraise of joy and praise	Rev. J. M. NEALE, D.D.	610
The sun has sunk beneath the wave	ANON	274
The sun is sinking fast	ANON	255
The winds were howling o'er the deep	Bishop REGINALD HEBER	536
The world is very evil	ST. BERNARD (Translated by Dr. J. M. Neale)	507
The year is gone beyond recall	ANON	312
They talked of Jesus as they went	THOMAS GRINFIELD	394
Thine, O Lord, is the kingdom	DEAN ALFORD	4
This night I lift my heart to Thee	BARTHOLOMEW	284
Thou art gone to the grave; but we will not deplore thee	Bishop REGINALD HEBER	332
Thou God of love! beneath Thy sheltering wings	ANON	338
Thou Judge of quick and dead	CHARLES WESLEY	351
Thou Son of God and Son of Man	ANON	190
Thou who art enthroned above	SANDYS	76
Thou, whose almighty Word	JOHN MARRIOTT	13
Through all the dangers of the night	ANON	233
Through the day Thy love hath spared us	THOMAS KELLY	281
Thus far the Lord has led me on	ISAAC WATTS	267
Thy goodness, Lord, our souls confess	THOMAS GIBBONS	5
"'T is finished!"—so the Saviour cried	SAMUEL STENNETT	427
'T is Heaven begun below	JOSEPH SWAIN	209
To God the only wise	ISAAC WATTS	134
To God, ye choir above, begin	PHILIP SKELTON	11
To Thy temple I repair	JAMES MONTGOMERY	66

INDEX.

	Author.	Page
Vital spark of heavenly flame	ALEXANDER POPE	344

	Author.	Page
Weary now I go to bed	Dr. H. W. DULCKEN	264
Weary of wandering from my God	CHARLES WESLEY	554
Welcome, sacred day of rest!	ANON	93
Welcome, sweet day of rest	ISAAC WATTS	82
We'll sing in spite of scorn	THOMAS KELLY	362
We plough the fields, and scatter	ANON	296
We sing His love, who once was slain	ROWLAND HILL	453
We've no abiding city here	THOMAS KELLY	151
We would come before Thy throne	GEORGE WOOLER	58
What are these in bright array	JAMES MONTGOMERY	503
What care the saints of God, if they	ANON	561
What means the water in this font	SPENCE	387
What sudden blaze of song	Rev. J. KEBLE	372
What various hindrances we meet	WILLIAM COWPER	61
When angels swell the heavenly choir	GEORGE WOOLER	550
When at Thy footstool, Lord, I bend	HENRY FRANCIS LYTE	39
When blooming youth is snatched away	ANNE STEELE	336
When gathering clouds around I view	Sir ROBERT GRANT	113
When I can read my title clear	ISAAC WATTS	150
When in the hour of utmost need	ANON.	42
When I survey life's varied scene	ANNE STEELE	121
When I survey the wondrous cross	ISAAC WATTS	428
When langour and disease invade	AUGUSTUS M. TOPLADY	105
When, marshalled on the mighty plain	HENRY KIRKE WHITE	364
Where two or three, with sweet accord	SAMUEL STENNETT	38
While shepherds watched their flocks by night	NAHUM TATE	365
While with ceaseless course the sun	JOHN NEWTON	319
Who are these like stars appearing	ANON	484
Who can, on the sea-shore	Dr. H. W. DULCKEN	15
Whom should we love like Thee	HENRY FRANCIS LYTE	527
Who would not leave this world below	ANON	140
Why do we mourn departing friends	ISAAC WATTS	337
With all the powers my poor soul hath	JOHN AUSTIN and THEOPHILUS DORRINGTON (Variation from Richard Crashaw.)	397

Ye golden lamps of heaven, farewell	PHILIP DODDRIDGE	498
Ye sons of men, with joy record	PHILIP DODDRIDGE	7

THE CHANDOS POETS.

Under this distinctive title will from time to time be published New and Elegant Editions of Standard Poetry.

Red Line Edition, New Type, crown 8vo, price 7s. 6d. cloth, or morocco, 15s.

The Poets of the Nineteenth Century.

With One Hundred and Twenty Illustrations by J. E. Millais, R.A., John Tenniel, F. R. Pickersgill, R.A., John Gilbert, Harrison Weir, &c., &c.

Engraved by the Brothers Dalziel.

Eliza Cook's Poems.

THE ONLY COMPLETE EDITION.

Revised by the Author, with many Original Pieces, Eight Steel Plates, and Portrait.

The Poetical Works of Longfellow.

With Original Illustrations by Cooper, Small, Houghton, &c.

Engraved by the Brothers Dalziel.

Legendary Ballads of England & Scotland.

Edited and Compiled by John S. Roberts. With Original full-page Illustrations, and a Steel Portrait of Bishop Percy.

Scott's Poetical Works.

With numerous Notes, Original Illustrations, and Steel Portrait.

Frederick Warne & Co., Bedford Street, Covent Garden.

FINE ART BOOK.

In a superb binding, colours and gold, One Guinea ; morocco elegant, £1 15s.

Embellished with Initial Letters, Vignettes, and page Pictures in Tints, with Gold Borders.

Golden Thoughts from Golden Fountains

Selected and Arranged by the Author of the "SPIRIT OF PRAISE."

Illustrated by J. Wolf, A. B. Houghton, W. P. Burton, J. D. Watson, W. Small, T. Dalziel, G. J. Pinwell, and others.

Engraved by the Brothers Dalziel.

PRESS NOTICES.

The drawings in "Golden Thoughts" alone make the book worth far more than its price.—*Westminster Review.*

The get up of the book is very beautiful. It is printed on rich cream paper, and adorned with exquisite borderings, initial letters, and full-page and demi-page engravings. It is the most dainty book of its class we have this year met with.—*British Quarterly.*

The book is printed by Messrs. Dalziel, and is certainly a first-rate specimen of typography; altogether it may be placed among the best works of its class which the season has produced.—*Art Journal.*

This is a capital selection of religious poems by old and current authors, that are very aptly and pleasantly illustrated by able artists.—*Athenæum.*

The editor has arranged the contents with considerable care, varying the monotony which is generally typical of such collections by introducing those golden thoughts with which the works of Jeremy Taylor, Bishop Hall, Richard Baxter, Bishop Butler, and others abound.—*Examiner.*

The letterpress is faultless.—*Times.*

This goodly volume, so beautiful within and without, with its charming pictures and its precious thoughts, is not only a most appropriate Christmas gift, but a treasury of perennial attraction.—*Sun.*

In this volume there has been much taste and labour bestowed in collecting the specimens.—*Saturday Review.*

This volume has a very handsome appearance, and has been printed with great care.—*Pall Mall Gazette.*

The printing of the book is of the very best.—*Daily Telegraph.*

Frederick Warne & Co., Bedford Street, Covent Garden.

Druck:
Canon Deutschland Business Services GmbH
im Auftrag der KNV-Gruppe
Ferdinand-Jühlke-Str. 7
99095 Erfurt